Dark Gate: Key to the Left Hand Path

Andhaku Amelatu

Dark Gate:
Key to the Left Hand Path

Nephilim Press © 2022

ISBN: 978-1-957758-00-8

Cover Art by Robert Cook
Sigil Work by Brian Snelling
Title Page Art by Natalie Pardy
Researched by Claire Lawrence and Richard S. Cavenett
Edited by Natalie Pardy, Amanda Maher, and Jason Johnson

I be not the shepherd nor the sheep. I need no permission, I seek no approval, I care not for your guidance nor your direction. For I carve my own path deep and wide.

—Jason Johnson

To Lucifer, my shining light.

Also to my long-suffering husband, Richard (may he rest in peace); my daughters, Tjanatja and Jessica; Janet and Terry, who are my oldest friends; my best friends, Natalie, Jay, Brian, Dario, Alton, Claire, Susie, Paul, Susan, Rob, Michael, Melissa, Amanda, and Miri.

Also to my sister Natasha.

Contents

List of Figures and Tables

CHAPTER 1

Satanism

S atanism is the worship of Satan in any number of forms but not necessarily the worship of devils or Demons. Devil worship is often confused with Satanism, but there are many ancient tribal groups that practice Devil worship *in absentia* of Satan. This is called Demonolatry (not to be confused with Demonology or the Christian study of Demons). Demonolatry is the practice of worshipping Demons, something you may find occurring in ancient African cultures, for instance, and, indeed, in modern Western culture as well.

To understand Satanism, you need to comprehend the difference between the left- and right-hand paths, and the real definition of light versus darkness. Let us first look at darkness versus light. I cannot stress enough that darkness is not about evil. I do not believe in evil as an entity or a force of nature; it is an act of choice or will. It is a construct developed by human beings as a function of religious morals, ethics and principles. Evil can exist within either the domain of light, or the province of darkness. Darkness is the absence of light, the absence of enlightenment, but also the place of hidden knowledge.[1]

In old English, there were three words that referred to darkness: *Heolstor, Genip,* and *Sceadu. Heolstor* meant "hiding place" and later

---

[1] Darkness [dahrk-nis], *noun* – the state or quality of being dark: The room was in total darkness. The absence or deficiency of light: The darkness of night. Obscurity; concealment: The darkness of the metaphor destroyed its effectiveness.

became *holster*. This bears a close similarity to the word *Occult*, which means "hidden." *Genip* meant "mist" or "veil"—the best approximation would be the word *secret*. It is still used in Germanic languages (e.g., in Dutch, *in het geniep* means "secretly"). *Sceadu* literally means "shadow." The word *dark* eventually evolved from the word *deorc*. None of these words that are the etymological roots of the word *darkness* implies that they are a source of evil. It is only later in the early history of the main Abrahamic faiths, around 1000 AD, that the term *darkness* became associated with evil. This makes it largely an idea born out of the minds of men as influenced by popular culture and religion. To associate Satanism with evil would be wrong, as it is correctly associated with the hidden elements of knowledge, as is the Occult in general.

Some will still not be convinced that darkness is not evil. It is a common ambiguity in texts that are clearly taken out of context. In science, darkness is merely determined as the absence of visible light. This is understood by scientists to be a fundamental and immutable scientific law. Light itself is part of the electromagnetic spectrum. From a scientific point of view light contains gamma waves, radio waves, electromagnetic waves, microwaves, infrared, ultraviolet, and X-rays. These all operate under many different resonances, temperatures, and conditions. All of this makes up the composition of light (20 percent). Darkness is therefore the absence of this in varying degrees (70 percent). There is much argument among scientists over the ambiguity of the definition of darkness—all agree that darkness and light exist on a sliding scale and can never be absolute. Nonetheless, they both serve a critical function in keeping balance in the universe. Darkness, therefore, is the absence of visible light (I stress here the absence of visible light)—see how these ties in with my definition of spiritual darkness?

From a spiritual perspective, the church portrayed darkness as evil in medieval literature. Darkness is a state of nonlight that denotes the non-visible, hidden, and secret elements. You need both dark and light in the universe to achieve balance in both the mundane and the spirit worlds. If there is one without the other, then our lives would be meaningless, empty, and we would be mere puppets in a dull, gray world. We are sensory creatures.

We all have the abilities to experience the entire spectrum of pleasure and pain. Predictability, this is what we exist for.

There are some Satanic movements that are predominantly what you would call evil, though most of the Satanic movement shuns these groups and their practices. These are the people who practice many forms of terrorism against Abrahamic faiths, and right-hand path faiths like Christianity, Wicca, and Buddhism. Their doctrine is akin to the doctrines of many Neo-Nazis and right-wing fascist groups. It is well known that they mandate human sacrifice. Many Satanists believe that this is not acceptable behavior, as it casts Satanism in a bad light. We believe that left-hand path and right-hand path faiths must coexist together as a critical function of balance.

It is not a fight of good versus evil, but a complementary existence between light and dark in order to produce balance in the universe. If there were only light and no darkness by which to see the virtues of light and no contrast, how boring would the world be!

The rhetorical use of darkness as a device was seen in Shakespeare. You will see references to Satan as the Prince of Darkness (King Lear: III, iv). Chaucer in the fourteenth century also wrote about works of darkness as evil. Note that these are popular fictionalizations and again, not fact.[2] However these depictions have been adopted by religion since medieval times. Next, we will discuss the left-hand path versus the right-hand path.

There is a broad difference between religion and faith and structure versus the solitary path. To paraphrase American novelist Jerry B. Jenkins, "The difference between religion and faith is that religion is where man seeks to find the face of God/Gods and faith is where deities reach down and touch man. Religion itself embodies a set of ideas, rules, artifacts and

---

[2]   Religious texts use the term *darkness* to make a visual point. See the Bible [Exodus 10:21, Matthew 8:12]. See the Qur'an [Naba 78.25]. Also review Greek Mythology where there were three layers of night surrounding Tartarus (the universe). Hindu texts refer to black or dark coloration with respect to balance and harmony with the Yang element. See the link http://symbolism.wikia.com/wiki/Darkness.

predetermined rituals utilized in attempting to commune with the divine."[3] In other words, it is an attempt at a systemic approach to faith, social control and social engineering.

Right-hand path faiths are those who have organized sets of rules. These have a prepackaged format and vary in degrees of adherence. Examples of right-hand path faiths are of course the Abrahamic faiths, Buddhism, Hinduism, and Sikhism. You can also say that Wicca and some Pagan belief systems are also right-hand path because they are just that, systems. Left-hand path faiths are those that are not part of a system of thinking. They are solitary. Among these, you can consider theistic Satanism, theistic Luciferianism, and Demonolatry.

Again folks, it's not about good versus evil. It isn't even about dark versus light, it's about individual verses systemic. Most left-hand path practitioners are solitary. They do not follow a systemic set of rules for what they believe. They can be polytheistic (believing in many Gods) or monotheistic (believing in one God).

Many new to the occult puzzle over the ultimate dichotomy of left-hand and right-hand pathways. I want to make a very special point here. An organism works as a whole. The human organism requires both left and right hands to function. This is no different in the spiritual world. I want to make it clear that the left-hand path and right-hand path do not refer to the false dichotomy of good versus evil. To think this is simplistic and foolish—it refers to two parts of a functioning and holistic unit.

The left-hand path is so called because its focus is based on individuality, a dismissal of social, moral, and religious dogma, liberation, self-thought,

---

[3] Re-lig-eon [ri-lij-uhn] *noun* a set of beliefs concerning the cause, nature and purpose of the universe, especially when considered as the creation of a superhuman agency or agencies, usually involving devotional and ritual observances and often containing a moral code governing the conduct of human affairs. a set of beliefs concerning the cause, nature and purpose of the universe, especially when considered as the creation of a superhuman agency or agencies, usually involving devotional and ritual observances and often containing a moral code governing the conduct of human affairs. The body of persons adhering to a set of beliefs and practices: a world council of religions. The life or state of a monk, nun, etc.: to enter religion. The practice of religious beliefs; ritual observance of faith.

self-actualization, and spiritual advancement. Left has always traditionally signified the sinister, from the Latin word *sinistra*. People have mistaken this over the centuries as bad or evil, as per our previous discussion. For example, some cultures wipe their bottoms only with their left hand and eat only with their right. It is easy to fall into false thinking about left versus right when you look at it in these basic terms, but it is not that simple. It is not about good and bad, but about separate but essential functions. You will find under this dichotomy some of the following as examples of left-hand path faiths:[4]

- Setism
- Cthuluism
- Luciferianism
- Satanism
- Necromancy
- Dark Paganism
- Chaos Magic
- Demonolatry
- some forms of Taoism, Hinduism, Aghoris, and some forms of Buddhism

The right-hand path covers faiths pertaining to **social adherence to conventions** and **taboos**.[5] It is a macro view of the world. This is a body of spiritual thought that guides those who may not be able to think for themselves and do not question. This is not always bad as these are the sources of our social cohesion and the social engineering that shapes us as a society. Social ethics, precepts, ideologies, and laws are formed in this way. These become social norms. These groups divide the concepts of

---

[4] See Barone Giulio Cesare Andrea Evola. The Yoga of Power: Tantra, Shakti and the Secret Way (1949) also see; Flowers, Stephen (1997). Also consider the Lords of the Left-Hand Path: A History of Spiritual Dissent. Runa Raven Press and Sutcliffe, Richard J. (1996). "Left-Hand Path Ritual Magick: An Historical and Philosophical Overview," in G. Harvey and C. Hardman (eds.), Paganism Today, pp. 109–37. London: Thorson's/HarperCollins.

[5] See D Evans, (2007). The History of British Magick after Crowley. Hidden Publishing. Page 204 and see Webb, Don; Stephen E. Flowers (1999). Uncle Setnakt's Essential Guide to the Left-Hand Path. Runa Raven Pr.

mind, body, and spirit. They have founding ethics based on the notion of lawful punishment for wrongdoing (e.g., the Threefold Law and the like). Not all right-hand path is Christian or Islam or Judaism; some are, in fact, part of the Occult. They serve a purpose in bringing collective groups of people together to worship under ancient systems of polytheism, and so forth. Under this aspect of the dichotomy, you will find Abrahamic core faiths, Fraternity of the Inner Light, Dharmicism, New Age religions such as Wicca, most forms of Neopaganism, Christian Gnosticism, right-hand path Tantra and Shinto, and so on.

Satanism is a left-hand path typology and is both a faith and a philosophy. It can be either monotheistic or polytheistic. Satanism is not always reverse Christianity. Some temples practice desecration of the holy sacraments and Black Mass. I have certainly tried this in the past, but it is not the province of all of Satanists. Based on my years as a theistic Satanist, approximately two–five percent practice these things. You see this often in France and around Europe. There are no sacrificing virgins at the altar, infants, or anything as horrid as that. Indeed, they may sacrifice animals at times, and certainly make blood pacts using their own blood, but they do not as a rule do the terrible things I have just mentioned. The percentage of Satanists who practice this way would be less than 1 percent, and they are shunned. When meeting in a Satanic circle, everyone is over the age of majority and is a willing participant. There are women who are called "secretaries" who are generally neophytes offering willing service at the altars, but not for anything dire. It is not like in the movie "The Exorcist." Demons are not fallen Angels; they are mercenaries that have sometimes been created by magicians or they are disembodied entities.[6] They are what is called a revenant, egregore, tulpa, or an animus. Some old Demons created by other cultures can be used in magic, but they roam independently of both Satanism and Abrahamic faiths. Demon possession is used in devil worship by devil worshippers, not by Satanists. Demons have been used by Christian Demonologists equally for example, John Dee was a prominent writer on the subject in the 1600s. He was a Christian, and not a devil worshipper or a Satanist.

---

[6] Refer to the Apocrypha, Enoch 15: 9–10.

There are two basic types of Satanism. There is atheistic satanism (note I used little "s"), which is a philosophy and not a belief in an entity. You will be familiar with the works of atheistic satanist Anton LaVey. The LaVeyans believe that the "self" is the highest form of deity. Satan is a symbol of independent thinking, a constant battle against conformity and the hallmark of the creation aspects of human nature. They do not worship Satan. They follow the ideas set out in Humanism via the notions espoused by philosophers such as Friedrich Nietzsche and the like. This is the predominant form of nontheistic satanist. The main organization for this group is the Church of Satan. There is a constant war in the Satanic community between atheists, who are very much into the costumery and melodrama of what they think satanism should be, and theists who believe in the entity and supremacy of Satan.

Theistic Satanists can be divided into several groups. There are Sumerians and those who believe Satan is an alien being, like the Cult of Cthulhu and then there are Gnostic Satanists,[7] Dionysians such as the Black Goat Cabal,[8] and Egyptians via the Temple of Set.[9]

Theistic Satanists for the mostly believe in the pursuit of the carnal. The Baphomet is the symbol used by Satanists because it was adopted by LaVey based on the writings of Aleister Crowley. Most of you are familiar with these articles. Baphomet is technically not even Satanic.[10] It became acculturated into Satanism because the Catholic Church used it to condemn the last of the Knights Templar. Baphomet is originally a word that can be translated to mean Mohamad. Baphomet was a borrowed symbol from both ancient forms of witchcraft and from ancient accounts written by Herodotus that refer to Egyptian beliefs. From that day, the symbol has been heavily used in Satanism as a symbol for wisdom and the transcendence from the physical to the spiritual (see appendix A—History and Anatomy of the Baphomet for more of a discussion on this). Most Theistic Satanists (not all) enjoy indulging in feasting, sex, and other proclivities. Many have rules about the

---

[7] See http://www.theorderofphosphorus.com/ for more information about adversarial Luciferianism.
[8] See http://theisticsatanism.com/bgoat/ for more information.
[9] See http://www.xeper.org/ for more information.
[10] See the appendix A – History and Anatomy of the Baphomet.

extent to which they can go to. In history, a famous Satanic group was the Hellfire Club (Order of the Friars of St. Francis of Wycombe) that existed in England in the 1800s. There were places that high-society men could practice their sexual proclivities from sadomasochism to homosexuality. Many of Britons most influential artists, poets, writers, and politicians were involved with this club, and purely to indulge their carnality.

Not all Theistic Satanists are about carnality. Some are about spiritual pursuits and the improvement of the spiritual self. This is where I stand as a Luciferian. Luciferians are not Satanists. Luciferians will be discussed in the next chapter.

True Satanism is not about 666, and Freemasonry has *nothing* to do with Satanism. They believe in the Supreme Architect and if anything, they are more of a Pagan belief system.[11] The alleged number of the beast, 666, is the number given to man. It was also the number assigned to the Roman Emperor Nero.

My own journey through theistic Satanism was quite interesting for me. After several years of worshipping our Satan, I decided that was time to seek a solid affiliation with a group that I could move from being a neophyte into much grander things. If anyone else is on this quest, be wary of what you read and what you believe. It is a veritable minefield out there.

I consulted with Father Satan on this mission, and the primary piece of advice I received and that resonated through me was to meditate and ask Father Satan to guide you to the right group of people, as there are many wolves out there. He told me to be wary and not to rely on the glitzy promises and hype that some leaders make or the assumptions in faith they forward—there are many divergent paths out there. Some of these are wolves seeking to prey on the young in faith for many selfish reasons, including money.

I asked Father Satan earnestly for criteria by which to judge the right choice for me; and this is what came to me:

1.   The path you choose, in order access to the darkest knowledge, must feel right and comfortable for you at the time. You will know beyond

---

[11]   See the Freemasons take on this via http://www.phoenixmasonry.org/ masonic_myths_ and _outright_falsehoods.htm

all that a path is the correct one, the dark light of the Black Flame will guide you in this quest. It will illuminate in your spirit like a light that has been turned on in the darkness—in other words, there will be no doubt. If you do not feel a school of magickal understanding is correct, then it is not correct for you currently, then do not take that path. You could be led back to this path later, however, even if it is to gain an understanding of it—keep an open mind and do not discount anything except where it is overtly inappropriate.

2. After reviewing all information, ask yourself if the leader has provided adequate substantiation for his claims from the collected esoteric, ancient, academic bodies of knowledge that are available. Note that not all written works are inspired by Satan's teachings, nor do they have his blessing. Not all ancient Grimoires are good.[12] In fact, many have been exposed as fraudulent. Before you read, ask Father Satan if the information is solid.

3. Ask yourself if the public communication of that leader is disseminating is all about sledging other paths or if it is about the objective of true faith? Leaders consumed with pulling other leaders down are on a path for their own advancement and no one else's. This is a recurrent issue in Satanism today. You may have to ask Father Satan to give you the gift of discernment for this at times, but also ask him to show you if there are any specific issues in the public eye that you can see. Be careful that you refrain from naming names, because a path may be right for a specific group of individuals, and just not for you at this moment in time.

4. Do the people in the affiliation share respect and love for one another and those of other paths? Are they accepting of outsiders? This is

---

[12] A classic example of this is the Necronomicon, which has questionable origins to many who study the occult in a formal academic setting. Some believe it was written by H. P. Lovecraft and others feel it is a genuine ancient Aramaic text—see L. Sprague de Camp, *Literary Swordsmen and Sorcerers*, 100–101. There is no real evidence to support either idea. Additionally, another example of a questionable work is the *La Poule Noire Grimoire* (*The Black Pullet*) written in the eighteenth century [see Spence, Lewis (2006). *An Encyclopaedia of Occultism*. 71.] Many early scholars believe that it is a work that escaped the burning of Ptolemy's library.

important! If they practice spiritual snobbery, then it should be an instant warning for you not to enter that group.

5. Are they making the claim that they are the only right way? Many groups do this, and there is a wide mixture out there of groups including those based on the core doctrines of right-hand path religions such as Christianity. Father Satan has taught me many times that the spiritual path is a rich tapestry of knowledge rather than a fragmented pile of pointless disorder. Differing paths satisfy differing needs within a person's individual psychosocial, spiritual, and intellectual development.

6. Are they making any claim that they are a leader who is a God incarnate or a vested power of Father Satan here on earth? These things are important because these claims put some of these groups into the category of cultists. Cults are one sided and therefore unbalanced, and making these types of grandiose statements is highly dangerous. Let's not forget the horror of scenarios like Jonestown,[13] the Waco siege,[14] and other cult lead horror stories of men who put themselves forward as the messiah or something similar. Do not fall prey to these kinds of people! They are persuasive and charismatic, but if you look closely at their arguments, they are hollow, unfounded, and even ludicrous.

7. Know the structure of Satanic faith and the left-hand path before you dive into any debate with leaders, so you do not appear foolish and that you can better discern the path you want to go down. There are those theists who believe in being adversarial and even destructive. Those who believe that the path existed as a function of Judaism, others Islam, others Christianity, others from different polytheistic lines such as Egypt and Sumer, and so on. These are not wrong, but if they do not speak to your spirit with a loud, resounding, and illuminating bang, then just leave them alone no matter how compelling the argument in their favor is. Remember: your path is about *your* learning and evolution as a spiritual person. Some groups

---

[13] Jonestown Cult Massacre—http://en.wikipedia.org/wiki/Jonestown.
[14] Waco Cult Massacre—http://en.wikipedia.org/wiki/Waco_siege.

are even Christianity in reverse. Again, this is not wrong, but may not be your walk. These groups have modelled themselves on the structure of the older organized religions, such as Catholicism, and perform rites like the Black Mass and desecration of holy books and so on. This is not a bad thing either it but may not be what *you* need for your path. Again, ask Father Satan to help you determine.

8. Do they practice any rite that could be deemed illegal or offensive (e.g., sacrifice of animals, children, or humans, in general)? Satan himself is beholden to laws—even if they are his own laws. No entity exists within a system of true anarchy or true chaos. Law and Chaos are two dominant metaphysical forces that exist on a sliding scale.[15] This is true in science as well. Everything in nature can be said to have a modicum of determinism within it, at least with its own code to exist by. Also remember we live in a universe that is bound together by laws—the laws of physics and science, laws of life. We must live within the law of land. We have to live in our neighborhoods and go to our jobs. We also represent the name of the Father, and things we can do can give him a bad name or cast an ill light on our path setting back its progress. Examples of those who have misrepresented the name of Father Satan are killers who have butchered in his name. Some of you may be too young to remember the Night Stalker: Richard Ramirez,[16] Adolfo Constanzo,[17] or Russell Williams.[18] There are many like this. While these people may be evil and even mentally disturbed, they are not real Satanists, despite what they call themselves.

9. Join online groups before joining their offline groups (where permissible). Ask questions. No question is too stupid. Read their documentation before you commit to their covens, temples, orders, and so on. If their documentation is exclusive and does not permit

[15] Law and Chaos—http://en.wikipedia.org/wiki/Law_ and _Chaos.
[16] Richard Ramirez—http://www.trutv.com/library/crime/serial_killers/notorious/ramirez/terror_1.html .
[17] Adolfo Constanzo—http://en.wikipedia.org/wiki/Adolfo_Constanzo.
[18] Russell Williams—http://www.henrymakow.com/elite_serial_killer_linked_to.html.

outside knowledge from the considerable body of occult work that exists out there, then it could be that the organization you are looking at is a cult.

10. Make sure that in these groups you feel warmth, love, and you are not turned away for saying anything silly. We all need to learn, and all must start somewhere. If you feel fear, then you should not be there. Predators can smell fear, even between us humans. You will fast become a target if you are new, frightened, or have an odd or eclectic reading repertoire.

11. Does the group have a political affiliation? If so, then it is likely that the group's entire purpose is simply a smoke screen for its political activities. There are a few groups out there like this. Most experienced Satanists know who these groups are and can guide you. First, you should ask Father Satan for guidance. Examples of these groups are the Order of Nine Angles and Joy of Satan Ministries.

12. Do the leaders practice what they preach, and deliver what they promise—or at least sincerely strive to achieve these things? I have had leaders of groups promise to deliver information to me that is purportedly fully syndicated and referenced. I am still waiting. This speaks volumes about their true motives.

13. Does the group teach sensible things (e.g., the sensible practice of Demonolatry and invocation for example)? Do they teach the correct methodology for safe invocation? Are these groups careful in their practice of dark magic? For example, some groups practice blood rites, which include the rite of drinking from a chalice mixed with human blood and urine, or even includes the use of menstrual blood. You may get sick from doing this, just as a matter of practicality. I recently read a legal document for a temple that said in one clause that it did not condone human sacrifice, but in another clause, it basically said that they would turn a blind eye if the killing was an act of vengeance against someone who hurt a group member.

14. Does the group ask anything of you that you do not want to give (e.g., excessive amounts of money, your firstborn child, sacrifices of items of wealth, denouncement of friends and family)? These are

warning signs and these groups are possibly cults and not bearing the direct blessing of Father Satan himself.

15. Does the group mix its paths? Generally, there will be some degree of path combination, but the degree to which it is done can cause a cancellation effect. For example, some literature suggests that our Demon friends may take offense to nine-foot circles, because in some forms they are, in fact, Demon traps and therefore disrespectful.[19] Yet others believe they need to be in a nine-foot circle before an invocation, and believe Demons need a license to depart.[20] These two practical underpinnings in one group will cancel each other out in terms of the effectiveness of any invocation or evocation undertaken. You may find mixed paths is a sign that the people running the group are uneducated in the ways of the Father and are ill informed or badly resourced. A good example of this is when you see groups that talk about hell and the inferno. This comes more from popular secular or mundane literature and popular characterizations of Satan as a scary, frightening beast,= and foul Demon lord. This is not how Satan should be portrayed. There is no black abyss (or punitive place called hell) outside of the Abrahamic faith pathways. Note this does not extend to some forms of polytheism where there may be a shoal or an underworld. Satan is here on this Earth right now, and he walks among us. Examples of popular literature that exemplifies this kind of thinking that has become acculturated into Satanic worship are works by Milton and the famous Dante's *Inferno*. Remember, brothers and sisters, these are *fictional* works or works of the mundane world—they are *not spiritual fact*. Some Demonolaters make this mistake; they base their Demonolatry on

---

[19] See Joy of Satan Ministries, Invocation and Evocation 2002— http://www. angelfire.com/empire/serpentis666/HOME.html.
[20] See F/ Goodman, Seal of Solomon In Magic Symbols, Brian Trodd Publishing House Ltd, London, 1989, 80. Also review Gray, William; "Exorcising the Tree of Evil: How To Use The Symbolism Of The Qabalistic Tree of Life To Recognise and Reverse Negative Energy", [Helios/Weisers/Kima Global], 1974/1984/2002, (originally The Tree of Evil).

Demons of myth and popular literature or media and not pay any homage to the true Demons of the old lore and faith.[21]

16. Does the group preach from a single book it claims is the only true work of Satan? Understand that not all works are authentic. Seek authentic sources for these, and read them before you venture in. Some groups may use these factors (and your failure to understand them) as a mark against you. It can be a dangerous interpretation of a more generalist work—a keen example of this is the hilarious book called *The Bible in Satan's Words* by Rev. John Pirog of the Coven of the Dark Goat (not to be confused with the Cathedral of the Black Goat or Dianne Vera's seminal body of work). It was supported by a Neo-Nazi Satanic war group and following its edicts would be dangerous, to say the least.

17. Lastly, Father Satan told me to sit back and watch. If there is strife and disunity coming from the group, then it is doing nothing more than seeking to unravel the community and confuse its followers—I refer to these as dark wolves. Satan has powerful enemies, not all of them are Christian—some exist within the realms of Satanism itself. Adversity also comes from other mundane sources such as personal ignorance, the laws of the land, other faiths[22] even misinformed government departments (FBI—Ritual Killing Crimes Unit comes to mind here and the infamous Satanic panic of the 1970s-80s). Not all dark forces come from the Satan. Many Demons and dark forces could be considered as mercenaries—Angels, as well, when it comes down to it. All Demonic forces bow to Satan, but not all of them are allied to him. Be careful, brothers and sisters—in these times, we need to take care with our path that we do not fall prey to the dark wolves. You want to seek involvement with groups whose only objective is to worship Satan, teach his ways, and manage his objectives. Never ever consider groups that are all about promoting themselves or are subterfuge for a more sinister mission.

[21] See *Deities and Demigods, Legends and Lore-The Acaeum* http://www.acaeum.com/ddindexes/setpages/deities.html.
[22] Refer to the Satanic Panic files of the FBI, there is so much adversity there

Now we get to the essentials of it all. What are the types of Satanists out there? There are many of them. It is believed that over eight hundred different Satanic groups exist. I am going to uncover the core groups using very simplistic analysis. I want to state two caveats here, however:

1. Firstly, nothing I am writing is designed to argue against any path. It is purely to illuminate and consolidate information for the neophyte.
2. Secondly, this is a very rudimentary dissection. For example, there is more than just polytheism and monotheism and pantheism. There is henotheism and many other forms of theism as subsets of the first. I want to only talk about generalities so as not to confuse.

I want to add also that Satanism should not be confused with other forms of Occultism (e.g., paganism). They may have some similarities but are not the same. This means that the magickal workings of these groups, rules and codes do not apply in Satanic worship. Some pagan groups are, in fact, right-hand-path groups or white lighters so to speak.

Now let's talk about the core types of Satanism out there.

Philosophical Satanists

Many will be familiar with the works of Anton LaVey. LaVey is not the only style of philosophical satanism out there, but there are some fundamental ideologies core to this group who calls themselves satanic. LaVey's understanding of the world lead to the creation of the First Church of Satan, which is now run by LaVey's daughter.

- Philosophical satanists do not believe in the supernatural but may believe in forces of nature. This means Satan is not an actual deity to them, just a force of nature or a term used to describe the adversarial current or energies in the universe.
- These are more correctly referred to as Atheists and Nihilists. The Atheists do not believe there is any kind of deity in the universe outside of self (Humanism). Nihilists believe the same but do not believe that there is any hope.

- To a philosophical satanist, Satan is nothing more than a symbol of rebellion, indulgence, pleasure, liberation, and individualism.
- There is a tendency to believe in self over a higher being, and in man as an animal.
- Philosophical satanists typically do not engage in worship, only in hedonism.
- Notable practitioners of this path are (of course) Anton LaVey, First Church of Satan, Church of Satan, Blanche Barton, and Michael Aquino. If you are only interested gaining experience with an atheistic view, then follow the works of these individuals and groups.

Theistic Satanists

We refer to the theistic Satanists as those who are traditional or spiritual Satanists. Some believe that to be a Satanist you need to be part of a hereditary line where its traditions and core principles are handed down to them from generation to generation (Order of the Brotherhood of Satan for example). The other type of theistic Satanist, is the one we are most familiar with—they are the Satanist that simply believes in Satan the entity in some form or another (e.g., As Lucifer, Enki, Samael, Set, Satan, Azazel, The Shaitan, Ha-Satan, Iblis, and many other names and points of origin). This does not preclude the use of a variety of different representations. These stem from differing cultures which bear no relevance at all to the historical and theoretical underpinnings of the origins of Satan (another dichotomy that is not really for discussion in this book). Theistic Satanists, of course, worship Satan. This means their words and all their codes of magick refer to Satanic principles [23] and not to pagan or other codes.

Coincidentally, the Bible only mentions Satan (capital *S*) approximately thirteen times, but it mentions *satan* (lowercase *s*) many times. Lucifer is only mentioned once, and its ancient origins suggested it meant *the howling ones*,

---

[23] See Müller, Max. (1878) *Lectures on the Origin and Growth of Religion: As Illustrated by the Religions of India*. London: Longmans, Green and Co.

and this was an error in translation of the general vernacular as opposed to transliteration that occurs with the translation of proper names.

What's the difference? The Hebrew word *satan* simply means "those who are adverse or who oppose." This does not imply an evil entity in any way. In fact, by this definition most here in this group would be considered in biblical terms as Satanists. This is probably why Christians incorrectly lump everyone who isn't Christian into the same basket. Be careful you do not also fall into this trap as well.

There are several types of theist. They can be broken down into the main categories of Polytheistic, Pantheistic, Gnostic Satanists, and Monotheistic Satanists. As I indicated earlier, there are several types of theism such as henotheism, which covers other subtypes as depicted in the works of Muller. I do not want to take up your time and energy on these definitions at the present time as they can be confusing and are highly arguable. We will talk about three types of theist.[24]

The Polytheistic Satanist

Typically, the polytheist believes in a bunch of different Gods and Goddesses from Demonology (e.g., Ashtaroth, Belial, Lucifer, and so on). There is what can be termed as "soft" polytheistic. In other words, they believe all the key Demons are facets or personalities of Satan (e.g., the four crown princes of Hell). The other typology is the "hard" polytheistic who believe there is a hierarchy of separate Demons residing under the leadership and patronage of Satan.

The Pantheistic Satanist

This group believe that Satan is the creator of the world. He is a source of all good. You will find the following groups may be more aligned to this

---

[24] See Taliesin McKnight—Types of Satanism, 2011—http://www.youtube.com/watch?v=Qa8ojRC56gc accessed February 9, 2012.

style of Satanism—Diane Vera, Cathedral of the Black Goat, and Satanic Red, to name a few.

The Monotheistic Satanist

The monotheistic group believe in only a single entity and the creation of their own utopia under this code. Some of the groups under this banner could be the Temple of Set, for example (who were originally derived out of LaVeyanism). They believe Satan had his origination in Egyptian mythology. This is their view. They believe that Set becomes Satan under this system. They do not believe in evil and have a form of initiated order. Another group under this banner can be the Pagan Satanists and the Luciferians. In Luciferianism, Lucifer is not Satan and represents enlightenment, evolution of consciousness, Gnosis and wisdom. This group believe that Lucifer and Satan are two different entities. Some writers of this type who believe that Lucifer represents enlightenment and evolution of consciousness are Michael Ford (adversarial Luciferianism) and perhaps Order of the Serpent, who believe the origination of Satan is in Sumer, predating Christianity and Abrahamic faiths by several thousand years. The Cult of Cthulhu is another example of a monotheistic system of Satanic believe that is different to other forms of Satanism that is based on a notion first born out of the head of H. P. Lovecraft in his short story "The Call of Cthulhu."[25]

These are the main typologies of Theistic Satanism. There are other typologies to that bear mention, and these are those groups who serve the master of pseudo-political Theism. Joy of Satan Ministries is an example of this kind of group. They are Demonolaters with a pantheistic pathway but is considered by many other groups to be a smokescreen for hardcore right-wing fascism. This type of group is also called a war group. They are socially adversarial in nature but not necessarily in their teachings.

---

[25]   See H. P. Lovecraft, "The Call of Cthulhu" in *Weird Tales*, published 1928.

Gnostic Satanists

Gnosticism relates to gnosis, enlightenment, and wisdom. Gnosticism is where people believe that there is a God (in this case, Satan) and a demiurge (in this case, Yahweh). This is called dualism, wherein there is a God and a demiurge, or two equally powerful and opposing forces. Not all Satanists are Gnostic Satanists in that many do not believe in the existence of Yahweh (the Christian God).

The Acosmic Movement

This movement is backed by the Temple of the Black Light or the Misanthropic Luciferian Order. This form is also called Chaos-Gnosticism. The anticosmic movement centers around the notion that chaos is both (a) infinitely dimensional and (b) pan-dimensional. The cosmos is made up of three dimensions that include a time dimension. They believe chaos is timeless; therefore, the philosophy of Chaospy is born. This belief encompasses the idea that chaos is not one dimensional and is formless in a never-ending, ever-changing dimensional space.

Satan in this view is the embodiment of chaos and chaos Gods and the evil demiurge (the Christian God) that keeps people away from Satan *vis*-à-*vis* the truth. Satan is the orchestrator and manager of chaos. Satan/Lucifer is the savior who will enlighten you and guide you out of the restraints of the demiurge to finally cross into acosmic chaos. Chaos powers are the destroyers of causal structures and cosmic bonds.

Causal versus Acausal Movement

This movement is espoused by the Order of Nine Angles. The ONA believes that it is a sinister tradition. It claims Satanism and the Left-Hand Path are causal forms. This means that they believe that challenges are used to aid the practitioner in spiritual development. It is a partly a Hermetic order and partly Theistic Satanist order with an admixture of Paganism in its path. Causal means acting as a cause. Acausal means no set rules and not linked to causality. They believe that Satan cannot be controlled and exists with other beings on an acausal continuum. The cosmos exists as a function of both the causal and acausal continuum. We cannot control the acausal but are kin to it because we have our own acausal energy.

All in all, categorization is difficult. So which is right? Well, I believe your spiritual development goes through stages. You might find at one time you may be warmed to polytheism, but you may evolve spiritually into another faith form. This is not uncommon as you gain knowledge, experience, and grow beyond what you have learned. Do not be dismissive of all these different typologies. Be aware that they exist and choose what is right for you now based on where your meditations and guidance from Father Satan lead you.

Reactive Satanism

I must mention this here because it is something that everyone has seen in society, and that is reactive Satanism. This form of Satanism is also called adolescent Satanism, where groups of youth and others formulate a basis for perceived Satanic behaviors as based on the biblical archetype of Satan and the reverse Christianity paradigm. This can be seen in groups like heavy-metal music fans circa 1968 and on, horror-movie enthusiasts, role players, the gothic subculture, and various gangs of youth.

Transcendental Satanism

This group formed as a result of its leader experiencing a dream after a session with LSD. This group believe that they are seeking ascension with a view to being reintegrated with their inner Satanic aspect. The Satanic aspect is a concealed part of the self that is distinct from consciousness. Believers can find their way to self by following a discretely formulated path.

Satan as a Front for Politics

The Satanic Reds formed a coalition that was based on the communist philosophy. Other groups like Joy of Satan Ministries and Order of Nine Angles have political agendas as well, in that they are based on fascist ideology. While these groups exist, they are largely shunned by the Satanic community. In the next section we will look at a dedication rite to Satan.

Dedication Rite to Satan

It is fitting at this point to briefly discuss what a dedication rite to Satan looks like. Note that dedicating your life to Satan is not selling your soul. He does not want your soul; he asks for your dedication.

What You Need

- a black candle
- a sterile needle
- a piece of paper
- a pen
- some incense (frankincense, myrrh, patchouli, sandalwood)
- a heat-resistant pot

Preparation

- Bathe in hyssop and saltwater.
- Meditate quietly for a few minutes.
- Light your candle and your incense.
- Write on the paper the following petition:

Before the immense Satan, I, (state your full name), renounce any and all past loyalties. I proclaim Satan as my one and only God. I promise to recognize and honor him in all things, without reservation, desiring in return, his manifold assistance in the successful completion of my goals.

- Prick your finger and place three droplets of blood on the paper and sign it.
- Recite the prayer out loud.
- Burn the prayer in the heat-resistant pot.
- Meditate until the candle burns down.

In conclusion, you can see that there is a wide array of mainstream as well as unconventional ideologies within the Satanic community. This chapter is meant to help the reader understand these groups with a view to navigating through them. Indeed, there are as many flavors of Satanism as there are Christian denominations and your choice is not an easy one.

The next chapter will place emphasis on Luciferianism and the different ideologies that exist within that paradigm. Luciferianism differs greatly to Satanism and should be viewed as a largely different group.

CHAPTER 2

Luciferianism

Lucifer is mentioned once in the Bible and the Tahnak.[26] In Hebrew, Lucifer translates into *Hêlêl ben Shachar*, which means literally "the Shining Son of Dawn" or "Venus." In earlier texts, Lucifer was lucifer with a little "l" and meant the *"howling ones."* This word was included in its lowercase form only and was, in fact, not a pronoun. In Greek mythology, Lucifer translates into **Phosphorus,** or **Eosphoros, and is analogous with the morning star, or Venus. The figure of Phosphorus is depicted as bearing a torch.** In mythology, Lucifer was cast down to Earth and shared his knowledge with mankind. Thus, he became the bearer of light. This is paralleled in Canaanite mythology and later in Greek mythology, where Prometheus came to Earth to share fire with man.

There is a group of scholars who believe that Lucifer predates Christianity. The earliest rendering could have been the God Attar in Canaanite mythology. Attar translates into Ashtar, who was depicted as Venus in the morning aspect. Attar was a warrior God who rebelled against Baal by believing that he could rule in Baal's stead. He was cast down and ordered to rule the underworld. Through this story, it is postulated that the Jews and Christians appropriated the legend and placed it in the Bible and made Lucifer analogous with Satan. Next, we will look at theistic Luciferianism.

---

[26] See Isaiah 14:12.

Theistic Luciferianism is a Gnostic religion where Lucifer is the original demiurge to Yahweh. Some believe Satan and Lucifer to be the same being. This is partially right, they are the same, but they are also different entities. Authors like Michael W. Ford refer to these facets as deific masks.[27] This is ultimately where one being has different facets or personalities to the other or in other words, each Demon is a differing facet of Lucifer. It is also believed that Samael is Satan. From a biblical point of view, they are the same entity.[28] Whether you are of the belief that they are different or the same will depend on if you are a hard or soft polytheist. Most theistic Luciferians, however, just believe in Lucifer as a single archetype who is effectively a liberator of mankind through the sharing of knowledge.

Luciferians, by default, acknowledge and worship Lucifer or knowledge and enlightenment. They do not necessarily recognize Satan as a deity or even acknowledge Lucifer as the Devil. There are three types of Luciferian, those who believe in the dark and adversarial energies, as adapted from Jewish and Islamic mysticism. The second type believe that Lucifer was God's most beautiful angel (similar to the Yezidis with Melek Taus). As the Bible says, he was an angel of light, the bearer of light.[29] Light is all about knowledge and learning and not about darkness and ignorance. The third type is the Atheistic Luciferian that believes in the betterment of the world and mankind through science and technology, self-enlightenment and self-deification. This group is a dichotomy that can be either Prometheans/Lilithians or Atheistic Luciferians.

As you have been reading, Luciferians and Satanists are two different beasts. I prefer to think of it as Satanists worshipping the hedonistic side of nature and Luciferians worshipping the more aesthetic side of nature. There are really several points on which they differ however (refer to table 1 below):

---

[27] See Michael W Ford, (2017) *Fallen Angels: Watchers and the Witches Sabbat*, Succubus Productions, Houston.
[28] See Isaiah 14:12, Luke 10:18, Ezekiel 28.
[29] See Isaiah 14:12

Table 1—Differences between Satanism and Luciferianism

• Satanism believes in reveling in the carnality and materiality of the world. The focus is on survival and self-preservation in the here and now.	• Luciferianism seeks to rise above carnality as it is the philosophical attainment of knowledge and inner power.
• Satanists revere Satan over Lucifer and see Lucifer just as one of the four crown princes of hell.[30]	• Luciferians worship the demiurge Lucifer as the whole or all, or at least the idea of him.
• Satanists just enjoy their lives and do not necessarily strive for ascension.	• Luciferians believe in enjoying their lives but believe that there is more beyond this and rise above materiality to seek spiritual ascension.
• Satanists see Lucifer and Satan as separate beings.	• Luciferians see Satan and Lucifer as different facets of the same being.
• Satanists are by and large anti-Christian in their outlook.	• Luciferians believe that Satanists focus too much on being anti-Christian in their outlook even though this does not apply to all Satanists.

Theistic Luciferians

As the Bible mentions, Lucifer was there at the time of creation and fell out with God and was cast down to Earth because he believed he could be equal to God and because he would not bow down to Adam.[31] He was not

---

[30] See Ephesians 2:2 where Lucifer was declared as prince of the power of the air.
[31] See Isaiah 14:12–15 and Revelations 12:7–9.

the Serpent in the Garden of Eden, this was not conclusively indicated in the scriptures, but he was used by God to test his believers.

Theistic Luciferians believe in striving for longevity, beauty, artistry, spiritual enlightenment, and the passing on of wisdom. They believe strongly in the higher self and attainment to greater spiritual gnosis. They are masters of energy work, psychic manipulation, and meditation, and are gentle, law-abiding people who do not practice any kind of violence.

Gnostic Luciferianism

Gnostic Luciferians believe in a range of differing left-hand path traditions. First and foremost, they believe that Lucifer is, in fact, a real deity and that there was a God who created the divine spark within each of us. They also believe in dualism in that that Lucifer is the rebel demiurge who sought to illuminate mankind with knowledge and who shattered the cosmic order of things. This is mixed with other traditions including modern esotericism and Thelema (the Neo-Luciferian Church and Fraternitas Saturni are examples of this).

Yezidis

While not Luciferians, the Yezidis bear a mention here because many believe the Yezidis to be like modern-day Luciferians and devil worshippers. However, they most certainly are not. There are some similarities in the stories that the Qur'an tells but they are merely coincidental, and I will explain why.

The Yezidis are common to the northern Iraq, Syria, and southeastern Turkey regions. They are both an ethnicity and a religion called Sharfadin. It is a monotheistic religion that worships Melek Taus (the peacock angel). The Yezidis believe in a kind of trinity just like in Christianity. They believe that there is a God but that he is distant from the world; that there is a ruler for this world (Melek Taus, an archangel) who was created out of the illumination of God. They also believe that their founder, Sheikh Adî, is the manifestation or reincarnation of Melek Taus. These three facets are what constitute the Godhead in Yezidi religion.

Melek Taus fell from the sky after he refused to bow down to Adam, and consequently, this is where the belief that Melek Taus is Lucifer came from. However, in Yezidi tradition, it is believed that God made him ruler over all men. The only group who were believed to have recognized Melek Taus were the Yezidis. The Yezidis believed they were the direct descendants of Adam (and not Eve). It was believed that Adam and Eve were encouraged to place their reproductive fluids into a jar for several months in order to reproduce themselves without intimacy. It was then said that Eve's fluid turned to insects and that Adam's fluids turned into a baby called Shehid bin Jer—the true descendant of Adam.

There is debate among the religious communities in the east about whether Melek Taus is Iblis or Shaitan because of the story where Melek Taus refused to bow down to Adam and was therefore cast down to earth. Many believe Melek Taus fell from God's grace. However, this is not the case as in the Yezidi story, Melek Taus was tested by God by seeing if he would bow to Adam after being instructed not to bow to anything in creation. This has caused the Yezidis to be persecuted by Muslims because they believed the Yezidis were engaging in devil worship, which they were not.

Atheistic Luciferians

Atheistic Luciferians exist as three main typologies, there are others, but they are small isolated groups that do not really bear mention here. The three main typologies are as follows:

1. Adversarial Luciferians
2. Prometheans
3. Lilithians

Atheistic Luciferians believe in working toward ascension through self-deification. They do not believe that Lucifer is an actual being but more of an archetype on which they can model themselves. The primary aim of the Luciferian is to strive to challenge oneself for self-betterment.

Adversarial Luciferians

Adversarial Luciferians believe that Lucifer, the bringer of light, is the adversary. They are against to concept of a "God" and organized religion and the sheep like following of such a "God."

The adversarial path is an initiatory system. Adversarial Luciferians can be Gnostic as well but are generally atheistic. Atheistic Adversarial Luciferians believe that Lucifer and the Demons are merely an archetype for self-driven ascension of the mind and worship of the self purely by will.

The Adversarial Luciferians believe in the adversarial current of the Qliphoth (see the chapter on the Qliphoth). This is based on the Sephirot tree often used in Jewish mysticism. They also believe that even if you believe in spirits you are accountable to yourself for the fulfilling of any work that you do. The schooling of the mind to accept oneself as a deity means you are freeing yourself of spirituality. Some organizations that are adversarial include the Order of Phosphorus, Temple of the Ascending Flame and the Greater Church of Lucifer.

Lilithians

Lilithians accept Lilith as the bringer of knowledge, feminism, and independence and they are closely aligned to Luciferianism. Lilith was first seen in Sumerian mythology (Lilitu) and was a Demon of the night who stole babies and who attacked men in their sleep, sexually draining them of power—the first succubus. Lilith is also believed to have existed before Eve as the first wife of Adam (according to rabbinic texts) where she produced children to Adam who were said to be Demons and was then thought later to be the wife of Samael.[32]

---

[32]   See the Talmud—Shabbat151a.

Lilith in the Occult is seen as the first mother. As such, she is seen as a teacher divine, and her link to the Qliphoth suggests she is pivotal in understanding the workings of the dark flame within us (see the chapter on the Qliphoth).

Many groups of Luciferians work with Lilith as do Satanists and Demonolaters. However, there are groups that exclusively take on Lilith as the archetype by which they model themselves, for example the Temple of Lilith.

Prometheans

Prometheus was a Titan who stole fire in defiance of Zeus, to bring it to the inhabitants of earth. His name in Greek means "forethought." He has been heralded as the bringer of knowledge and enlightenment. The story of Prometheus almost has Christ-like qualities in that Prometheus stole the fire to illuminate mankind and was punished by Zeus by being chained to a pillar and having his liver pecked out by carnivorous birds. The sun would rise, and the next day, Prometheus would be back on the pillar fully restored only for it to happen all over again. Here, we see that Prometheus dies and rises again, giving himself as a sacrifice for the people of Earth. Heracles kills the carnivorous birds and delivers Prometheus to Zeus.

Prometheans deal with the question "Where is God?" and "How can we enlighten mankind through science, technology, philosophy, and theosophy and other psychosocial factors?" While they are Luciferian in typology, they are not necessarily Luciferian in practice or theosophy.

The Luciferian community is somewhat smaller than the Satanic. However, there are just as many divisions as with the Satanic community. The Luciferian community, like the Satanic community, is divided between theism and nontheism. There are branches that strictly don't belong to the community such as Prometheans but despite this they fall under the Luciferian umbrella if that makes sense? Next, we will look at a dedication rite to Lucifer.

Rite to Lucifer

- Face your altar to the east.
- Draw a circle with salt.
- Place a white candle at each elemental point.
- Invoke the elemental Demons (see appendix B—Dedication Rite to a Patron/Matron Demon) working in a clockwise fashion. Leave Lucifer until last.
- Burn sandalwood incense for effect.
- Anoint each candle with the oil of Lucifer (carnations, cinnamon, or clove oil, musk oil, patchouli oil, vanilla oil, all mixed on a Thursday in the hour of Jupiter).
- Light the candles in a clockwise fashion, leaving Lucifer to last.
- Carrying an incense burner and a ritual dagger, approach each point and kneel, reciting Lucifer's enn (Renich Tasa Uberaca Biasa Icar Lucifer).
- Wave the dagger through the smoke.
- Invite the fifth element Satan from the center of the circle.
- Kneel at the altar and pray to Lucifer something like this:

> *"I pray thee, Lucifer, bestow upon me the strength of your enterprise. Your light shall be my defense and guide me through this life. I humbly pay homage to thee in my offer of incense that you may know my respect for your vast strength. I offer requests of knowledge and reflection that I may engage your creation to do so. Hail, Lucifer, Lord and Master of Air."*

- Requests of concentration, knowledge, intellect and purification are burned at the altar in a fireproof bowl.
- Crush the ashes to a fine powder.
- The ritual is closed thusly: "Hail, Lucifer, Lord and Master of Air. We thank thee for being present at our ritual. We bid you go in peace."
- Disperse the ashes into the wind.

This rite to Lucifer is for the theistic Luciferian to dedicate oneself to Lucifer.

In conclusion, many Luciferian typologies were discussed here. Not all of them have a religious association to them. Some are by far largely about science and technology while few others seek to honor Lilith or Prometheus. The next chapter discusses Demonolatry in its varying forms. Demonolatry is the love and worship of Demons and is a lot older than Satanism and Luciferianism. Each Demon is viewed as a separate entity that assists the practitioner in rituals and magic.

CHAPTER 3

Demonolatry

D emonolatry is a unique area in the left-hand path. It constitutes the worship of Demons. Demonolatry is not to be confused with Demonology, which is the Christian study of Demons. Demonolatry believes primarily that Demons are a misunderstood group of entities that are largely benevolent and that worship of these through the Patron/Matron system assist the practitioner in magick and celebratory rites, like invocation.

Demonolatry is a polytheistic ideology that forward the idea that several entities termed as "Demons" are in fact the old Gods. The etymology of the word is as follows:

- The original word was in Greek, and it was *Daimon.*
- In Latin, it was *Daemon.*
- In middle English, the word changed to become *Demon.*

In Latin, the word means "divinity, guiding spirit, tutelary, and genius." It was not until circa 1200 that the word became synonymous with "evil spirits" because of the change into old English where the word came to mean "evil spirit," no doubt brought on by the church. Demonolatry is all about self-authorization or self-empowerment. This statement encapsulates Demonolatry nicely, the "whole" referring to Satan but not in the same way that Satanists of Luciferians may view him, as to demonolaters, Satan represents the "all."

The Demonolatry typologies are based on the different pantheons of Demons that are followed. These can include the following:

- Goetic Demonocracy, or those believing in the Demons of the Solomonic grimoires (but not through evocation, through invocation only)
- Khemetic Demonocracy, or those believing in the Gods of ancient Egypt as the Demons of this Demonocracy
- Dukanté Demonocracy **(1963),** which is a highly debated hierarchy developed by Richard Dukanté and pulled from a variety of other mythologies
- Collin De Plancy's *Dictionaire Infernale* (1863)
- Sir William Fletcher Barrett's *The Magus* (1801)
- Grimoire of Pope Honorius III (1600s)
- Johan Weyer's *Hierarchy of Hell* (1515–1588)
- Sebastien Michaelis's *Histoire admirable de la Possession et conversion d'une penitente* (1613)
- Peter Binsfeld's *Demons of the Seven Deadly Sins* (1589)

Demonolatry is largely Hermetic in its origins in that it encompasses the ancient occult traditions of alchemy, astrology and theosophy. Demonolatry is older than Christianity, starting around 3000 BC.

There are two types of demonolaters, the first being the theistic demonolaters who believe that Demons are real entities. There is some crossover here with Satanism and Luciferianism in that some Satanists and Luciferians are demonolaters. However, not all demonolaters are Satanists and Luciferians. Satan is considered to be the "fifth element," or the ALL, or a cosmos of all energies. Some of this group are generational in that the knowledge of Demonolatry has been passed down from generation to generation. The second group are termed modern demonolaters who believe that Demons are pure energy forces that assist in spiritual growth and magick. This is somewhat similar in approach to the nontheistic Satanists and Luciferians who study Lucifer and Satan as representations rather than entities.

Demonolaters choose to work with one specific Demon over the course of their practice. This is called having a Matron/Patron Demon. Generally, this comes to you through gnosis of some sort or via varying forms of divinatory practice. Other Demons become tributary to the Matron/Patron Demon.

Demonolaters practice invocation over evocation, believing that Demons cannot be controlled or forced to appear to do the magicians bidding.

- Invocation: Basically, this means prayer or petitioning. In the case of Demonolatry this is done using enns as tools to call forth Demons. Enns are basically sentences written in Demonic. The first enns were seen in the works of Demonolater Alexander Willit in AD 1585.[33] Their origins are otherwise unclear, but they have remained unchanged across groups that work with them.

- Evocation: To call forth by commanding or by means of control. A good example of this is from the Solomonic grimoires where the triangle of art is used to call forth a Demon and trap it. This is considered to be somewhat disrespectful to demonolaters.

Next, we will discuss finding your patron/matron demon and the differences between the patron/matron, mentor, and guardian. A patron/matron stays with you constantly and a mentor comes to teach you something then goes again. Guardians speak for themselves but largely provide the practitioner with extra protection and support. Lucifer and Satan can be guardians but cannot be patrons. With a patron you will feel drawn to them. The same goes with a mentor and a guardian. You can work with a patron/matron and many mentors at the same time. The choice of patron/matron is a very personal thing and your chosen patron/matron should offer you balance.

My Patron came to me during meditation. I have also worked with Gamigin, Haures, and Orobas recently as mentors. Haures and Orobas were teachers I was drawn to for about five years, and I worked with them successfully. Gamigin came to me in a dream after meditating on sigils in July 2018. A sigil is an inscribed symbol considered to have magickal properties. Each Demon has their own sigil. The standard Goetic sigils in

---

[33] See appendix C—Demon Correspondences

this book are from the *Ars Goetia*. They allow practitioners to focus on the energy of the entity that they are working with. Sigils are sometimes encircled to represent Satan's all-encompassing energies.

There are several ways to acquire a Patron/Matron:

- You will feel drawn to them.
- Meditation on sigils.
- Life symbols like dreams and omens.
- Divination—some people use pendulums to work out who to follow.
- Asking the entity in person while undertaking invocation.
- Knowing your element via a natal chart, so for example if you are a fire sign with a rising in an air sign but are highly creative you might consider Belphegor or Flereous—see the table below for more ideas on matching a Demon to your sign. You must know what each Demon does before you assign yourself to them, so it doesn't hurt to do a little research. See Correspondences.

Once you have chosen your patron/matron, you should do a dedication rite to them in order to complete the process. See appendix B—Dedication Rite to a Patron/Matron Demon for a commitment rite.

Table 2—Demons by Zodiac

Sign	Demon
Aries *March 20—April 20* *Fire*	• Agares (Earth) • Bael (Fire) • Halphas (Fire) • Malphas (Air) • Marbas (Air) • Phenex (Fire) • Vassago (Water)
Taurus *April 21—May 21* *Earth*	• Focalor (Water) • Gamigin (Water) • Raum (Air) • Valefor (Earth) • Vepar (Water)

Sign	Demon
Gemini *May 22—June 21* *Air*	• Amon (Water) • Andrealphus (Air) • Barbatos (Fire) • Paimon (Water) • Sabnock (Fire) • Shax (Air) • Vine (Water)
Cancer *June 22—July 23* *Water*	• Aim (Fire) • Bifrons (Earth) • Buer (Fire) • Gusion (Water) • Haagenti (Earth) • Sitri (Earth) • Uvall (Water)
Leo *July 24—Aug 23* *Fire*	• Balam (Earth) • Beleth (Earth) • Crocell (Water) • Eligos (Water) • Furcus (Air) • Leraje (Fire)
Virgo *Aug 24—Sept 23* *Earth*	• Alloces (Fire) • Bathin (Earth) • Botis (Water) • Camio (Fire) • Marchosias (Fire) • Murmur (Fire) • Zepar (Earth)
Libra *Air* *Sept 24—Oct 23*	• Gremory (Water) • Marax (Earth) • Orobas (Water) • Ose (Air) • Purson (Earth)
Scorpio *Oct 24—Nov 22* *Water*	• Amy (Fire) • Ipos (Water) • Naberius (Fire) • Orias (Air) • Vapula (Air)

Sign	Demon
Sagittarius *Nov 23—Dec 21* *Fire*	• Bune (Earth) • Glasya-Labolas (Fire) • Ronove (Air) • Volac (Earth) • Zagan (Earth)
Capricorn *Dec 22—Jan 20* *Earth*	• Astaroth (Earth) • Berith (Fire) • Cimejes (Earth) • Forneus (Water) • Haures (Fire)
Aquarius *Jan 21—Feb 19* *Air*	• Amducius (Air) • Andras (Air) • Belial (Fire) • Decarabia (Air) • Foras (Earth) • Gaap (Air)
Pisces *Feb 20—March 20* *Water*	• Andromalius (Fire) • Dantalion (Water) • Furfur (Fire) • Seere (Fire) • Stolas (Air)

Moving forward, we will look at the basics of Demonolatry practice. You can split Demonolatry practice into two sections, religious practice and that of magick. The religious practice includes invocation or prayer, worship, and celebration. The holidays are designed to get the practitioner closer to the Demons worshipped. There seems to be different holidays depending on the pantheon you follow.[34] In addition to these holidays, the Demonolater would include a holiday for their Matron/Patron Demon. In addition to these holidays, there are other days that are used to celebrate:

- marriages
- funerals
- initiatory rites

---

[34] See Connolly S., *The Complete Book of Demonolatry*, USA, 2006.

- rites that are a result of pacts
- prayers for self-empowerment

It is like any other religion that honors its Gods and Goddesses and partakes in celebrations of life events. For a list of possible Goetic holidays consult with appendix C—Demon Correspondences. Next, we will discuss demonolatry in relation to hermeticism.

To understand demonolatry, you need to understand hermeticism and its tenets. Hermeticism is a set of religious philosophies that combine the use of alchemy, magick, and astrology. It is based on the works of Hermes Trismegistus, which is thought to be an amalgam between Hermes and Thoth. Hermeticism is very old and has existed since late antiquity. It is thought to have first emerged in Alexandria where it was thought to draw together Judaism, Christianity, Hellenic philosophy as astrology, and ancient Egyptian religious beliefs in terms of magic. These writings were of great influence in the Renaissance and the Reformation and had a lot of influence on modern Western esotericism. The primary characteristic of Hermeticism is the search for hidden wisdom and knowledge and that the cosmos existed as a series of vibrations of the "All."

The three pillars of Hermeticism are called the three parts of wisdom of the whole universe:

Alchemy—the operation of the Sun where there is the transmutation of metals into gold.

1. Astrology—the operation of the Moon where the movement of the planets have a meaning beyond physics.
2. Theurgy—the operation of the Stars where there are two different types of magick that are opposites of which alchemy is the basis:
   - Demonolatry—magick using Demons.
   - Theurgy which is magic, in the case of demonolatry, using Demons and Demonic powers.

The aim of theurgy is to gain unification with the universal "All" through ascension and gnosis.

Classical beliefs in Hermeticism are basically as follows:

1. Ultimate Reality—where everything is mental (idealism) or real (materialism). All entities are vibrations in ultimate reality, such that the only difference between different states of physical matter, mentality, and spirituality is the frequency of their vibration. The higher the vibration, the further it is from primal matter.
2. The Elements—earth, air, fire, water, and spirit.
3. Reincarnation—the possibility that there is life after death.
4. Morality—the dichotomy of good versus evil is central to Hermeticism.
5. As Above So Below—whatever happens in the cosmos also happens in the material plane.
6. The Creation Legend—the basic elements emanated from the "All."

So how does all this link into Demonolatry? See table 3—Demonolatry and Hermeticism below.

Table 3—Demonolatry and Hermeticism

Hermeticism	Demonolatry
• **Alchemy**	• Alchemy is used in the creation of oleums and in the use of oleums in ritual magic. Plus, in the transmutation of energy.
• **Theurgy**	• Not groveling to Demons, but it is working with them to honor them and find enlightenment and self-actualization through ascension and gnosis.
• **Astrology**	• Astrology is used in the creation of rituals and magic.
• **Ultimate Reality**	• Demonolaters believe that they are working toward the ultimate ascension through gnosis, to the "All."
• **The Elements**	• The practice of Demonolatry magick and ritual is based on elemental magick.

Hermeticism	Demonolatry
• **Reincarnation**	• This is an individual belief that people either believe or disregard.
• **Morality**	• The theurgy component is based on Demonolatry and the worship of Demons and their use in magick practice.
• **As Above So Below**	• As Above So Below, As Within So Without.
• **The Creation Legend**	• The emanation of vibrations from the "All" is the basis of the creation of the cosmos.

As Demonolatry is a hermetic practice the magickal practice involves elemental magic, spell work, alchemy and divination. The Demonolatry magickal practices happen strictly within the confines of a rite or ritual. They use circles not for protection, but to balance energies. You can see an example below in figure 1—Balanced Elemental Circle. Appendix B—Dedication Rite to a Patron/Matron Demon shows how to create a balanced elemental circle.

Figure 1—Balanced Elemental Circle

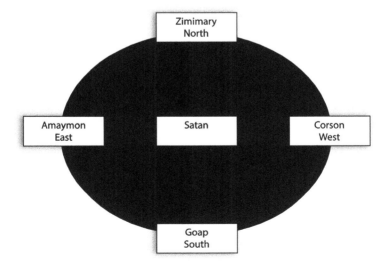

Demonolaters practice varying forms of magick that include the following:

- Planetary magick—using planetary alignments and planetary hours to cast spells and do rituals. Each Demon has its own planetary alignment, cardinal point and astrological sign (see appendix C—Demon Correspondences). Also, most invocation is tied to a moon phase that is linked to full and dark moon correspondences.
- Elemental magick—the elements being fire, water, air, earth, and spirit. Each Demon has its own element that is used in altar facing and ritual.
- Using oleums—these are special oils made by the Demonolater to dress candles and sometimes to imbibe for magickal practice. They are generally made from herbs, roots, and carrier oils.
- Sigil magick—the creation and use of Demonic sigils and personal sigils. Sigils are an inscribed or painted symbol considered to have magickal power. See the chapter on Sigil magic. Sigils are burned after use to empower the ritual request and as an offering to Demons. The sigil is usually prepped with a few drops of the demonolaters blood or sexual fluid to make it more powerful.
- Blood magick—use of one's own blood without sacrifice to give magick special empowerment and meaning. This is done in the least negative way possible.
- Lucid Dreaming, out-of-body experiences and astral-travel magic. See the chapter on meditation and energy manipulation.
- Power meditation and energy manipulation. See the chapter on power meditation and energy manipulation.
- Servitor creation, where a servitor (also called an egregore, thought form, or tulpa) is a being created by using powerful energy to be used for a special purpose such as protection.
- Sex magick—use of one's sexual fluids and the energy created by arousal and orgasm to attain magickal goals.
- Execration magick also referred to colloquially as "dume," hexing, baneful magic, fulmination, imprecation, or cursing. This is not taken lightly and is generally done only under special circumstances.

- Necromantic practices such as working with or talking to the dead to achieve a magickal goal.
- Some demonolaters even practice sympathetic and intuitive magick as well using other pathways such as Hoodoo although this is not common.
- Divination using scrying mirrors, stones, cards, pendulums, and Ouija boards. See the chapter on divination.
- Blessing and cursing of objects or using tag locks (like hair and nails or an object belonging to another that has significance).

In conclusion Demonolatry as a practice and as a school of magick has been on the rise over the last few years. This could be due to the proliferation of reading materials generated by Demonolatry authors like S. Connolly, William Briar, and J. Thorp. this is also because of the explosion of the internet. Demonolatry as a practice is being incorporated into most mainstream left-hand path practices, including Satanism and Luciferianism. The next chapter looks at mythology and the role that mythology has played in the occult today.

CHAPTER 4

Mythology and Its Role
in the Occult Today

Theis chapter discusses several types of mythology that have been blended into modern-day occult practices. These include Sumerian, Canaanite, Jewish, and Egyptian mythologies. Each of these will have a cursory discussion in this chapter.

Sumerian or Akkadian Mythology

The use of Sumerian mythology has become an accepted part of the Occult over recent years, especially in the practice of theistic Satanism. The many legends that follow in Sumerian mythology that vary widely from region to region. During Mesopotamian history, however, there are parallels that can be drawn between the modern-day depictions of Satan and the ancient Mesopotamian and Babylonian counterparts that were taken by Christianity and adapted for biblical inclusion. Many of the deities in the Sumerian pantheon, and there are many, were deemed to be Demonic by modern Christians, but in fact, they are just spirits that were worshipped by the Sumerians.

Some believe that Enki is Satan. They reject the typical name of Satan as a biblical representation of the deity and choose to adopt Enki because it predates the history of the Bible and is the earliest recorded history of mankind. There is a large body of work that stretches from 1854 until now that attempts to support this theory.[35] However, it is worth noting here that these theories are equally disputed because of translation issues and other factors, such as overlapping mythologies.

Enki was the demiurge in Sumerian mythology and was pitted against his half-brother Enlil, who was the king of Gods. Enki was the God of wisdom, mischief, crafts, and fresh water who lived at the bottom of the oceans. He is the God of magick and defeated his grandfather Apsû and created the Earth people. Enki was in the story of the Great Flood, where he saved mankind by telling Atrahasis to build an ark before the waters rose.

Enki is thought to mean "Lord of the Earth," *En* meaning "Lord" and *Ki* meaning "Earth."[36] There is some dispute over the origins of Enki. Some believe he is a Semitic deity, and others still believe he is purely Mesopotamian. Enlil created the Mesopotamian equivalent of Eden and then created man. It is thought that Enki was the serpent in the Garden of Eden because the word for Snake is *nahash* which means "to decipher" or "find out." Hence, it is believed to be Enki, God of Wisdom. Enki and Enlil forge human alliances, and the result is a war between Enki's people and Enlil's people around 2000 BCE. Enki's people being the Egyptians and others and Enlil's people being the Semitic tribes. The war between Enlil and Enki was of epic proportions. Enlil was responsible for the following:

- originating the Semitic invasion of the other races
- causing the "confusion of tongues" which destroyed Sumer
- causing the Sodom and Gomorrah story
- bringing on the great flood

Enki has aspects, one of which is Dagon/Dagan (Zagan in later mythology)—a half-man, half-fish God. The representation of the essence of human DNA (sperm), fertility, and sexual strength. He was thought to be the father of Baal (Hadad) in Canaanite mythology. See the discussion below on Canaanite mythology. Dagon is mentioned several times in the Bible.[37]

---

[35] See http://voiceofsatanism.com/2010/09/21/origins-of-satanism-why-sumeria/.
[36] See https://en.wikipedia.org/wiki/Enki.
[37] See Judges 16:23, 1 Samuel 5, 1 Chronicles 10:10, I Maccabees 10:83b–84.

Marduk (Enki's son) was thought to later replace Enlil in the Babylonian mythology. Next, we will take a look at the creation story in Babylonian mythology.

The Enûma Eliš and the Babylonian Point of View

The *Enûma Eliš* was a series of seven tablets that outline the creation story from the Babylonian point of view. They are freely available on the internet to read and quote the creation story something like this:

Tablet 1—Apsû and Tiamat partner to create the first Gods. Lahmu and Lahamu were created. Then, next, Anshar and Kishar were created. From Anshar came Anu. From Anu came EA or Nudimmud. The new Gods disturbed Tiamat. Mummu advised Tiamat to kill them, but she was loathe to. EA composes a spell to halt this after discovering what was going on. EA puts Apsû to sleep. EA took Apsû's halo and claimed Mummu. EA slays Apsû. Tiamat creates eleven chimeric creatures with weapons to battle the Gods. Tiamat creates Kingu the God King. The tablet of destinies is given to Kingu to make his power unchallengeable.

Tablet 2—EA hears of Tiamat's plan for revenge and talks to Anshar. Anshar tells Anu to speak to Tiamat to calm her, but it doesn't work. Anshar proposes Marduk be the champion of the Gods against Tiamat.

Tablet 3—Anshar speaks to his advisor and asks him to fetch Lahmu and Lahamu. Anshar tells Lahmu and Lahamu the story of Tiamat's plans. Lahmu and Lahamu enter into a contract with Marduk.

Tablet 4—Marduk is given a throne, vestments, scepter, and weapons with which to fight Tiamat. Marduk sets a trap using the four winds to trap Tiamat. Tiamat becomes enraged by the trap and the accusations leveled at her by Marduk regarding Kingu being her consort. Marduk uses a net from Anu to try and trap Tiamat. Tiamat tries to swallow Marduk, but the evil wind enters her mouth and stops this. Marduk fires his arrow and slays Tiamat. Marduk splits Tiamat into two halves. From one half, he makes the sky. He makes places for Enlil, Anu, and EA to reside.

Tablet 5—Marduk makes constellations in the sky for the Gods as likenesses. Marduk creates night and day. Marduk gives the tablets of destiny to Anu.

Tablet 6—Marduk uses Kingu's blood (from the sacrifice of Kingu) to create man. Marduk divides the Gods into "above" and "below." Marduk is then given titles.

Tablet 7—This tablet is dedicated to reading the titles given to Marduk.

Tiamat the Dragon Queen is the Goddess of creation and the chaos of the primordial abyss. She mated with Apsû to create other Gods in Sumerian mythology, and she features prominently in both Sumerian and Babylonian mythologies and has parallels in Canaanite and Semitic mythology as well. She is worshipped by Satanists, Luciferians, and demonolaters alike.

The primary objective of the Black Flame is to ascend back into the womb of Tiamat in the primordial abyss. The primordial abyss within us is the Sitra Ahra, the opposite side to holiness (the Sefirot) within the Qliphoth of the Kabbalah. The next section will look at Lilith, another important figure in the occult.

While Lilith is not an archetype for Satan, she is worshipped by Satanists, Luciferians, and demonolaters alike. Lilith in Sumerian history was the daughter of the underworld Gods Nergal and Eresh-Kjgal and handmaiden to Inanna. Lilith belonged to a class of female Demons called Lilitu. Lilith was the Demon of the night and known for being a Succubus and stealing babies, according to Sumerian mythology. She is later translated into Semitic mythology, where she became the first wife of Adam. She refused to become subservient to Adam and was thus cast aside and became the consort of Samael. Lilith is a far cry from these archetypes in modern worship where she is seen as the doyen for independence among women.

Many of the key figures of the occult stemmed from Akkadian mythology and are still worshipped today. The next section will look at Jewish mythology.

Jewish Mythology

Jewish mythology is close to our understanding of what Satan is today. Both Satan (as Samael) and Lilith carry across from Sumerian mythology into Semitic mythology. This was of course borrowed by Christians, who incorporated Samael as Satan into biblical references. Samael (the poison of God) is important in Talmudic and post-Talmudic literature as the dreaded ha-Satan, who seduces and destroys mankind with the permission of YWHW. Samael was the angel of death responsible for bringing souls to account before YWHW. He is also thought to entice people into sin. Samael had as his consorts, Eisheth Zenunim, Na'amah, Lilith, and Agrat bat Mahlat.

This is a simplistic look at Jewish mythology, but again, you see the key characters emerging, changed through history. The next section will look at Canaanite mythology.

Canaanite Mythology

In Canaanite mythology, you have Baal and the Philistine Beelzebub, Lord of the Flies. Both are worshipped as Demons in modern-day Demonolatry. Beelzebub was depicted by Christian Demonologists as one of the seven crown princes of Hell. In ancient Philistine mythology, Beelzebub was the God of the city known as Ekron. Beelzebub is associated with Baal. Baal was a collective term for many Gods that meant "Lord." There were several Gods in Canaanite mythology that had the prefix name of Baal. It wasn't until later that the Jewish peoples adopted a mythos concerning Baal into their set of beliefs. This later transposed into the biblical Baal that is read in today's Bible.

In Canaanite mythology you also have Dagan who is the supreme ruler of the sea, fishing, grain, sexuality, and strength. Dagan has syncretism with El and with the Sumerian God Enki. Yet other sources credit him with being an aspect of Enlil, Enki's brother. Nonetheless, the fish aspect of Dagan became a representation of sexual strength where the qualities of mind, soul, and spirit are placed. The next section will discuss Egyptian mythology and its role in the Occult. Again, there are arguments among practitioners of these paths as to who is what, but I will cover the basics.

Egyptian Mythology

Finally, we will discuss Egyptian stories that made the cut into occult hierarchies. Within Satanism (The Temple of Set and Demonolatry (Khemetic demonolaters), there are those who follow the Egyptian mythological traditions. It is firmly held that Set (Seth, Setesh, Sutekh, Setekh, or Suty) is the archetype for Satan. In Egyptian mythology, Set is the demiurge who butchered his brother Osiris. Isis reconstituted Osiris's body in order to fall pregnant to him. Along with Set, Apep (Apophis), and Thoth are also considered to be archetypes for Satan as well. These will all be briefly discussed below.

Set is the Egyptian God of Chaos, desert storms, foreigners, and violence. Set was a consequence of the union between Geb (earth) and Nut (sky). Note the parallel with the Akkadian myths in the previous section. During the third intermediate and late periods, Set, as the God of foreigners, was demonized as foreigners became associated with oppression and ruin (e.g., the Assyrians and the Persians). So it came to be that Set's defeat by the God Horus was a point of celebration for ancient late Egyptians. Hence, Set became demonized.

There is some disagreement in the community about whether Set was the archetype of Satan, or Apep (Apophis), who is the dark serpent. Apep challenged Ra the Sun God and was defeated by Set. Apep was also Apophis and was the God of chaos and Darkness. Apep was enemy to the light (Ra) and Ma'at, which was considered to mean order and truth. Apep was born of Ra's umbilical cord. His existence in mythology, not as a primal force but as a function of Ra's birth. This meant that concept of evil in Egyptian mythology is as a function of the individual's own struggle. Apep was depicted as a giant serpent with a head made of flint. Apep's seed is thought to represent the Black Flame in Satanic and Luciferian pathways.

Thoth is also worth mentioning here. There was a movement in the late 1960s that saw Thoth placed in the limelight as the true demiurge in Egyptian mythology. Thoth was basically the God of Wisdom and the moon. He was also thought to have been responsible for maintaining the universe, organizing time and responsible for magic. One of his consorts was the famed Ma'at, who stood with Thoth on the other side of Ra's barge.

Thoth gave Isis the words to reconstitute the butchered body of Osiris. Thoth also was thought to have invented writing and calendars. Thoth was thought to be Hermes in Greek mythology. He is also believed to be linked to Enki in Akkadian or Sumerian mythology because of his connection to water.

Whether you consider Set, Thoth, or Apep as the demiurge and prototype for Satan is up to you, the reader. There are parallels in other mythological sets. However, they are too numerous to mention here.

In conclusion, the oldest civilizations worshipped Satan-like deities that have been revived in the modern era. Whether you choose to believe in this as the correct depiction or not is largely up to the path that is presented to you by Satan himself. The next chapter will look at the black flame and how that impacts on your spirituality. It will also explore the term gnosis and will expound on working with the Qliphoth.

CHAPTER 5

The Black Flame, Gnosis and Working with the Qliphoth

This chapter will explore the Black Flame, Gnosis and working with the Qliphoth. It is worth noting here that appendix E—Demons, Chakras and Cardinal Points has a discussion of the Chakra system in order to understand some of the elements in this chapter, you will need to read that.

The Black Flame was an expression first used by Michael A. Aquino in the 1970s. At the time he was part of the Church of Satan which later split and the Temple of Set was formed. The Black Flame became a centralized ideology within the Temple of Set and was deemed to be a gift from Set, the true God of sovereign existence. The Black Flame is a well-known concept in the left-hand path now. In fact, it is the most important concept among Satanists and Luciferians alike.

The black flame is the primordial aspect that burns inside the depth of the left-hand path practitioner. So what is the black flame in simple terms? Well, it is the divine spark within each of us constituting intellect, desire, imagination, inner light, and divine consciousness. It is an inner driving force that seeks to strengthen our will and gives us the ability to ascend back to our origins within Satan/Lucifer. It separates the animals from humans. The black flame is symbolic; and it is represented in the seal of infernal union between Samael and Lilith surrounded by the power of the ALL or Satan/Lucifer. See the figure below.

Figure 2—Seal of the Infernal Union

The divine spark or black flame is fueled by gnosis or spiritual knowledge of ourselves and of the universe. It is the primordial energy within us that gives us spiritual power. Since Lucifer/Satan is the embodiment of wisdom, this should come to us naturally as we learn and grow, and it gives us the impetus to advance to where we ascend back to the womb of Tiamat.

The black flame is the gnosis/Da'ath that is the gate to the Sitra Ahra. The Sitra Ahra is the outer darkness on the way back to Tiamat's womb. In other words, it is a reference to the Qliphoth, or the opposing force in the Kabballah, which will be discussed in detail. The diagram below shows how the Self or Ego (the dayside, or mundane mind) as it is connected to the black flame through the unconscious, or night-side mind. This is, in turn, connected to the cosmos or the void.

Figure 3—The Black Flame In Relation to Self

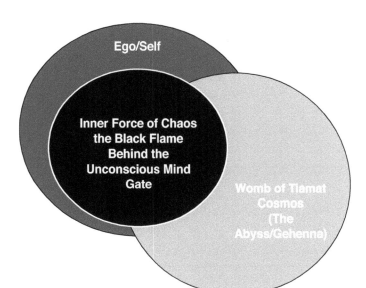

The light and dark aspects of self are a part of the Black Flame within. All aspects of you are encompassed within the aspect of "Self," which is driven by the Black Flame within.

Michael Ford writes inexhaustibly about the Black Flame. He defines it as the gift of individual awakening. He also defines it as the Black Light of Iblis as a gift from Shaitan, or Set, where it is considered a source of individual consciousness, intellect, and divinity. This gift was first evident in Tiamat the Goddess of the abyss. This process is accessed via meditation, dream working, and astral projection.

There is another theory proposed for the Black Flame that involves the four crown princes of hell as they are attached to individual elements and sets of qualities. The table below shows these designated elements and qualities. What this means in terms of the Black Flame is that all these factors (elements and qualities) are what the Black Flame inspires. We will briefly discuss gnosis next and the Qliphoth.

Table 4—Demonic Elements and Qualities

Prince	Element	Qualities
Satan	Fire	• Will • Ego • Rebellion
Lucifer	Air	• Intelligence • Truth • Awareness • Enlightenment • Imagination • Inner Light
Belial	Earth	• Strength • Lust • Hedonism • Power • Self-sufficiency • Accomplishment
Leviathan	Water	• Emotion • Passion • Sexual Desire • Chaos • Power to create and destroy.

Understanding Gnosis

Gnosis is spiritual experiential knowledge or knowing. The word originated from the Greek word γνῶσις, meaning "knowledge." Gnosis is also commonly called Da'ath. You will hear people talking about gnosis quite a lot in the left-hand path. It is knowledge we do not learn or read or study for. Rather, it comes from within ourselves and usually pertains to knowledge through spirituality that encompasses the whole person. Personal experiential knowledge is not transmissible. It comes to us and us alone. Real spirituality is based on your own efforts to understand the truth behind everything.

Working with the Black Flame will cause gnosis, as will working with the Qliphoth. This usually happens through meditative practice, dream, and astral workings. The next section will discuss the Qliphoth and how to work with it.

Working with the Qliphoth

In ancient Jewish mysticism, there is a concept called the Kabballah, which is used to explain the way in which creation (the finite) interacts with God, the *Ein Sof,* or the infinite. This concept dates back to the Assyrians and was adopted by Jewish mystics during medieval times. The modern esoteric concept of Kabballah has since been adopted by the modern occult. The Kabballah has two aspects, the Tree of Life and the Qliphoth, or the Tree of Death.

The Tree of Life is about the creation of the human soul and has ten nodes, or Sephiroth, which represent different archetypes and aspects of God. The Tree of Life is depicted below in figure 4—The Tree of Life. Each node, or Sephiroth, can be an angel, a deity, celestial body or quality. The Sephirot is both a process of creation that emanates from God and represents the creation of the universe as a function of his will and one of ethics where each node is a quality such as truth, justice, and kindness, for example, and a righteous person will work their way up the tree by doing acts of righteousness. The columns in the diagram are also called pillars, and they represent a quality, electrical current, or type of ritualistic magic. The Tree of Life will not be discussed in detail in this book as the interest here lies in the Qliphoth, or Tree of Death, as it is pivotal in the left-hand path.

Figure 4—The Tree of Life

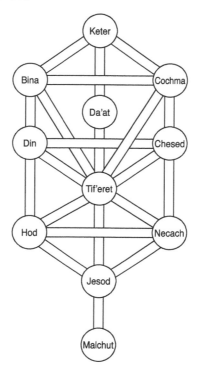

The Qliphoth, on the other hand, is the Tree of Death/Tree of Da'ath. It is the waste that is associated with creation and banished from the tree of life. Lilith is said to have tempted Eve to eat of the tree of knowledge (the Qliphoth) in order to entice man to Godhead. This is the left hand of the Kabballah. Each Sephiroth is the polar opposite to the Holy Sephiroth on the Tree of Life, and it is thought to represent evil or impure spiritual forces. This collectively is also called the *Sitra Ahra*. We discussed the Sitra Ahra earlier with reference to the Black Flame. The Sitra Ahra is the way back through the subconscious mind to the abyss or the womb of Tiamat. In the original Kabbalistic cosmology, the Qliphoth were shells surrounding holiness that represented obstacles to holiness.

So what does this all mean. Some believe the Qliphoth (Figure 5—The Qliphoth) to be husks or shells left over from an attempt at creation by God, the leftovers being a result of a divine force too powerful for the Sephiroth, and these husks, or shells, are inhabited by Demons. Others believe that the Qliphoth is a shadow of the holy Sephiroth in the abyss. Some also believe that the Qliphoth is the exact mirror opposite of the Sephiroth. This makes the explanation of the Qliphoth very confusing for the reader. So we will take a simple look at the Qliphoth as an opposing mirror opposite of the Holy Sephiroth. Table 5—Sephirot Characteristics below is a cursory look at this.

Figure 5—The Qliphoth

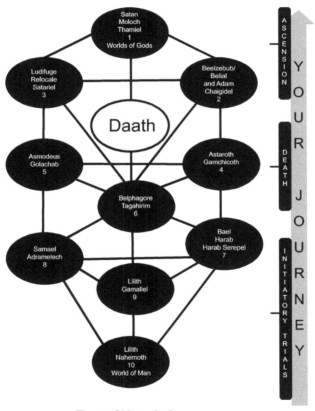

Tree of Knowledge

Table 5—Sephirot Characteristics

Demonic Force	Planet Per Sephirot	Holy Sephirot and Characteristics	Qlippa and Characteristics
Satan/Moloch	Pluto	Kether • Unity • Perfection • Crown	Thamiel • Division/Duality • Twins of God • Cut off from Creation • Aggressive tension • Demonic powers seeking to destroy God's harmony/unity
Lucifuge Rofocal	Saturn	Binah • The great revealing one who bestows the absolute onto the created • Understanding	Satariel • Demonic work to conceal God's perfection • Death of creative energy
Beelzebub	Neptune	Chochma • Wisdom	Chaigidel • Confusion of the Power of Creation • The hinderers • Obstruction of creation
Asmodeus	Uranus	Gevurah • Righteousness • Strength	Golachab • Burning destruction • The flaming ones • Its wrath against life and creation • Fury • War • Attraction and Repulsion • Lust • Suffering
Belphegor	Sun	Tiphereth • Beauty • Balance • Integration • Spirituality • Miracles • Beauty	Tagahirim • Revolt • Dissension • Derangement • Loneliness • Despair

Demonic Force	Planet Per Sephirot	Holy Sephirot and Characteristics	Qlippa and Characteristics
Astaroth	Jupiter	Chesed • Source of bounty • Mercy • Mildness	Gamchicoth • Devourers who waste the substance of thought and creation • The smiting ones
Samael	Mercury/ Mars	Hod • Complex working of the will of the absolute • Splendour	Adramelech • Poison of God • Desolation of God • The Left-Hand • The deceivers • Dissolution of intellect • Shadow Treaty of the Soul
Lilith	Moon	Jesod/Yesod • The place form becomes matter • Foundation	Gamaliel • Polluted of God • The obscene ones
Bael	Venus	Necach/Netzach • Openness • Natural Love • Perpetuity • Victory • Endurance	Harab Serapel • Ravens of dispersion • The corrosive ones • Fear • Transience • Desolation • Weakness
Lilith	Earth	Malchut • Pleasant • The physical manifestation of the Will of God • Kingdom	Nahemoth/Naamah • Excitation of the mind to cause strange desires • All worldly pleasures • Womb of the queen of the night • Netherworld of the soul • The opening of the gates to the Sitra Ahra

Apart from the Qlippa that are present the Qliphoth has twenty-two joining paths called the Tunnels of Set. These connect the Qlippa and are filled with vampires and spirits of varying types.

The journey through the Qlippa represents a descent into the underworld, metaphysical death, rebirth, and ascent to Godhood. Your journey starts at the bottom of the Tree of Death with several trials you must undertake and pass. You then move to Da'ath which is the period of gnosis or death to self. Da'ath is the door that leads from the first triad to the second and third. You finally reveal your shadow self and learn your special inner skills and where you recreate yourself in order to ascend to Godhood. This can take a long time to achieve and is not for the impatient. You can in part achieve this through meditation and astral travel. It will be a process of facing your worst fears, nightmares, and weaknesses and overcoming them before you can ascend to the next trial.

Working with the Qliphoth means calling on each sphere for empowerment over a long period of time—say a year. I have seen it recommended that you can do one Qlippa a month. Once you have worked your way through the ten Qlippa, you can work your way through the twenty-two Tunnels of Set.

1.   Nahemoth

Nahemoth is the start of your journey as an initiate. It represents all worldly pleasures and is why it is called the opening of the gates of the Sitra Ahra. It is the start on the path to death of the old, gnosis, and life of the new. The calling on this sphere will open the way to the Sitra Ahra, elevate the consciousness of the practitioner by awakening the third-eye chakra and causing the practitioner to start the trials of the spheres. This will be a working with Lilith/Na'amah and will involve calling upon her name to open the way to ascension. The process of calling her will come through astral travel and meditation.

You need to ensure you have the following:
1. Red and black candles
2. Athame and chalice
3. Red wine offering
4. Frankincense incense
5. A sigil of Lilith imbued with your own blood
6. Your third-eye chakra anointed with your own blood
7. Ritual tools as per your usual workings

Figure 6—Sigil of Lilith

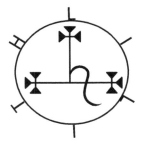

You sit and meditate and focus on your breathing in the darkness. It is often thought that doing this in a wooded area at night is best. Relax your mind and chant to Lilith to open the Sitra Ahra for you. Lilith's enn is **"Renich biasa avage Lilith lirach."**

While you are chanting, be aware of your Kundalini rising from the base of your spine (your Muladhara chakra) up through your chakras to the third eye. Imagine you are inside a warm dark place. Visualize yourself standing before Lilith in a completely black space. Visualize her opening the way for you to go through the gate of your unconscious mind. Ask her for direction. Lilith will open her womb to you. You may feel uneasiness, or you may get a strong emotional impulse. When you are done with your meditation, write down everything you saw and felt. Thank Lilith for her being with you.

2.   Gamaliel

This sphere relates to the polluted of God and the obscene ones. It is again we see the utilization of Lilith in the Tree of Death. This is the place the debris of matter lays, where there are shifting sands. You may find you are exposed to aspects of self you do not want to accept. Here you will be introduced to lunar magick as Gamaliel is a reference to the dark side of the moon, witchcraft and sexual alchemy. This sphere has its place in the realm of dreams and, oftentimes, those that we deny or relegate to the subconscious mind.

You invoke Gamaliel in much the same way that you invoked Lilith. However, with this particular sphere, you would benefit from undertaking sex magick, either alone or with someone, to open up the portal to Gamaliel.

Again, for this exercise, you will need these items:

1. Black and red candles
2. Athame and chalice
3. Red wine offering
4. Frankincense incense
5. A full dark moon
6. A sigil of Lilith tainted with your own blood or sexual fluids
7. Ritual tools as per your usual workings.

Before you meditate or use dream work, try sexual abstinence and sleep deprivation for a couple of days. Your meditation will focus on the Svadisthana, or Sacral Chakra. If you choose to practice sex magick to invoke Lilith, you wait until the crescendo of climax to call out to her asking her to open the portal to Gamaliel. Your blood and sexual fluids will be an offering. Incubi and succubi may come to you. Do not give in as you can be seduced and left as a shell. Otherwise, you will meditate on Lilith's sigil and ask her to open the portal to Gamaliel. Visualize yourself standing in front of Lilith in a dark place with endless sand, chant Lilith's enn, and then request that she open up the way to Gamaliel. Lilith may appear as a spider woman or a vampire Queen. Imagine stepping through a doorway into a room. Explore that room. Meditate on it for a while. Write down everything you saw and felt. Especially note any dreams you have after the ritual has ended. Close the ritual and thank Lilith for coming.

3. Adramelech

Adramelech relates to Samael the consort of Lilith. Samael is the poison of God, the desolation of God, the left hand, and the deceiver, according to ancient texts. He tempts with occult knowledge. The practitioner will face a deconstruction of all of their personal artifacts until nothing remains. Indeed, your personality will be deconstructed, and you will be made to rethink everything you know. In this way insanity becomes knowledge.

This sphere represents the working of the will of Samael. One partakes of the poison of God to reduce the foundation of intellect so you can enter a treaty with your shadow self. Lilith and Samael work together and are the combined male and female energies of the Qliphoth. You would use Kundalini yoga to access this sphere or meditation with a focus on the male and female energies of the Kundalini, whereby you raise up Samael and Lilith through you together.

You would use for this meditation:
1. Blue or red candles
2. Sandalwood or lavender incense
3. Music as an offering to Samael
4. Athame and chalice
5. The sigil of Samael infused with your own blood or sexual fluids
6. Your usual ritual tools

Figure 7—Sigil of Samael

You would use Kundalini yoga to open Adramelech. If you are not keen on yoga, try meditating on the Kundalini Serpent, allowing it to rise from the base of your spine through to the top of your head. Once you have achieved the uncoiling of the Kundalini Serpent, you then invoke Samael to open the portal to Adramelech. Samael's enn is *"Jach Eleh Adonnay Samael."* Visualize standing before Samael. Ask him the way through to Adramelech. Visualize walking through a door into a darkened room. Explore the room. Write down your impressions and feelings. Close the ritual and thank Samael for coming.

4.   Harab Serapel

This sphere is the opposite of Netzach and is ruled by the "Black Venus." Here the ravens of death and dispersion are contrary to the doves of peace in the Netzach in the Tree of Life. This sphere is identified with fear, transience, war, desolation, and weakness. You would engage this sphere for help in battles in life. Also, this sphere helps you become one with your inner Demon. This is the sphere of dark emotions for the practitioner. The raven is the symbolic bird here that brings baptism to the practitioner. This is a direct parallel to the doves of peace seen as the symbol for the Holy Spirit.

This will be a working with Bael, whereby the practitioner calls upon Bael to start the trial through a process of astral travel and meditation. This will essentially be a process of death and rebirth. Your trials will help you overcome your weaknesses with this sphere.

For this sphere, you will need to meditate using the following:
1.   Yellow or black candles initially but put them out for the meditation
2.   Fern as an offering
3.   Frankincense incense
4.   The sigil of Bael imbued with your blood
5.   Your regular altar tools

Figure 8—Sigil of Bael

Meditate in complete darkness. Focus on your breathing, invoke Bael using his sigil and his enn. Bael's enn is **"Ayer Secore On Ca Bael."** You will be faced with your fears and weaknesses. Confront all your fears and weaknesses one by one and allow each rendition of yourself to become as a living and separate entity and absorb it into yourself. This should make you feel free once you have completed this, and your fears and weaknesses will become diminutive to you. Once you have achieved this, close the ritual and thank Bael for coming. Note down anything you see or feel during this process.

5.   Tagahirim

Tagahirim is the sphere of Belphegor, it represents the "Black Sun." The Sun is the symbol of the complete self. This sphere means revolt, dissension, and derangement or imbalance. Any allies that you had in your journey will leave you at this point, and you will face loneliness, despair and possibly imbalance. The point of this is to (a) light the way with the black flame from within; and (b) acquire the concept of Self-divinity and power.

What you need to meditate on and summon Belphegor with is as follows:
1.   Green candles
2.   Lemon balm incense
3.   Your regular altar tools
4.   A sigil of Belphegor imbued with your blood
5.   Lemon peel as an offering

Figure 9—Sigil of Belphegor

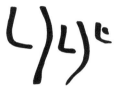

Meditate on Belphegor's sigil chanting his enn—*"Lyan Ramec Catya Ganen Belphegor."* Ask Belphegor to open the way to Tagahirim. Ask him for protection as you walk through the Garden of Shadows. Visualize walking through a door in the garden. Focus on your surroundings and explore. Imagine becoming one with the shadows, your body falling away and being replaced by pure energy. Visualize a figure emerging before you—this figure is yourself. Imagine the figure being connected to your shadow by tendrils of light. Both these aspects, the shadow and the bright light, are reconciled as self. You can now focus on your problems and work through them. When you are done, you will feel a lot of power. Use this to have your queries answered. When you are done write down your impressions and your thoughts, write down what you saw. Close the ritual and thank Belphegor for coming.

6.   Golachab

Golachab is ruled by Asmodeus under the guiding light of Uranus. It means burning destruction, the pit of fire, wrath against life and creation, the bringer of the apocalypse, violence, and the flaming ones. It is the most dangerous of the shells that the practitioner will encounter. In encountering this sphere, you will face internal issues such as fear, taboo, anger, and violent emotion.

To attune to this sphere, you will need the following:

1. Yellow candles
2. Frankincense incense

3. Mint for an offering
4. Your regular ritual tools
5. The sigil of Asmodeus imbued with your blood

Figure 10—Sigil of Asmodeus

During the meditation for this sphere you will traverse nine hells of Asmodeus before coming to the throne, which is where Asmodeus sits. You will invoke Asmodeus using his enn—*"Ayer avage aloren Asmoday Aken."* The first hells you will encounter during meditation will be these:

1. The gate—about submitting yourself to the fire of change
2. The path of fornication—Asmodeus is the Demon of lust here, so this is about enduring pleasure.
3. The wilderness—This is where you bring your enemies to suffer and where you yourself suffer from self-inflicted torture.
4. The treachery—about prey and predator
5. The labyrinth—about letting go of self
6. Hall of judgment—about balance and karma in waking life
7. The mire—learning not to trust the physical senses
8. The hunting fields—about power you achieve and develop on the path, mastery of life and death
9. The throne—about gathering and raising energy

Again, jot down your experiences within this Qlippa before moving on to the next.

7.   Gamchicoth

This is the realm of Astaroth under Jupiter. It is also called the devourers and the smiting ones. This sphere rules over the spheres below it and represents the conceptualization of ideas. This is where the practitioner faces the last trial before the abyss. At this point the practitioner has been stripped of everything and is pure enough to enter the abyss. The last three spheres are Satariel, Chaigidel, and Thamiel. This is the triad that represents divine consciousness. During meditation on this sphere, you become the smiter, destroying the laws and principles of the world. Astaroth is the devourer. His breath being instrumental in this process. This sphere is about stripping all aspects of self and the conscious to reveal the naked and pure practitioner unencumbered by ego, identity, personality, and self. This is the first step toward rebirth and divinity of self and to the knowledge hidden from the conscious mind.

What you need for this meditation is the following:
1.   Green candles
2.   Sandalwood incense
3.   Laurel for an offering
4.   Your usual ritual tools
5.   A sigil of Astaroth with your blood on it
6.   You should be devoid of clothing if you wish.

Figure 11—Sigil of Astaroth

Here you meditate on the candle flame and envision walking into the door of Gamchicoth. You visualize yourself naked, destroying the last remnants of Self. Chant Astaroth's enn—**"Tasa Alora Foren Astaroth."** You picture putting all of these things into a box and burning it with fire and hand the ashes to Astaroth to devour. Imagine yourself standing in the heart of the void. Once you are done with the meditation, write down your thoughts and feelings. Close the ritual and thank Astaroth for coming. Note down all you experience before moving on.

8.   Da'ath

The Da'ath is the abyss. You are entering the Da'ath to absorb knowledge. This is gnosis. This is the gate between the conscious and the subconscious mind, between knowledge and the unknown. During this period the practitioner's soul will be transmuted into a black diamond. All the things that limit you from becoming divine will be polished off. Here you call upon the keeper of the gate to show you the way into the light of the Black Flame—the entry point to the Sitra Ahra. Choronzon is the keeper of the abyss. You would do an invocation to Choronzon using Sandalwood incense, seven red candles and the sigil of Choronzon with your blood on it. Activate the sigil by meditating on it.

Figure 12—Sigil of Choronzon

Here you are focusing on the Vishuddi, or throat Chakra. Visualize yourself alight with the Black Flame. Visualize standing before a mighty raging river. Imagine going down to the waters and bathing from head to foot. This is the baptism of your reborn self in the black waters of the abyss. Imagine you are a scroll and tendrils of energy are coming from you. Visualize these tendrils absorbing information. Make sure you are completely relaxed. As you visualize this, a person is coming toward you. Speak to them. Ask them to illuminate you with knowledge. This is Choronzon. Sit for a while and meditate. As you finish, thank Choronzon for coming and close your ritual. Write down your feelings and impressions.

9. Satariel

This shell is the womb of the Queen of the Sitra Ahra. Lilith the spider Queen resides here and the sphere itself is ruled by Lucifuge Rofocale/Focalor under Saturn, which is associated with disease and death. It is known as the concealer of God's perfection and the death of creative energy. This is where Lilith weaves the threads of destiny on the lower astral levels. Here the practitioner is asking for guidance through the confusion to truth, guidance into the heart of the Sitra Ahra.

For this meditation exercise you will need these items:
1. Green candles
2. Sandalwood incense
3. Water in a chalice
4. A rose for an offering
5. Your usual ritual tools
6. A sigil of Lucifuge Rofocale imbued with your blood

Figure 13—Sigil of Lucifuge Rofocale/Focalor

Meditation on the sigil of Lucifuge Rofocale/Focalor is done here using his enn—**"En jedan on ca Focalor."** Visualize yourself standing in the middle of a spiderweb surrounded by threads that are attached to you. Take your knife and cut these threads to symbolize cutting away your old world. This is where the Eye of Lucifer opens and all is revealed. Meditate on your Kundalini serpent and visualize Lilith the Spider Queen coming forward to show you the way through this sphere. Ask her to guide you. When you are done, write down your experiences and close the ritual thanking Focalor for coming.

10. Chaigidel

This shell is the province of Beelzebub under Neptune. This shell means confusion of the power of creation, the hinderers, obstruction of creation, and the place empty of God. This sphere is where freedom is granted from the restrictions of the El. There is a dark masculine force of creation/re-creation imbued in this sphere. The whole universe is destroyed and recreated here, and thus, the practitioner here must become Adam/Belial.

To do this meditation you will need the following:
1.   Some earth in a bowl
2.   Frankincense or myrrh incense
3.   Dark red candles
4.   Your usual ritual tools
5.   The sigil of Beelzebub and Belial imbued with your own blood

Figure 14—Sigil of Beelzebub

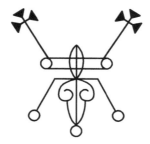

For this meditation, you need to focus on the sigil of Beelzebub and invoke him, using his enn—"**Adey vocar avage Beelzebuth.**" Visualize becoming Adam/Belial. Naked before a throne in a dark cave where Beelzebub will appear before you. You ask him the way through Chaigidel. When you have finished this meditation, write down your impressions and experiences. Close the ritual and thank Beelzebub for coming.

11. Thamiel

Thamiel represents is the crown of the Qliphoth and the duality of God. This realm is split into two and is ruled by Moloch and Satan. These are like the two-faced God Janus, one face, that of Satan, looks toward what has been destroyed, and the other (Moloch) faces what you, as a God, can create. This sphere is the polar opposite of Kether, where the Sephirot means unity and perfection. This sphere is where the path into the abyss becomes open to the practitioner known as the black diamond. The practitioner was prepared as the black diamond during the machinations of Da'ath and the transmutation of the soul. The black diamond is the multifaceted truth. It is the final path to Godhood and self-liberation. This is about final liberation from the Abrahamic God and taking up the mantle of self-deification under the tutelage of Satan and Moloch.

This meditation is quite simple in that you merely sit between two candles. One in front and one behind. The purpose of this is to cast a double shadow representing the twin Godheads of Thamiel. You focus on the shadows also as part of yourself. Focus on raising your Kundalini serpent from the base of your spine through breath and open your third-eye chakra. Breathe until you are in a trance like state. Ask Satan and Moloch to guide you through into the abyss to the black diamond. This could take a while. Once you have achieved full awakening, take the crowns of the Sitra Ahra and place them on your head. Once you have finished this meditation, write down your thoughts and feelings. Close your ritual and thank Satan and Moloch for coming.

***

In conclusion, the Black Flame is of pivotal importance in the occult. It is defined as a primal energy or force that is made up of the subconscious mind and advances us toward ascension by sparking gnosis, creativity and divinity. It is retrieved through meditation, astral travel and dream work. The Qliphoth is also of prime importance in the left-hand path. Practicing meditation on the Qlippa and reaching a final point of ascension is necessary to remake yourself in the image of Satan and cast you into the black diamond of the abyss of Godhood. The next chapter discusses meditation and energy manipulation as a tool for the practitioner to learn and use for magick and ascension. The chapter will also discuss astral temples, astral travel, servitors, and dream work.

CHAPTER 6

Meditation and Energy Manipulation

I n this chapter we will talk about energy manipulation and meditation. Meditation is almost essential in the left-hand path for so many things. You will see a lot of meditation so get used to doing it every day. This chapter will discuss meditation and energy manipulation, astral travel, dream working, and servitor creation.

To meditate means to focus one's mind using breathing techniques, in silence or with the aid of a mantra (chant), for spiritual reasons or in order to relax one's mind. There are several types of basic meditation used in the left-hand path to achieve certain goals. The simplest ones are chakra cleansing, centering, grounding, and shielding.

Grounding

Grounding is where you make a connection to the Earth. The Earth is filled with free electrons and making your bare feet touch the Earth allows a full and free flow of electrons from you to Earth. This is also called Earthing. In meditation, it is the practice of sitting upright with your feet firmly planted steadfastly on the ground. During this time, you visualize your feet are roots going deep into the surface of the Earth. It promotes well-being and allows you to connect with all things in the Earth. It is essential where you feel displaced and where you feel that you are out of sorts or where you have too much energy build up from rituals and workings. It is the foundation of any energy work you will do, and you should do it daily and after any ritual or working you do to leech off excess energies. It only takes a few minutes.

Exercise One: Walk through a park or on a beach barefoot and allow the Earth's energies to come up through your legs all the way up to the top of your head. Push your energy out through your feet if you have too much of it. Your energies get recycled in this way back into the Earth, cleansing and purifying them.

Exercise Two: Remove your shoes and socks and sit on a chair. Visualize your feet planting into the Earth like tree roots. Imagine the cycle of energy from the Earth cycling through you and your energy cycling through the earth. Push your excess energy out through your feet and toes into the Earth.

Exercise Three: Carry a stone or crystal in your pocket. When you are feeling that your energy is in excess, allow the stone or crystal to absorb your excess energy.

Next, we will discuss shielding.

Shielding

Shielding is where you protect yourself from harmful energies, such as negative people, places, or bad feelings in general, by placing an energy barrier around yourself that cannot be penetrated. This is especially important in warding off magickal or psychic attacks or those who would seek to drain energy from you. Essentially, there are a couple of ways to do this.

Exercise One: Focus on your energy core and expand it out to where it covers your whole body. Envisage tendrils of negative energy trying to leech energy from you or trying to send you negative energy. They cannot because you are shielded in a bubble and will bounce off the bubble and go back from whence they came.

Exercise Two: Visualize a bubble of energy forming around yourself. Imagine arrows trying to hit it but bouncing off and going back to where they came from. Chances are your attacker is not shielded and you are sending the negative energy back to them and creating harm for them not for you.

Centering

Now, we will look at centering. Centering is knowing where you are in time and space; it is finding equilibrium within your inner space to help you deal with your outer space. Centering is also gaining focus, which is important for ritual work. Centering is important in magick and is the beginning work for energy manipulation. It is where you calm your emotions and your breathing down to a point where you become more aware of what is going on around and inside of you. This should be done before any ritual work because it is important to be fully aware of what you are experiencing, and you should be focused before you start your work. When you are centered, you are neutral. That is, there are no negative feelings or positive feelings. You are focused and not scattered, and there is no resistance.

There are four centers in your being. These are the physical center where you collect information through your five senses. The next is your emotional center, which is centered around your heart and relates to your feelings. The next center is the mental center, which is where you think, and the final center is the spiritual center, which is where the higher self stays.

Exercise One: You sit and focus on your breathing. You make your breathing regular and slow. Clear your mind of all thoughts—do this for about fifteen to twenty minutes. Rub your hands together lightly and slowly bring them twelve centimeters apart (approximately five inches). Feel the energy between them like a ball. It may take a few times to feel the energy ball between your hands, that's ok. Just make sure you are in a quiet space with no interruptions. Visualize the ball expanding and contracting like a balloon full of air. Expand the ball until it covers you completely. Draw the energy ball into yourself via the heart chakra or the solar plexus.

Exercise Two: Focus on your breathing until it is slow and regular. Breathe from your belly. Bring your awareness to your physical sensations, emotional sensations, spiritual sensations, and your mental chatter. Imagine that you're a tree. Your head, arms, hands, and fingers are the branches. Your legs and torso from the trunk, and your feet sprout roots far down beneath the ground. Feel how heavy your feet get as they take root.

Exercise Three: Sometimes, it helps if you are moving. Calm your breathing down until it is slow and regular and walk slowly staying present with every step. Synchronize your breathing to your steps.

Chakra Cleansing and Balancing

Next, we will discuss chakra cleansing and balancing. You have seven major energy centers in your body, called Chakras. There is a dissertation on Chakras in appendix E—Demons, Chakras and Cardinal Points. For many reasons, Chakras get blocked, and the energy flow diminishes. It is an unhealthy state to be in as certain parts of your life fail to function correctly as a result of blockages. The process of getting the Chakra energy flowing again is called Cleansing and Balancing.

The figure below gives an in-depth look at each chakra and how it is impacted by blockage. You will notice physical effects, mental effects, and emotional effects. Basically, where these effects are present, there is a blockage, and you need to address it. For example, if your root chakra is blocked, you will experience constipation, inability to let go of problems, fearfulness.

Chakra cleansing and balancing can remedy blocks and get your energies flowing correctly, which will improve your health and your mental and emotional states. This will in turn make your spiritual state better, and you will have more successful ritual work and indeed, everything in your life will improve. When Chakras need balancing, they are often spinning out of time or in reverse directions or have even stopped. Balancing is very important. The exercise below shows you how to cleanse and balance a chakra.

How I do chakra balancing and cleansing is as follows:

1. Sit quietly with few distractions. You can play meditative music. I like shamanistic drums.

2. Focus on your breathing until its slow and steady. Do this for a few minutes until you are calm and relaxed.

3. Focus on your root chakra that sits between the legs.
   a. It is a dirty-red color and is spinning slowly in a clockwise fashion.
   b. You will notice the color red is off, or there are dark bits in your chakra center.
   c. As you are breathing out, visualize these black pieces spinning out of the chakra and leaving your energy field until the chakra glows bright red again.
   d. Visualize this chakra spinning faster and faster as it is freed from blockages.

4. Focus on your Sacral chakra at the base of your spine.
   a. This chakra is orange and is spinning slowly or not at all at this stage.
   b. You will notice the color orange is dirty and has blocks of black in it.
   c. As you are breathing out, visualize these black pieces spinning out of the chakra and leaving your energy field until the chakra is glowing bright orange again.
   d. Visualize the chakra spinning faster and faster as it is freed from blockages and until it matches the speed of the root chakra.

5. Focus on the Solar Plexus chakra as it is located above the naval and below the umbilical cord.
   a. This chakra is a dirty-yellow color and is spinning slowly.
   b. This chakra has dark blockages in it.

    c.   As you exhale, visualize these dark blockages spinning off and being flung outside of your energy field. Do this until you notice it is bright yellow and clear.

    d.   Visualize the chakra spinning faster and faster until it matches the other two Chakras you have cleansed and balanced.

6. Focus on the Heart chakra, which is in the center of the chest.

    a.   This chakra will be a dirty green and will spin slowly.

    b.   Visualize the dark blockages in it.

    c.   As you exhale, visualize the dark blockages spinning off and being flung outside your energy field. Do this until you notice it is a bright-green color and its speed matches the other chakras cleansed earlier.

7. Focus on the Throat chakra. This chakra is blue.

    a.   Visualize the throat chakra as dirty and having large blocks of darkness in it.

    b.   As you are breathing out, visualize the dark blockages spinning off until the chakra is bright blue and clear. See it spinning faster and faster as it is cleansed until it matches the speed of the chakras cleansed previously.

8. Focus on the third-eye chakra between your eyes.

    a.   Visualize your third-eye chakra as foggy and indigo in color.

    b.   As you are exhaling, exhale all the fog and blockages in your third eye and watch it spin faster and faster until it spins with the same rhythm as the other chakras you have cleansed.

9. Focus now on your Crown chakra, which is on top of your head and is purple.

    a.   Visualize this chakra as foggy as well and darkened by blockages.

    b.   As you are exhaling, breathe out the negatives and fogginess of this chakra until it is bright purple and spinning at the same speed as your other chakras.

10. Visualize a bright light coming down from your crown to your feet, filling your chakras with illumination and magickal energy. Visualize this for several minutes as you focus on your breathing and keeping the rhythm of the chakras spinning.

Figure 15—Chakra Chart

CHAKRA CHART							
	1	2	3	4	5	6	7
	Root Chakra	Sacral Chakra	Solar Plexus Chakra	Heart Chakra	Throat Chakra	Third Eye Chakra	Crown Chakra
Location	Base of torso	Below the naval	Above the naval	Middle of the chest	Throat	Between the eyes	Top of the head
Colour	Red	Orange	Yellow	Green	Blue	Indigo	Violet
Mental	Foundations, inability to let go, failure to be grounded, lack of abundance.	Creation, interaction, relationships.	Intention, ambition, will, independence, confidence.	Self love, isolation, nurture, renewal, and growth.	Self expression, communication, innovation, and emotions.	Wisdom, insight, intuition, intellect, and mind empowerment	Perception, wisdom, divine connection, inspiration, and vision.
Physical	Back, legs, intestines, teeth and bones, vitality, and immune system.	Lower back, bladder, sexual organs.	Digestive and adrenal systems. Stomach, gall bladder, and pancreas.	Lungs, heart, thymus gland, respitory functioning.	Throat, vocal cords, neck, jaw, lungs, breathing	Eyes, sinus, nose, brain, ears, pineal, and pituitary glands.	Skull, skin, upper brain, nervous system, and the pineal gland.
Emotional	Protection, security, trust, and survival foundation	Passion, sexuality, attraction, creativity, isolation.	Power, spontaneity, anger, frustration, joy, full.	Love, trust, grief. Forgiveness, empathy, and compassion.	Sharing, expressing, choice, planning and creativity.	Intuition, inspiration, truthfulness. Dreams, Perceptiveness.	Clarity, divine acceptance and nervous conditions.
Imbalances	Fear, anxiety, poor boundaries, recklessness, hoarding and poor focus.	Emotional instability, fertility issues, pride, selfishness, urinary infections.	Victim mode, diabetes, chronic fatigue, liver, and digestion issues.	Asthma, circulation, blood pressure, heart lungs, and immune system.	Sore throat, voice issues, neck, ears, thyroid, PMS.	Headaches, insomnia, dizziness, anxiety, vision, and nervousness.	Mental illness, confusion, alienation, depression and lymphatic.
Essentials Oils to help restore balance.	Frankincense, myrrh, clove and cedarwood.	Orange, sage, bergamot. Patchoulli, ylang-ylang, cinnamon.	Lemon, basil, grapefruit, clove, ginger.	Cypress, Geranium, Eucalyptus, Jasmine and Peppermint.	Lavender, Chamomile, Sandalwood, Basil, Marjoram	Sandalwood, Sage, Patchouli, Rosemary, Myrrh.	Rose, Sandalwood, Lavender.

You can use meditation for a variety of things such as increasing focus; increasing magickal ability; focusing more power; healing your mind, body, and spirit; contacting Demonic entities; and much more. You must get into the habit of practicing mindfulness in your meditation and therefore record your all of your experiences and sensations so that you have a reference point on which to reflect. The next section will discuss energy manipulation and how energy manipulation can be useful in magick.

Energy Manipulation

Energy manipulation is the raising of energy, projecting of energy, sensing and absorbing and manipulation of energy. It is where energy can be changed from one form to another—for example psychic energy to kinetic energy. One thing you need to remember is that no new energy can be created; there is a finite amount of energy in the universe. Energy can only change forms. This is a law of thermodynamics.

Raising energy involves taking one form of energy and changing it into another form with a view to using it in magick. For example, in baneful magick and execration magick, you may wish to raise the energy from hate or anger in order to achieve the level of energy you need to perform a curse.

Exercise One

- Relax and get into a meditative state.
- Choose an emotion. As you meditate, raise the energy of that emotion within you.
- Imagine what that energy looks like to you.
- You may wish to chant or rock or dance to achieve this.
- You may play music to match the mood as well.

Exercise Two

- Use your breath to raise your energy.
- Every time you breathe in visualize your energy raising.
- Visualize the energy and yourself like a battery filling up with this energy.

Projecting energy is where you focus on moving your energy, via visualization, into an object or a situation. This is an essential part of spell work and used in rituals. This is straight forward and you can use the following exercises to help you with this.

Exercise One

- Use an object to project your emotions into via visualization.
- Pour your energy into the object.
- Visualize the object filling up like a battery.

Exercise Two

- Use a spell you have written.
- Pour your energy into the spell you have written.
- Visualize the spell coming alive with the energy.
- Visualize your outcome and project it onto the spell.

Next, we will discuss sensing energy. Sensing energy requires a deep meditative state. Once you have achieved this, you then extend your vision to see energy in all its forms and sense energies around you. You will be familiar with this in terms of aura work. This is where you see the aura of energy around a person—it will be very colorful.

Exercise One
- When you have programmed your objects to have different energies, you try to sense the energies you have imbued into the objects.
- You can do this with people too. You can sense their energies.
- Meditate and get your mind into a receptive state, when you are ready you just touch the object to feel its energy.
- When you think you know what you are sensing check to see if you are right.

Exercise Two
- Sit in a room filled with people.
- Be relaxed to where you can see energy fields around people.
- Discern the energy the person is carrying and how it changes when it encounters other people.
- Look past the person to see their energy field. This may take some practice.
- Try and use the energy to guess what the person is feeling.

Once you have learned to sense energy then you can begin to absorb energies. You can also absorb energy from people and objects by simply sending out your energy tendrils from the stratosphere of your aura to absorb energies from the stratosphere of their aura.

Exercise One
- Meditate on your object/person or situation.
- Envision the energy being soaked from your object into your hand.
- Carry the object for an entire day.
- Feel its energies often.

Exercise Two

- In a crowded room, visualize yourself with tendrils of energy coming out of your aura.
- Visualize taking energy from other people using these tendrils.
- Try and absorb their negative energies.
- Process and cleanse this energy from your heart chakra.

We have already discussed energy manipulation in quite a bit of detail. Here are some exercises to help you with energy manipulation.

Exercise One

- Sit in a meditative state.
- Being in a dark room helps.
- Gather your energy from your solar plexus or even your heart chakra.
- Form it into a ball.
- Imagine the ball of energy being cupped in your left hand. Feel it.
- Move the energy to your right hand. Feel it.

Exercise Two

- Sit in front of a lit candle in a still environment.
- Focus on the candle flame.
- Visualize moving the flame with your energy.
- Exercise your will and move the flame with your energy. This may take a bit of practice.

In the remaining sections in this chapter, we will look at astral temples, astral travel, lucid dreaming, and servitor creation.

Astral Temples

Next, we will look at astral temples, astral travel, and lucid dreaming. Astral temples are places you create during meditation and astral travel to do ritual work in. They are visualizations created through a force of will, and they are effective for those who cannot have an altar for ritual workings or who find it difficult to do ritual workings for a variety of reasons, such as when there are too many people around. To create your astral temple, you would do the following:

- Sit perfectly still, calm and relaxed.
- Focus on making your breathing regular and slow.
- Visualize walking through a forest on a leaf-littered path down beside a small creek.
- You see a large tree. It has a huge door in its trunk big enough to walk through. The door can be locked using a key that only you have. You may have to astral travel to search for the key, and the key may be music, words or an actual key that you can keep, locking and unlocking this place of peace that you create.
- Walk into the tree. Inside, there is a giant room and over by the wall is an altar.
- Decorate your altar with the tools you visualize using.
- Make your space as visually appealing as possible. Decorate it with lit candles and sigils of those Demons you want to work with. Be as detailed as possible.
- Write down what your Astral Temple looks like and how to get there.
- Be careful not to divulge to anyone where your key is or how they can get to your astral temple unless you are sharing the temple with someone and have an agreement to do so.
- Each time you go to use your astral temple, be sure to bathe ritually with a hyssop, sage, and saltwater before entering. Bath salts are ideal for this purpose.
- When you are using your temple for rituals ensure you create a balanced elemental circle (see appendix B—Dedication Rite to a Patron/Matron Demon, which has an example of a balanced elemental circle).
- Develop a personal call back mechanism such as clicking your fingers or a word in which you can come back to the mundane world.
- Practice mindfulness, that is where you record every aspect of sensation you feel when in your astral temple.

- You can use rhythmic music to help you get into this place with meditation or astral travel/dream work.

Astral Travel

Astral travel, sometimes called Lucid Dreaming, Out-of-Body Experience (OBE), Astral Projection, and Dream Walking, is something that is quite difficult to achieve without practice. Astral travel is an out-of-body experience where the practitioner trains their mind and spirit to separate and travel into different planes of existence. Astral planes are different frequencies you can travel on other than the mundane, or Earthly, plane. There are lighter frequencies and darker frequencies you can travel along. Some are dangerous because of astral leeches, but know that you will not die and your body will not be stolen. In order to master astral travel, you need to master your subconscious mind through meditation.

To master astral travel, you first need to master meditation and lucid dreaming. The lucid dreaming teaches you how to control your dreams. You have probably heard of the red-ball technique where you consciously tell yourself it is a dream by willing a red ball to bounce into your dream. This is lucid dreaming. It is where you separate the subconscious and conscious mind.

Meditation in this case is about breath control. You will find that controlling your breathing will help you to maintain focus and allow your body to shut down enough and relax enough that you can get the desired effect. You do this by the following:

- breathing in for the count of four (or four heartbeats)
- holding for the count of four (or four heartbeats)
- breathing out to the count of four (or four heartbeats)
- drawing energy into different parts of your body until you reach your toes
- allowing your mind to be free of thoughts but focusing on each breath and each heartbeat until you feel yourself float
- doing one final repetition of breathing

You do this for twenty or so minutes before you attempt astral travel. At this point, you have activated every chakra in your body and you are relaxed to the point where you are near sleep. Visualize your astral body floating outside of your physical body. There is a silver cord connecting your astral body to your physical body. At this point, think about what you would like to see and where you would like to travel to. Keep in mind that you will successfully travel to your destination and that you will be safe. You do not want to travel anywhere in the dark frequencies, because astral leeches will attach to you and come back into your waking life, causing havoc and destruction.

You will find, as you near sleep, you will notice tingles and pricks as your astral body leaves your physical body. Note these indications well as they are generally a sign you will be traveling soon, and your astral body is separating from your physical body. You may visualize a rope leading to the ceiling, actively push yourself up and along this rope hand over hand to force the separation. This is forcing the hypnogogic state between wakefulness and sleep.

Astral projection can be caused by many things, including the following:
- intention—where you are willing yourself into astral projection
- physical trauma—such as surgery or an accident
- spontaneous traveling—unwilled traveling as is most common
- mind-altering substances—the use of hallucinogenic material
- physical exertion—like Native American Indian sun dancing or a Buddhist meditation

Astral projection can be used for a number of things but mostly to affect your life in the physical realm by manipulating your energies in the astral realm. It can be used to explore the nature of the universe; meet other beings, including your own self; assist other beings, including your own self; and learn from the masters.

Note that you need to be in a safe and comfortable environment before you travel so that it is conducive to proper travel without risk. Examine and face your fears before traveling, also ensure you are warm and have limited noise in the background. Ensure your room is dark and welcoming. Also ensure there are limited distractions so turn off any technology, such as mobile phones and televisions.

There are laws for astral worlds just as there are laws for the physical world. These laws include (a) the law of karma, which returns quicker in the astral planes than it does on Earth; (b) there is duality between good and evil present in the astral world; (c) manifestation is instant and that includes your fears; (d) like thought and action attracts like thought and action and experience in the astral; and (e) there are all levels of beings and experiences, just like on Earth.

It is important that you develop your inner-awareness skills. This way you can avoid unnecessary interactions on the astral plane. Your emotions will guide you in what you see and feel and will teach you what to stay away from. You can also seek assistance from other astral bodies in the astral plane as well.

The astral plane is made up of seven levels. These are depicted in the table below. This depiction is but one depiction as posited by Professor Frederick Myers from Cambridge University in 1885. This was included for the interest of the reader, but it is generally accepted across the board.

Figure 16—The Astral World

The Earthly Plane—This is where we are now. It is the mundane world.

The Astral Plane—This is made up of upper and lower. The lower levels are dark and are where souls are cut off from love and hope. The upper level is lighter where spirits are in transit to other planes.

The Plane of Illusion—This is where life imitates the earthly plane, but it is stagnant, and souls either must move to higher planes and grow or go back to earth and grow.

The Plane of Idealized Form—This is where all ties are cut to the earthly plane. Thoughts and knowledge are expanded. Reincarnation is no longer necessary. This is where true freedom is found.

The Plane of Flame—This is where the soul takes on a fiery form, vibrates and resonates with other souls who seek to grow in understanding.

The Plane of Light—This is where all souls who have lived through all aspects of the created world live. They are evolved souls. Emotion is absent, and these souls are pure white light.

The Plane of the Spirit Realm—Where the soul becomes one with the creator, whoever you deem that to be.

In the following sections, we will be looking at dream work and servitor creation.

Dream Work

Dream Work is where the practitioner uses dreams as a source of intuitive interpretation and divination for their waking life. It is any dream-based exercise you undertake consciously based on your dream life. This is not to be confused with dream magick, where you manipulate your dreams in some way to affect a magickal outcome.

Dreams reflect our conscious and subconscious waking processes. They can be both insightful and predictive in nature and hence can be used for divination purposes and to construct dream magick. To this end, it is recommended that the practitioner keeps a dream journal to help them to remember dreams. Writing them down on waking or heading to sleep will help with manipulation and use of dreams.

There are several factors that can stop us from remembering our dreams in our waking lives. For example, if we are struggling to deal with uncertainty in our lives our dreams become ambiguous and are easily forgotten. Likewise, if we tend to focus more on the future and not in the now, dreams become focused in the future and dreams that move away from the now tend to be forgotten more readily. Focusing on outcomes only will make dreams non-goal oriented and easily forgotten. If we tend to ignore intuition, dreams will also ignore intuition and creativity then our dreams will become mundane and will be easily forgotten. Finally, if we suppress negative thoughts and emotions, our dreams become more about those negative thoughts and emotions, and as a result of this, repression dreams will be forgotten. So changing our daytime habits will make our dream memories more successful. An effective way to achieve this is by using meditation before sleep to clean negative thoughts and emotions, focus in the now, and clarify uncertainty.

Dreams happen during rapid eye movement, or REM, sleep. They generally occur just before you are ready to wake up. Restatement of dreams generally occurs best when you are just waking up or just going to sleep. This is the ideal time to write dreams down. Relax yourself and stay calm without intention so that dreams come back to you more readily.

Some tips to help you with dream recollection are presented in the sections below.

1. You need to follow a series of steps during the daytime that include reading about dream interpretation, conducting reality tests every day, repeatedly telling yourself that you will remember your dreams, replace the words *sleep* and *sleeping* with *dream* and *dreaming*, and expressing your dreams creatively either by writing or drawing.

2. In your going-to-bed phase, place a dream diary and pen next to your bed, lie in a relaxed fashion on your back, conduct dream nurture, and let all your thoughts go and allow yourself to fall asleep. Dream nurture is where you are as relaxed as possible so dreams come back to you.

3. Finally, during the waking phase, stay in the position you woke up in, allow your mind to return to your dream, and finally write

it down, including all feelings, sensations, and the flow of events in your dream.

Once you have written down the plot of your dreams you need to objectify that dream for easier interpretation. Be careful not to over interpret your dreams by asking yourself a series of questions:

1. What are the *main* symbols of your dream?
2. *What emotions* do the dream symbols provoke in you?
3. Does the dream present any solutions?
4. What is your *dream self* doing in your dream?

The next step is dream interpretation. You can locate several dream-interpretation services on the internet these days. There are also many books on the subject. It would be useful if you were to purchase a book on dream interpretation or use a reputable site such as www.dream-moods.com. Write down your dream interpretation of the main symbols in your dream. Note that not everything is a main symbol. Once you have your dream interpretation, then you need to relate it to your everyday life. This can be a life-changing experience. You will find some dreams are insightful, and others are predictive. Predictive dreams fulfill the necessary toolset for dream divination. In the next section, we will look at servitor use and creation.

Servitors

Servitors go by many names, tulpa, egregore, and thought forms, to name a few. They are constructs created by the practitioner to carry out a magickal function in the mundane and spirit worlds. A servitor is a magickal being you create, charge, and send out to accomplish a magickal purpose, whether it be for protection, accumulating wealth, cursing, gathering energy, or whatever you choose it to do. It uses your subjective reality and energy to complete any purpose you choose, even worship. To make your servitor, you do the following:

1. Seek Lucifer for a name for your thought form. This must be kept secret.
2. Choose or draw an image of your thought form.
3. Write down your statement of intent for the servitor. Include a list of its powers you want it to have (e.g., one of mine has the power to attract money through savings, bargains, and plain outright receipt of cash).
4. Create a logo for your servitor.
5. Charge the servitor by visualizing it until you actually see it. Also focus on its logo and repeat its name to yourself for ten to thirty minutes. You can choose to do this under a full moon or during the hours of Jupiter during the day or both. Keep doing this for three days. Don't visualize it as being too big. Small is adequate as the larger they get the more energy they need, and they can exhaust you. The power of sex is a good way to embody or charge your servitor.
6. Continue to meditate on your servitor and its purpose. See it achieving your purpose and coming back to you.
7. Cast your servitor or send it out to do your bidding. This is as simple as strongly willing and commanding it to go and do what you want. Use its name. Focus your energy on sending it out to do your work. Believe in it. You can also focus your energy using sexual energy to give you the boost of power you need to launch your servitor.

Once your servitor has achieved its purpose simply stop thinking about it, and it will disappear. Never leave a servitor hanging around, or others will see it, and it will cause problems (such as haunting). A high burst of positive energy from you will dispel your thought form or any seeking to harm you through them. Believe me when I tell you some magicians send servitors out there to damage other people.

***

In summary, this chapter has presented the reader with a variety of tools and techniques for meditation, grounding, shielding for protection and chakra cleansing. The chapter has also focused on dreamwork, astral travel and the creation of servitors. All these things the reader will come across during their studies of the occult, no matter what path you are following.

The next chapter will deal with divination. Divination or scrying is where you use certain tools to provide insight into any number of situations, past, present and future. The chapter will provide tools and techniques for some divinatory techniques and it will provide some divination exercises.

CHAPTER 7

Divination

D ivination, or scrying, is the art of gaining insight into a subject using supernatural means. It is as old as civilization itself. There have been many forms of divination developed over the centuries, from cards to shells to telling fortunes by entrails. There are many types of divination the reader will be familiar with, such as tea-leaf reading, palmistry, and tarot cards. We will discuss a few here but before we do here are some tips that are universally applicable to divination. When you are using divinatory tools try the following:

1. Have a quiet environment with no electronic devices nearby.
2. Meditate on your question.
3. Burn candles and incense.
4. Anoint your third eye with Tiger Balm.
5. Don't doubt your abilities.
6. Write your results.

There are many types of divination. The main types I will be discussing here are pendulums, Ouija boards, pyromancy, astrology, and black mirrors. First up, we will discuss pendulums, which are arguably the simplest form of divination.

The Pendulum

The pendulum method of divination was first established in Rome during the late Roman Empire. It involves dangling an object on a piece of string so as to tell your fortune or communicate with spirits. It can also be used to locate objects that are lost or hidden. This method of divination was a precursor to the Ouija Board. You set up letters, "Yes," and "No" on paper and place them on a steady surface. Once you have done this, you should construct and consecrate your pendulum. The best pendulums seem to be made from crystals on a chain.

To consecrate your pendulum, you simply pass it through sage smoke, rinse it with saltwater and dry it in the moonlight. Say a few words over it like "I offer this instrument to Leviathan as an instrument of communication, that its words may be true." You can also use other Demons to consecrate it as well such as Alloces, Orobas, or Astaroth. You can also offer it to all four of them if you wish. To use the pendulum, you simply do the following:

- Hold it in your hand. Either hand is okay. Keep it steady.
- Ask it what "yes" is. Let the pendulum swing. Notice the direction it swings in and note it down.
- Ask the pendulum what "no" is and let it swing. Notice the direction it swings in and note it down.
- Once you have established "yes" and "no," start by asking simple yes/no type questions. Be sure to meditate on your question before you begin. If it doesn't work, then put it away and try again at some later stage.
- You can also use letters of the alphabet and numbers to communicate with the pendulum once you become more adept with it.

The pendulum is very good for communicating with Demons. It is also great for finding things that are lost and hidden. They are even used for healing and dowsing. I find the pendulum is the simplest way to communicate and very effective. I find myself using my pendulum several times a day to answer questions people pose to me and also to find things that are lost.

In the next section, we will look at the Ouija board.

Ouija Boards

The Ouija board has been much maligned over time, usually as a function of popular media. However, its usefulness as a tool in divination is quite profound. The Ouija board first came into existence as a toy in 1891 and grew in popularity with the rise of Spiritualism, as a more serious artifact of the occult.

Before you use your board, you must cleanse and consecrate it. Sprinkle it lightly with saltwater and smudge it with sage smoke. Rub sage oil into the board and the planchette. You can also drip candle wax onto the planchette and engrave a Demonic sigil of your choosing into the wax. I use a sigil decal on mine. I find that is effective, and most printers will print decals if you have the right medium in which to print.

Using a board is quite simple, and it is best operated alone. It is useful for contacting Demons and the spirits of the dead. Note well, though, that not all Demons like the use of the board or respond to it. Essentially, to use the board, you must enter a deep meditative state whereby you block out all extraneous distraction and noise. You relax and place your fingers lightly on the planchette and allow it to gently pull. It will spell out words and answer yes/no questions. Start slowly and simply at first and build up to more complex questions. In the next section, we will discuss pyromancy, which is divination by fire.

Pyromancy

Pyromancy is the attempt to divine the future or communicate with spirits by looking at fire and smoke from fire, using the shape it emits to discover answers. It originated in ancient Greece, and the word can be broken down into its Greek roots—*pyros*, meaning "fire," and *manteia*, meaning "divination." You can get different responses depending on what you burn. People throw salt into fire, burn plants, and laurel leaves.

Begin fire divination with a candle. Rub the candle with an oil like Sage or depending on the purpose for which you are divining. For example, if you are divining for love, you may want to consider using rose oil. Carve a Demonic sigil

99

into the side of the candle, an incantation or a word of power. Light the candle and stare into the flame of the candle in a deep meditative state. Observe the colors, intensity, shapes in the smoke and in the flame, and write them down. Also ask the candle yes/no type questions and see how the flame moves for each response. The colors you would use depend on the purpose of your question:

- White—all questions
- Purple—spirituality, position, and authority
- Blue—sickness, health and recovery
- Green—family, children, money, jobs
- Yellow—relocation, passing tests, communication
- Orange—physical actions, activity
- Red or Pink—love and relationships
- Pink—friendship

If you are working with a larger fire, wait until the embers begin to die down. Sprinkle some salt onto the embers and watch the flames for twenty minutes. Observe the pops and crackles, the color and intensity of the flame, and look for symbols in the fire. If you see a big symbol, take note of it because it is important. The images are predictions and portents. A clear flame with no smoke is a sign of good fortune. To see a windmill or a fountain, you will experience change for the better in the future. If the fire suddenly goes out, it spells disaster. If you see flowers in the embers, it is a sign of disappointment forthcoming. If the flame crackles loudly and is quick to kindle, this is a good sign. If the flame crackles softly and was slow to kindle, this was not a good sign. This was a brief dissection of pyromancy. There are many books covering the subject. Next, we will delve into astrology and the study of the stars in relation to magick.

Astrology

One of the biggest forms of divination utilized today, and proliferated by popular media, is Astrology. Astrology is another ancient method of divination that has developed across the globe and has been popular for many thousands of years as a way of predicting events and as a tool in magick. Astrology is the study of the sun, moon, and planets and how they are positioned to effect changes for life here on Earth, predict character and effect magickal outcomes. In magick, astrology is used to determine altar configuration, colors used, correspondences, and timeliness in casting and performing rituals.

I felt it was necessary to include astrology in this book as it is pivotal in magickal workings. Note that I will not be delving into natal astrology at any great length here as it is a subject that would consume a whole book. Instead, I will focus on the magickal qualities of astrology and how it can be utilized by you the magician.

The planets correspond to Demons of the Goetia as well as the Qliphoth and Chakra systems. While the planets move, their relationships to each other does not change at all. However, they do move over time. Each planet is a source of specific power. Planets correlate to minerals, plants, herbs, metals, and colors.

- ☉ Sun rules Leo—Vitality, Life, Ego, Creativity. Depicts the macrocosm and microcosm. Tiphereth in the Qabalah and Tagahirim on the Tree of Death. Colors are orange and yellow. Metal is gold.
- ♃ Jupiter rules Sagittarius—Abundance, Expansion, and Wisdom. This planet represents Chesed in the Tree of Life and Gamchicoth on the Tree of Death. Colors are blue and violet. Metal is tin.
- ♂ Mars rules Aries—Assertiveness. Associated with the power of will. It is associated with Geburah in the Tree of Life and Adramelech in the Tree of Death. Colors are red and scarlet. Metal is iron.
- ☿ Mercury rules Gemini and Virgo—Intellect, Logic, Perception, and Communication. It represents a channel between layers of being. Mercury represents Hod in the Qabalah and Adramelech in the Tree of Death. Colors are orange and yellow. Metal is mercury.
- ☾ Moon rules Cancer—Emotions, Moods, Intuition. Depicts spirit and soul. It also depicts the unconscious and subconscious mind. Colors are violet, white, and blue. Metal is silver. In the Tree of Life, it rules Jesod, and in the Tree of Death, it rules Gamaliel.
- ♆ Neptune rules Pisces—Dreams, Illusions, Delusion, Spirituality, Oneness, and Addiction. This planet represents true vision and

delusion. This correlates to Kether on the Tree of Life. Colors are blue and aqua. Metal is cobalt.

- ♀ Pluto rules Scorpio—Power, Transformation, Obsession, Alchemy, Healing, Life, and Death. This planet is correlated with Daath on the Tree of Life and Thamiel on the Tree of Death. Colors are white and gray. Metal is Bismuth.

- ♄ Saturn rules Capricorn and Aquarius—Structure, Restriction, Time, Authority, Discipline, and Limitation, Magick such as binding, loosing, cursing, and hexing. This planet correlates to Binah on the Tree of Life. It rules Satariel in the Qliphoth. Colors are black and indigo. Metal is lead.

- ♅ Uranus rules Aquarius—Revolution, Rebellion, Individualism, Eccentricity, Humanitarianism, Science, and Invention. This planet represents the divine spark and the higher self. This planet correlates to Chokmah on the Tree of Life and Golachab on the Tree of Death. Colors are brown and beige. Metal is zinc.

- ♀ Venus rules Taurus and Libra—Pleasure, Romance, Love, Femininity, Beauty, and Art. Venus represents the transmutation of the sun's power here on Earth. It is associated with Netzach in the Tree of Life and Harab Serapel in the Tree of Death. Colors are emerald green. Metal is copper.

Over the years, many asteroids and other bodies have been found. These are sometimes used in astrology as well—it depends largely on the astrologer.

The zodiac signs are important to discuss here. These are not the constellations but 30 percent segments that portray the journey of the sun through the sphere of the year. Because of the slow wobble in the Earth's rotation, the stars move 1 percent every 72 years, so the constellations in the sky do not match up with the signs of the zodiac. The northern spring equinox marks the beginning of Aries and moves from there. The vernal equinox is the point of origin for the degrees of longitude used in astrology. In fact, the changes in the seasons mark the changes in energy. The flow of the signs is counterclockwise. Each of the signs has an element, a modality and a polarity.

Polarity means that the sign is either extroverted (+) or more introverted (-). Modality implies the following:

1. **Cardinal signs**—enterprising and bring about change. Aries, Cancer, Libra, and Capricorn are cardinal. The outpouring of creative energies coming into being. This correlates to the desire of the magickian.
2. **Fixed signs**—consolidate and preserve change and are focused and determined. These signs are Taurus, Leo, Scorpio, and Aquarius. This represents homeostatic balance of energies.
3. **Mutable signs**—flexible and adjust to change readily. These signs are Gemini, Virgo, Sagittarius, and Pisces. This represents the divine will to evolve.

The elements are as follows:

1. **Fire**—Brings vitality, excitement, and intensity.
2. **Earth**—Brings stability and common sense. They get things done.
3. **Air**—Brings intellect and sociability.
4. **Water**—Brings strengthened emotions and intuition.

The elements are self-explanatory in their use in magick. Each Demon and each spell utilize an element in its execution and summoning.

Table 6—The Zodiac Dates, Polarity, Modality, and Element

Sign	Zodiac	Dates	Polarity	Modality	Element
♈	Aries the ram	March 21—April 20	+	Cardinal	Fire
♉	Taurus the bull	April 21—May 21	-	Fixed	Earth
♊	Gemini the twins	May 22—June 21	+	Mutable	Air
♋	Cancer the crab	June 22—July 23	-	Cardinal	Water
♌	Leo the lion	July 24—August 23	+	Fixed	Fire

Sign	Zodiac	Dates	Polarity	Modality	Element
♍	Virgo the virgin	Aug 24—Sep 23	-	Mutable	Earth
♎	Libra the scales	Sep 24—Oct 23	+	Cardinal	Air
♏	Scorpio the scorpion	Oct 24—Nov 22	-	Fixed	Water
♐	Sagittarius the archer	Nov 23—Dec 21	+	Mutable	Fire
♑	Capricorn the goat	Dec 22—Jan 20	-	Cardinal	Earth
♒	Aquarius water bearer	Jan 21—Feb 19	+	Fixed	Air
♓	Pisces the fish	Feb 20—March 20	-	Mutable	Water

Each sign has a thought form associated with it that can be used in magick. Each thought form takes on the qualities of the sign itself. Each of the twelve signs is representative of human consciousness and personality type.

There are the twelve houses or sectors that make up the circle of the year that represent areas of your life and are related to how the Earth spins around its axis. These wedges, or sectors, can vary in size unlike the signs. Effectively, astrology maps the movements of planets through these houses. They are akin to the clock and measure seconds, minutes, and hours. The houses mark the position of the planets in degrees.

It is worth mentioning ascendants here. The ascendant is the rising sign of your birth, or the sign climbing over the eastern horizon at the time of your birth. I am a Leo, but I was born at 9:00 a.m., so my ascendant is in Libra. The ascendant marks the start of the twelve houses for you as an individual. It shapes the persona that you show to the world. So if you were born at dawn, your rising sign will be the same as your sun sign. The twelve houses start with your ascendant sign. If you are not sure of when you were born, then you just take your ascendant from dawn or midday.

Table 7—Astrological Houses

House	Mundane Concepts	Magickal Association
First	Self-absorption, personal projection and appearance	House of Aries. Determines the qualities of the human energy field or magickal persona.
Second	Values, self-worth, finances and assets, and security	House of Taurus. Outlines the magickal powers the magician has naturally.
Third	Travel, local network, siblings, and communications	House of Gemini. Telepathy, chanting and voice skills. Ability to sense magickal energy.
Fourth	Foundations, family, ancestors, and home atmosphere	House of Cancer. Ancestral magick, magickal lineages.
Fifth	Self-expression, children, identity, security, and play	House of Leo. Magickal ritual and creativity in ritual. Animal magnetism, charisma. The role of leaders in magick are determined at this time.
Sixth	Service, working environment, health, and integration	House of Virgo. Magickal oaths, pacts, and duties. Balance between the mundane and spiritual.
Seventh	Partnership, dealings with others and adversaries	House of Libra. Concerns how you work with others in your path. Mediumship and channeling. Relates to how you interact with deity.

House	Mundane Concepts	Magickal Association
Eighth	Other resources, inheritance, secret powers, and death	House of Scorpio. Shadow work dominates here. Cycles of death and rebirth covered.
Ninth	Long-distance travel, higher education, and the law	House of Sagittarius. Deals with higher mind, prophecy, relationship with religion.
Tenth	Ambitions, author-ities, goals, and professional expression	House of Capricorn. Place in growing and tending the world. Goals of incarnation being achieved.
Eleventh	Social affinities, groups, friendships, and political visions	House of Aquarius. Lodges, covens, egregores, belief structures of ideologies and traditions.
Twelfth	Withdrawal, isola-tion, the divine and inner worlds	House of Pisces. Higher Self, Holy Guardian Angel/Demon.

The Aspects

The next consideration is the aspects. This refers to planetary interactions with each other. They are either harmonious or inharmonious, supportive or challenging. Planets are said to be in aspect to each other when they are a given distance apart as measured in degrees.

Remember: signs are thirty degrees apart, and the planets will represent some degree differential from the sign or will wax or wane toward that perfect differential. There are several standard aspects that need to be considered.

- The Conjunction (!)—0°, where the mixing of planetary energies is intense. This is a neutral aspect in that it can be either favorable or unfavorable.

- The Sextile (*)—60° where planets are 60° apart or two signs apart plus/minus 6°. This is favorable and inspires communication and harmony, but these must be actively encouraged.

- The Square (#)—90° or three signs apart, in the same modality but varied elements. It is the most challenging and denotes hardship but promotes growth and learning.

- The Trine ($) 120° or four signs apart, same element but different modality. This is a harmonious aspect whereby characteristic talents become evident.

- The Opposition (") 180° or six signs apart. Where planets are directly opposite to each other on the zodiacal wheel. This is a complex and challenging aspect. There will be great effort with little results.

- The Semisextile (%) 30°, which suggests a low-grade positivity between planets.

- The Quintile (Q) 72° brings with it spiritual awareness.

- The Quincunx/Inconjunct and 150° where planets are of different elements and modalities. Planets in this aspect are underutilized.

Below is an example of a natal chart showing the aspects, planets, signs, houses, and the ascendants. I have pointed out what symbols are present but won't go into detail as to the interpretation as that can be gained by understanding the different symbols within. You will get a cursory idea from reading books on interpretation of astrological symbols.

Figure 17—A Natal Chart

Xajjia Satanas

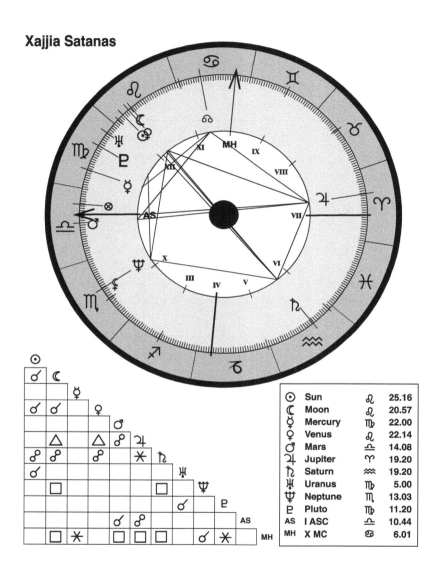

		Sun	♌	25.16
☉	Sun	♌	25.16
☾	Moon	♌	20.57
☿	Mercury	♍	22.00
♀	Venus	♌	22.14
♂	Mars	♎	14.08
♃	Jupiter	♈	19.20
♄	Saturn	♒	19.20
♅	Uranus	♍	5.00
♆	Neptune	♏	13.03
♇	Pluto	♍	11.20
AS	I ASC	♎	10.44
MH	X MC	♋	6.01

So let's examine this briefly. First, it shows the sun sign is Leo with an ascendant in Libra. The moon sign is also in Leo.

• There is a conjunction between the Sun and Moon, Sun and Venus.

- There is an opposition between the Sun and Saturn.
- There is a conjunction between the Sun and Uranus.
- The Moon is in the eleventh house, and there is a conjunction between the Moon and Venus and a trine between the Moon and Jupiter.
- There is opposition between the Moon and Saturn.
- There is a square between the Moon and Neptune.
- Mercury is in the twelfth house with Venus in Leo, Venus is in the eleventh house.
- There is a trine between Venus and Jupiter, an opposition between Venus and Saturn.
- Mars is in the first house and is in Libra. There is an opposition between Mars and Jupiter and a conjunction between Mars and the ascendant.
- Jupiter is in Aries and the seventh house. There is a sextile between Jupiter and Saturn and an opposition between Jupiter and the ascendant.
- Saturn is in the fifth house with a square between Saturn and Neptune.

These are just a few observations from the natal chart provided. There are a lot more that the reader can discern for themselves. This was just an example of a natal chart, although we are not covering natal charts in this book. It is extremely complex and requires a thorough understanding of Astrology and a lot of time to examine all of the possibilities.

Some other considerations in astrology that are important are retrograding planets as they will affect magickal outcomes. For example, Mercury in retrograde will affect communication, retrogrades for Venus will not bode well for love and relationships, and retrogrades for Saturn can mean that magickal workings will not be successful. Jupiter retrogrades mean it is not a good time for finances, and Mars in retrograde will mean relationship issues may arise and assertiveness may be questioned. Think about these as you are doing rituals and working with magick.

The planetary hours are most pivotal in magick workings as they are the correspondence of time. The hours you will use will correspond to your purpose in magick. Below is a table of the planetary hours for the southern hemisphere. It will differ for the northern hemisphere, so if you are reading this and you are from the northern hemisphere, refer to the internet for more information.

Table 8—Southern Hemisphere Planetary Hours—Daytime

Planetary Hours of the Day							
Hour	Sunday	Monday	Tuesday	Wednesday	Thursday	Friday	Saturday
1	Sun	Moon	Mars	Mercury	Jupiter	Venus	Saturn
2	Venus	Saturn	Sun	Moon	Mars	Mercury	Jupiter
3	Mercury	Jupiter	Venus	Saturn	Sun	Moon	Mars
4	Moon	Mars	Mercury	Jupiter	Venus	Saturn	Sun
5	Saturn	Sun	Moon	Mars	Mercury	Jupiter	Venus
6	Jupiter	Venus	Saturn	Sun	Moon	Mars	Mercury
7	Mars	Mercury	Jupiter	Venus	Saturn	Sun	Moon
8	Sun	Moon	Mars	Mercury	Jupiter	Venus	Saturn
9	Venus	Saturn	Sun	Moon	Mars	Mercury	Jupiter
10	Mercury	Jupiter	Venus	Saturn	Sun	Moon	Mars
11	Moon	Mars	Mercury	Jupiter	Venus	Saturn	Sun
12	Saturn	Sun	Moon	Mars	Mercury	Jupiter	Venus

Table 9—Southern Hemisphere Planetary Hours—Nighttime

Planetary Hours of the Night							
Hour	Sunday	Monday	Tuesday	Wednesday	Thursday	Friday	Saturday
1	Jupiter	Venus	Saturn	Sun	Moon	Mars	Mercury
2	Mars	Mercury	Jupiter	Venus	Saturn	Sun	Moon
3	Sun	Moon	Mars	Mercury	Jupiter	Venus	Saturn
4	Venus	Saturn	Sun	Moon	Mars	Mercury	Jupiter
5	Mercury	Jupiter	Venus	Saturn	Sun	Moon	Mars
6	Moon	Mars	Mercury	Jupiter	Venus	Saturn	Sun
7	Saturn	Sun	Moon	Mars	Mercury	Jupiter	Venus

Planetary Hours of the Night							
Hour	Sunday	Monday	Tuesday	Wednesday	Thursday	Friday	Saturday
8	Jupiter	Venus	Saturn	Sun	Moon	Mars	Mercury
9	Mars	Mercury	Jupiter	Venus	Saturn	Sun	Moon
10	Sun	Moon	Mars	Mercury	Jupiter	Venus	Saturn
11	Venus	Saturn	Sun	Moon	Mars	Mercury	Jupiter
12	Mercury	Jupiter	Venus	Saturn	Sun	Moon	Mars

Hour of the Sun: This hour is useful for workings pertaining to employment, public speaking, improving social status, approaching authority figures, improving health.

Hour of the Moon: This hour is useful for workings that relate to temporary change, for increased intuition, and for all domestic activities. You will also need to be aware of magickal practice during moon phase. See the discussion below on moon magick.

Hour of Mercury: This hour relates to abstract thinking, mental alertness, contracts, or any activity related to communication.

Hour of Venus: This hour relates to love, financial investments, reconciliation, mediation of disputes, achieving calm after stress, and to work toward peace.

Hour of Mars: This hour good for activities and exercise, boldness, courage, active enterprise. Mars can be confrontational depending on your mood.

Hour of Jupiter: This hour is useful for workings pertaining to success and money matters. The only downside would be where a tendency toward overindulgence or excess.

Hour of Saturn: This hour relates to getting organized, getting work done and being productive, breaking bad habits and addictions, accepting executing responsibilities, and for contemplation and meditation. This is a great time for magickal workings to be executed such as bindings, hexing, and casting spells in general.

You can get apps for your smart phone that tell you the planetary hours. It is not necessary to work them out yourself.

The next thing to consider in magick is the moon phase. Waxing versus waning moons is important for specific outcomes. My rule of thumb is to cast spells and perform rituals on a waxing moon if you want positive change and related to projects that require success, loosing, healing, and blessing. Waning moons are good for getting rid of negatives, such as bad habits, cursing, and binding. The full moon is good for any type of spell and enhances spell energy immensely.

The moon influences each of the twelve zodiac signs. The following magickal workings are recommended during the time moon enters different zodiacal signs:

- **Moon in Aries**—Time to begin new things. It is the best time for short term results.
- **Moon in Taurus**—Great for protection and warding work
- **Moon in Gemini**—Great moon for using divination and astral travel
- **Moon in Cancer**—Great time for honing psychic abilities
- **Moon in Leo**—Best time to hone leadership qualities
- **Moon in Virgo**—Great for breaking of bad habits
- **Moon in Libra**—Good for contracts and negotiations, pacts with entities, and resolution of differences
- **Moon in Scorpio**—This is a great moon for breaking negative magickal workings, summoning, and banishing.
- **Moon in Sagittarius**—This is the time to expand your consciousness and work on your higher self.
- **Moon in Capricorn**—In terms of magick, it is good for loosing and binding magick.
- **Moon in Aquarius**—Great time to enter oaths/pledges
- **Moon in Pisces**—Great for dream work and past life regression therapy, trances and meditation

There are candle colors, gemstone, metal, and herb correspondences that go with the zodiac signs. This is useful in magickal working with the planets and signs. See the table below:

Table 10—Zodiac Correspondences

Zodiac Sign:	Colors:	Herbs	Crystals/Gems	Metals
Aries	Crimson, Pink, Red, White	• Basil • Nettle • Chervil • Wormwood • Geranium	• Bloodstone	• Iron
Taurus	Olive, Pink, Red, Yellow	• Mint • Thyme • Violet • Marshmallow • Catnip	• Sapphire • Malachite • Jade • Dioptase • Amber	• Copper
Gemini	Blue, Brown, Red, Yellow	• Dill • Parsley • Anise • Lavender • Marjoram	• Agate • Chalcedony • Stibnite • Red Fire Quartz • Harlequin Quartz	• Mercury
Cancer	Brown, Green, White	• Sage • Aloe • Lemon balm • Bay • Parsley	• Emerald • Citrine • Moonstone	• Silver
Leo	Gold, Green, Orange, Red, Yellow	• Sunflower • Lemon Balm • Chamomile • Tarragon • Eyebright	• Onyx • Zircon	• Gold
Virgo	Beige, Black, Gold, Mauve, Rainbow	• Caraway • Dill • Mint • Horehound • Marjoram	• Carnelian • Chrysoberyl • Aventurine	• Mercury

Libra	Black, Blue, Green	• Catnip • Elderberry • Thyme • St. John's Wort • Bergamot	• Peridot • Jade • Aventurine • Tourmaline	• Copper
Scorpio	Black, Brown, Magenta, Vermillion	• Basil • Sage • Catnip • Coriander • Nettle	• Beryl • Aquamarine • Rose Quartz • Rhodochrosite	• Plutonium
Sagittarius	Blue, Gold, Red, Violet	• Sage • Basil • Borage • Saffron • Chervil	• Topaz • Turquoise	• Tin
Capricorn	Black, Brown, Gray, Red	• Rosemary • Tarragon • Caraway • Chamomile • Marjoram	• Ruby • Hematite • Onyx • Jet • Obsidian	• Lead
Aquarius	Blue, Gray, Green	• Comfrey • Rosemary • Fennel • Violet • Valerian	• Garnet	• Silver • Uranium
Pisces	Blue, Green, White	• Basil • Lemon balm • Borage • Sage	• Amethyst • Sugilite • Fluorite • Chrome Diopside	• Platinum

Each Demon is associated with a Zodiac sign, an element, a day, and a planet. See appendix C—Demon Correspondences. It is important to incorporate this into your magickal workings as well where applicable. For example, Duke Aim is associated with Nov 4–12. This Demon is associated with the direction south, the planet Neptune, and the sign of Cancer. So working with Aim when Neptune is in Cancer would be favorable. Also working within the phases of the moon, for example if you are doing an invocation of a Goetic spirit it would behoove you to do this ritual within the first fourteen days of a whole moon on even days. This would be the same for dark moons for execration magick.

That concludes our cursory discussion on astrological symbology. Next, we will talk about the construction and use of the black mirror. Black mirrors come under scrying which means to focus meditatively on a shiny surface until a vision appears. It is ultimately using clairvoyance as a method of communication and prediction.

Black Mirrors

Making a black mirror is simple to use and construct. You need the following items:

- A small picture frame with the back removed and the glass intact
- A can of high-gloss enamel black spray paint
- Somewhere to spray the surface and dry the item
- Newspaper to catch the excess spray
- A small sigil decal of your patron Demon. Mine is Gamigin/ Samgina.
- Some sage oil to anoint the mirror when complete
- A black velvet cloth to cover the mirror when it is done so as to keep prying eyes from looking into our plane of existence when not in use
- A decal of a scrying demon to place on the mirror frame to boost its power

To make the mirror, you simply apply three coats of black enamel high-gloss spray paint to the back of the glass, allowing it to fully dry between coats. Make sure you have plenty of newspaper down on the ground to avoid spraying your floors and walls with the paint. Once it has dried, I leave mine for three days to fully dry and then reassemble the picture frame, placing the painted side of the glass down into the frame so the natural glass side is pointing outward in the frame. You then decorate the frame with the decal, rub the frame with sage oil, and cover it with the black velvet cloth when not in use. Dedicate your mirror to your patron or to Leviathan, Alloces, Orobas, or Astaroth, who are the Demons of divination. This prevents "other" spirits from coming through and trying to connect. If you are using the mirror for necromantic purposes, you will need to dedicate it to Gamigin, Baalberith, or Babael.

When you use the black mirror, you need to light incense and a candle that is placed behind you and the black mirror. You will need to get into a deep meditative state, even do a ritual beforehand. You sit and stare into the mirror until images start to appear. Write down what you see. Feel free to commence asking questions of the mirror. Start with simple yes/no questions first and build up to more complex ones. Remember not to falter in your ability if you fail at first, as this takes some practice and requires dedication and a keen eye.

In conclusion, I have endeavored to cover some pivotal divination methods here that relate directly to magickal practice. There are many forms of divination that are not covered here, including palmistry and other forms of divination. The next chapter will cover spell work and the different types of magick utilized in the left-hand path.

CHAPTER 8

Spell Work

Magick and spell work are the crux of the left-hand path. You cannot have one without the other. This chapter will discuss and demonstrate different types of magick that you will come across in the left-hand path and what they entail.

Magick is the power of influencing events and situations by utilizing mysterious and sometimes supernatural means. Magick is made up of three components which are desire, will and intent. Events cause us to want to use magick in the first place. Then these three ingredients when applied to events will affect change. See the figure below.

Figure 18—Magick Mechanisms

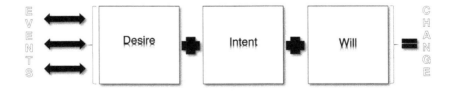

For example, if you are suddenly finding yourself low on cash you create the desire for more money. When you apply your intent (e.g., "I intend to have more money") and you make it a force of your will and do everything to help that along, you will affect the mechanisms of change. This change can happen in a number of ways: (a) it may be that you find five dollars on the ground on your way to work; (b) you might find that someone bequeaths an estate to you; (c) or simply it may mean you become more efficient at budgeting and reduce your spending; or (d) you simply increase your income by means of a pay rise or promotion. This is magick. It seems mundane, but that is how it works.

There are many ways you can do magick. These ways differ in delivery only and are not necessarily right or wrong. I will discuss the types of magick here in the next few pages in the hope you will gain a preliminary understanding of each type of magick. Before we discuss the differing styles of magick commonly in use, we will look at spells and what they entail.

What Are Spells?

Spells are the use of words to create charms and incantations used in magick to affect change. These are the carrier mechanism for magick in that they embody desire, intent, and will. Spells may contain more than just desire, intent, and will. They may contain correspondences or things used to make a spell effective. This may include herbs, colors, incense, and timing elements, such as moon phase and planetary alignments.

How Spells Work

The moment you start preparing for a spell is the moment it starts working because of your intent and will. Your planning phase is like you are actually casting the spell, so be very careful with preparation and planning.

Spells work principally by affecting the mind of the caster. It is a tool of psychology. By casting a spell, you are actualizing desire and imposing your intent and will on something to affect change.

Rules of Spellcasting

1. Specificity—Spells must be specific. This means that it is not enough to say I want a cat, you have to specify what cat, what color, what type, and so on.
2. Timeliness—When the spell is to be completed by.
3. Key operators—Who is involved in making the spell happen.
4. Where—Where the results are delivered to.

Now that we have a handle on what spells are and how they work, we can look at the differing types of magick in use today. We will begin our discussion with candle magick.

Candle Magick

Candle magick is probably the simplest form of magick. Candle magick harnesses the transformative powers of fire to affect change. Candle magick is a form of sympathetic magick where you have a candle standing as a proxy for a person or thing. You can also use the candle as a correspondence in spell work. It is a versatile and effective method of doing magick. For example, if you have a candle with your name on it, it can be used for healing and wealth creation. This is sympathetic magick, which is discussed below.

With candles, we talk about candle colors as being useful for differing types of candle-magick spells. The table below lists a few colors and their significance.

Table 11—Candle Color Significance

Candle Color	Magickal Significance
White	Truth, purity, sincerity, power and cleansing, spirituality, wholeness, generosity, outgoingness, prophecy, clairvoyance
Yellow	Persuasion, confidence, unity, success, creativity, development of occult powers, invocation, inspiration, concentration
Green	Finance, luck, abundance, cooperation, generosity, fertility, ambition, greed, envy, harmony, peace, health, healing
Blue	Health both mental and physical, change, truth, inspiration, immortality, loyalty, serenity, sincerity, devotion, kindness, patience, fidelity, honesty, peace, harmony in the home
Red	Sex and strength, courage, energy, impulsiveness, willpower, conceit, vitality, magnetism
Pink	Honor and love, affection, service, spiritual awakening, unselfishness, leadership, diplomacy, femininity
Orange	Encouragement, attraction, joy, enthusiasm, friendship, stimulation, self-control, adaptability, intellect, receptivity, organization
Brown	Hesitation, uncertainty, neutrality, balance, concentration, indecision, telepathic power, study, communication, thrift, earthiness
Purple	Spirituality, tension, overcoming obstacles, dignity, ambition, idealism, psychic ability, progress, independence, protection, pride, honor
Black	Loss, discord, confusion, adversity, protection from evil, shield from the evil eye, repel black magick

Different sources list different meanings for each of these colors. These are what I use in magic. Now what I usually do is anoint candles with essential oils depending on what I am doing. For example, sage oil is used for cleansing and purity. Some essential oils I use are listed below.

Table 12—Essential Oils

Essential Oil	Magickal Purpose
Acacia	Meditation
Allspice	Determination, energy
Almond	Wakefulness, prosperity
Anise	Clairvoyance
Apple Blossom	Happiness and success
Basil	Harmony
Bayberry	Luck, money
Benzoin	Peace of mind
Bergamot	Prosperity, protection
Camphor	Psychic powers, breaking up relationships
Carnation	Healing
Cinnamon	Protection, sexual stimulation, meditation
Cinquefoil	Luck, money, wisdom
Clary Sage	Cleansing, purification
Cloves	Aphrodisiac
Coriander	Love
Cumin	Peace and harmony
Cypress	Peace, protection, consecration
Eucalyptus	Healing, banishing
Frankincense	Purification, exorcism
Geranium	Protection, courage
Ginger	Passion
Honeysuckle	For the mind, promotes memory
Hyacinth	Mental health
Hyssop	Cleansing and purification, breaking of hexes
Jasmine	Love, attraction
Lavender	Healing, cleansing
Lemon	Cleansing
Lemongrass	To aid psychic powers

Essential Oil	Magickal Purpose
Lilac	Past lives
Lotus	Blessing, consecration, meditation
Mint	Prosperity
Musk	Sex
Myrrh	Purification, breaking hexes
Nutmeg	Sleep, third-eye awakening
Orange	To make someone in the mood for marriage
Patchouli	Money, wealth, wards off evil and negativity
Peppermint	Opening the third-eye chakra
Rose	Love, attraction
Rosemary	Healing and for common sense
Sandalwood	Protection
Sesame	Hope
Tea Tree	Healing, banishing
Vanilla	Sexual attraction
Violet	Love
Ylang-Ylang	Irresistibility to the opposite sex

You can make these oils yourself by steeping the ground plant matter into a carrier oil such as grapeseed oil. These keep for a while and the potency is quite good, it is in fact better if you are making these oils yourself as commercial oils tend to be watered down.

Candle magick is a very substantial and very simple magickal technique. Candle magick can be a form of sympathetic magick. Some things I tend to do when using candle magick is, I write abbreviated names or situations on the side of the candle to give it more potency. I then rub the corresponding oil onto the candle in a downward motion. I set up my altar so I have the right incense that corresponds to the oil used and then begin the working.

The types of candles used will be dictated by the type of magick. Generally, I use taper candles. However, I have been known to use candles in the shape of a person (male or female) depending on the subject's gender. You can buy these from specialty shops or make them yourself. Since I am in Australia, I have to source these from overseas. You can make the casts yourself out of plaster and pour candle wax into them.

Your candle-magick ritual will include research on the hours of the day and planetary correspondences mentioned in the last chapter as well as other astrological factors, moon correspondences, and perhaps seasonal factors. To set up your ritual, you will need to do the following:

- Make sure you shower with Hyssop soap or Lavender before your ritual to cleanse yourself.
- Work on the correct day of the week. For example, Fridays is associated with Venus so you would do a love working on a Friday. See table 14—Days of the Week.
- Work your spell during the correct planetary hour. For instance, you would work a general spell for money during the hour of Saturn (see the previous chapter for more information).
- Make sure you have the correct moon phase for working. Waxing and full moons/new moon for positive workings such as healings, loosing magick, blessings, and consecrations. A waning and full moon/new moon for reversals, banishings, bindings, or hexing.
- Have a quiet spot where you will not be disturbed. I have my altar setup facing north under a window, so I feel the effects of the moon. Sometimes in the right weather, if you live in a country area, you can set your altar up outdoors.
- Setup your altar facing north with a cloth, incense and oils (see figure 19—Candle-Magick Altar Layout). Make sure your altar is consecrated and cleansed before you use it by either sprinkling saltwater on it or burning sage over it.
- Have your candles at the ready with names or abbreviated situations carved into the side of them from the bottom up. For example, if you were doing a money working you would simply write wealth on the side of the candle.
- Rub your candles with the corresponding oil that you wish to work with according to the purpose of the spell. Start from the middle and massage the oil in a downward motion and then from the middle upward.

- Have your astral candle present on the altar to the left of the incense burner. This is the candle that represents you and is often aligned with your zodiac sign (see the table below).
- Your candle represents fire on the altar, and incense represents air. Have a bowl of water on the altar and a bowl of salt to represent Earth.

Table 13—Astral Candle Colors

Zodiac Sign	Candle Color
Aquarius	Yellow and Blue
Pisces	Blue and Green
Aries	Pink and Orange
Taurus	Blue and Gold
Gemini	Red and Blue
Cancer	Red and Green
Leo	Pink and Orange
Virgo	Pink and Gold
Libra	Pink and Gold
Scorpio	Yellow and Blue
Sagittarius	Red and Orange
Capricorn	Red and Gold

Because authors cannot agree on what your own astral color is, it is practical to choose your own color. This could be a color you like, or one revealed to you during meditation. Also, sometimes if you are representing someone else in a candle, think about the colors they commonly wear and use those as a representation of the other person.

Figure 19—Candle-Magick Altar Layout

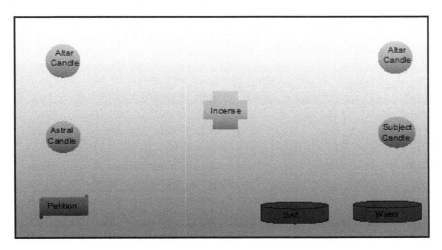

There are different types of candles for different purposes. Here are some examples, for instance:

- Bayberry scented candles—for blessing homes
- Beeswax candles—Color vibration is not used with these candles, instead they are used for special candle-magick ceremonies for protection and spirituality.
- Cat candles—for simple candle spells related to money, sex, and luck
- Devil candles—used in exorcisms
- Figure or image candles—used to represent your astral self or your own image and also used in a sympathetic manner to cast spells on others. They act like a poppet and can be quite powerful if used in conjunction with the color vibration candles.
- Reversible candles—usually a colored candle dipped in black wax so it has a black wax coating. Burning these is used for burning away negative influences.
- Sabbatic goat candles—used for strengthening your spiritual powers
- Wishing candles—for making dreams come true
- Skull candles—used exclusively for hexing

- Witch candles—in the shape of the witch and used for potent love spells

Table 14—Days of The Week

Days of the Week	Ruling Planet	Magickal Association
Monday	Moon	Ancestral workings, dreams, healing, childbirth, instinct, memory, property, theft, purity
Tuesday	Mars	Enemies, initiations, loyalty, marriage, protection, prison, war, wealth
Wednesday	Mercury	Communication, debt, fear, loss, travel, contracts
Thursday	Jupiter	Desires, harvests, honor, marriage, contracts, money
Friday	Venus	Family, friends, beauty, love, growth, harmony, sexuality
Saturday	Saturn	Real estate, freedom, gifts, sowing, tenacity
Sunday	Sun	Gardening, creativity, hope, money, victory

Now that we have the theory it is time to look at an actual candle-magick spell examples. I will give an example of two candle-magick spells: one that is a simple money spell and the second that is a more complex spell for love.

Money Spell Using Candle Magick

What You Need
- Cleanse all candles with saltwater.
- A green candle with WEALTH carved into the side of it rubbed with patchouli oil.
- Two white altar candles
- An astral candle representing yourself

- Patchouli incense
- A paper with your petition on it saying, "Please bless me with $10,000 by June 2019."
- A bowl of salt for your altar
- A bowl of water for your altar
- This spell will be carried out during the hour of Jupiter on the day of Jupiter which is a Thursday during a waxing moon.
- A small gold cloth bag with mint and parsley in it. You pass this through the incense and over the candle flame and carry it with you always.
- Remember at all stages to infuse your intent and will into the spell.

Love Spell Using Image Candles

What You Need
- Two pink image candles sitting on opposite sides of the altar
- Two white altar candles
- One astral candle to represent yourself
- A bowl of black rock salt
- A bowl of water
- Your petition: "By love, I bind these two, so mote it be."
- Rose oil for anointing the image candles
- Jasmine incense
- The timing correspondences would be Friday during the hour of Venus on a waxing to full moon.
- A red ribbon

You first need to cleanse the candles. You then light all the candles and anoint the image candles with oil according to purpose. Light the incense and the astral candle. You then move the candles closer to each other while reciting the incantation above several times. Then after you have moved the image candles closer, you tie them with a red ribbon. Put them out and place the tied candles in a safe place. Close the ritual. Remember to put your intent and will into the spell. The next section will deal with other forms of sympathetic magick.

Sympathetic Magick

Sympathetic magick is where you have an item that you use as a proxy for a person or thing. You work your magick on the proxy in the hope that it affects the person or thing in such a way that you get the outcome you desire after the application of will and intent. An example of this is the famous poppet. Poppets are mistakenly called "Voodoo" dolls. They are basically a worldwide phenomenon that has been attributed to Voodoo because of popular media. Essentially, every culture has a form of sympathetic magick. You can virtually use anything to represent a real person or thing. Matchsticks, candles, poppets, pegs, branches of trees, the list goes on.

I am going to describe how to use poppets. Poppets can be made of stocking or socks, cloth, candle wax, wood, or clay. You can fill them with herbs and tag locks (items belonging to the person such as photos, hair, and nails) that suit the purpose for which you make the doll, and whatever you do to the doll is done to the person who is the target of the doll. I have used poppets with a great deal of success over the past few years and I prefer them to many other forms of magick. We will discuss how to do a healing spell using a poppet here for someone who suffers headaches and stomach problems.

What You Need
- An old stocking that you can cut up and use for the poppet
- A tag lock (hair, a photo, or nail clippings from your target)
- String
- Herbs corresponding to purpose (see appendix G—Herbs and Their Magickal Use), in this case healing, so we will use Angelica, Arrow Root, Eucalyptus, Fennel Seeds, and Garlic.
- Candles according to purpose. For this purpose, we will use blue candles and lavender oil to anoint the candles.

- Incense according to purpose. For healing, we will use lavender incense.
- Timing correspondences are a waxing to full moon, the hour of the Sun on a Monday.
- Some pins to pinpoint where the sickness is. In this case, it is the stomach and the head.
- Saltwater in a bowl
- Some straw for image magick and luck.
- Copal Resin to represent the heart of the poppet
- A needle and thread
- Wool
- Colored pens to decorate your poppet

Method
- Focus your intent and your will.
- Cleanse and consecrate your tools and the candles with saltwater.
- You will make the poppet and tie off the head, arms, and feet with string. You will stuff the head with straw. In the center of the body, you will place the tag lock and the herbs previously suggested. The tag lock links the poppet to the person who is the target of the spell.
- You will place the copal resin in the center of the body where the heart is.
- You will sew up the poppet, so it is complete and recite this incantation over it: "Breathe life into ye as I sew ye well. Ye are [person's name] alive with the fire of life, so mote it be."
- Decorate your poppet with a face and hair made of wool.
- Breathe life into the mouth of the poppet.
- Place pins in the head and stomach to signify where the illness and pain is. Slowly draw the pins out of the poppets to signify the pain going. Focus your intent on the pain leaving the body.
- Recite this incantation: "Headaches be gone. Stomach be well. Health will come. Time will tell."
- Imagine the person recovering from the pain and meditate on the poppet for a time. Place it on your altar where you can see it. Be careful not to smother it or place it in a box. It is a living creature now.
- Close the ritual.

Poppets can be used for just about anything, finding a job, money, healing, revenge, hexing, cursing, binding, loosing, or even for sex and love. They are a simple concept that has existed since 1100 BCE across all cultures and religions. They are probably the most well-known form of sympathetic magick. The next section will look at Chaos magick.

Chaos Magick

Chaos magick emerged in the 1970s. It is based on the works of Austin Osman Spare. It is basically success magick, or results-based magic. It claims results over and above traditional magick systems. Belief is the main tool of chaos magick. It rejects the notion of absolute truth that denies the use of superstition and overthrows the idea that magick is a supernatural system. They believe that magick is only successful because of the belief of the practitioner and this brings about change. The belief-based system strips away other, older systemic approaches to magick and is left with belief as the main tool of magic. The means of getting there is up to the practitioner. There are several key components to chaos magick.:

1. Belief as a tool—Nothing is true, and everything is permitted, a rejection of all fixed models of reality. Older systems are just road-maps that do not have value in themselves but are just a means to achieving an end.

2. Kia and Chaos—Kia is like a universal hive mind of which the individual human consciousness is an aspect. It is the source of consciousness. Through the conscious mind, desires grow into obsessions that result in fixed outcomes. This is an outworking of magick through the individual consciousness. Chaos is the force that caused life to emerge from nothingness. All individuals have this as a hallmark of their existence. This means that kia plus chaos gives magickal outcomes because will and perception are perpetuated into the universe to become magick. There are four models of explanation for this:

    (1) Within the spirit model, the practitioner projects their intention onto spirit helpers to affect a magickal outcome.

(2) Within the energy model, the practitioner projects their chi toward specific objectives.

(3) Within the psychological model, the practitioner projects the symbolism of their consciousness toward producing goal attainment.

(4) Within the information model, the practitioner transmits information toward a knowledge base to produce specific effects.

Within chaos magick each tradition is stripped down to its bare bones, which means any magickal tradition can be utilized to obtain an outcome. However, there are some tools specific to the practice of chaos magic:

1. Gnosis or the altered state of consciousness. There are three types of gnosis:

   a. Inhibitory gnosis, which is deep meditation and trance, sensory deprivation and relaxation.

   b. Ecstatic gnosis, which is mindlessness brought about by intense arousal.

   c. Indifferent vacuity, in which spells are cast incidentally (e.g., doodling sigils).

2. Sigils and sigil use, where sigils represent desire or intent. This helps the mind yield a result by forcing it into the subconscious where the conscious mind forgets it and the subconscious mind works on fulfilling the desire.

3. The cut-up technique, where written text is cut up to make new text. This allows the construct to be broken down in the conscious mind and are reflective of future events.

4. Synchro-mysticism, where a deliberate set of synchronicities (i.e. patterns repeat and are associated with similar outcomes in your life). Magickal results consist of meaningful coincidences. The universe speaks in a symbolic language.

In other words, chaos magick allows the practitioner to create their own magickal system, his own methods, ethics and uses of magick.[38] See the chapter on sigils and sigil creation for examples of Chaos Magick. The next section briefly discusses elemental magick.

---

[38] See Jaq Hawkins, Understanding Chaos Magic (Milverton: Cappall Bann Publishing, 2006).

Elemental Magick

Elemental magick pertains to the use of air, water, earth, fire, and spirit in workings. The whole universe is made up of the elements. The basic premise of this type of magick is that you affect change through will and intent, using the elements. We are familiar with the elements when we call forth an elemental circle and call earth to the north, air to the east, fire to the south, water to the west, and spirit from the center. The elemental spirits are powerful vibrational entities that exist in a different ethereal plane. In Astrology, they are fixed cardinal points that are mutable in nature.

The earth element represents all that is final in magick. It is solid and tangible. This represents the physical body. The characteristics of earth are as follows:

- **Direction**: North in the northern hemisphere and south in the southern hemisphere.
- **Color**: Green, black
- **Time**: Midnight, winter
- **Plane**: Physical
- **Senses**: Touch
- **Zodiac**: Taurus, Virgo, Capricorn
- **Magickal Tools**: Crystals, pentacles, altar
- **Ritual Work**: Wealth, prosperity, surrendering self-will, empathy, stability, healing

Candle magick is considered to be earth elemental spell work as well as sympathetic magick (depending on how it is used). Here is an example of an earth elemental magick spell for finding a job:

What You Need
- Brown and purple candles and candle holders
- Astral candle to represent you and a candle holder
- Frankincense incense
- Mint oil
- Powdered dragon's blood

- Brown stones such as river stones
- Something sharp to carve the candles with

Method
- Face your altar north in the northern hemisphere and south in the southern hemisphere.
- Rub the mint oil into the brown and purple candles. As you rub chant the following: "Employment come to me. Make it swift. So mote it be."
- Roll the candles in powdered dragon's blood.
- Write on the candles JOB or EMPLOYMENT.
- Time this for a waxing to full moon.
- Place the three candles on the altar in a triangular fashion.
- Place the stones next to the candle holders.
- Light the astral candle and say, "I will do everything to find a job."
- Light the brown candle and call on the creative powers of Earth.
- Light the purple candle and state, "My desires come to me this night."
- Focus your will and intent into the spell and meditate on a good job outcome for yourself.

Below is a protection spell utilized as a form of earth magic.

What You Need
- Brown candle
- Black candle
- Your astral candle
- Sandalwood incense
- Geranium oil
- Dried and crushed Aloe, blackberry, and blueberry

Method
- Your altar faces north in the northern hemisphere and south in the southern hemisphere.

- You massage geranium oil into both your brown and black candles and then roll them in the dried and crushed herbs. As you massage the candles and roll them in herbs, you recite the following incantation: "Protection to me and mine, so it shall be. Banish all that's bad, so mote it be."
- Write "Protection" in the side of your brown candle and then write "Banishment" in your black candle. You light your candles and place them at opposite ends of the altar. Meditate on the candles and picture a wall of rock surrounding you and all that is yours. As the bad energy hits the rock, it is banished by the black candle.
- Light your astral candle and place it at the northern front of the altar. Light your incense and have it in the middle of your altar.
- Mediate again and picture yourself and your loved ones being surrounded by a titanium shield. Arrows bounce off this shield and are banished or returned to sender. Also picture your feet growing the roots of a tree and growing down deep into the earth. This is simple shielding and grounding as discussed in a previous chapter.
- Snuff out the candles. Let the incense burn down. As the incense burns down, you feel protected and peaceful.

Next, we will discuss the element of Air. Air represents all that cannot be seen that is gaseous and light matter. This represents the mental body or the mind. The characteristics of Air are as follows:

- **Direction:** East
- **Color:** Yellow or silver
- **Time:** Dawn and spring
- **Plane:** Mental
- **Senses:** Smell
- **Zodiac:** Gemini, Libra, and Aquarius
- **Magickal Tools:** Wand, incense, visualization
- **Ritual Work:** Business, legal problems, travel, information, logic, creativity, divination, mental health, revealing the truth, finding lost objects

For spell work. I will use the following example of a spell for legal matters.

You Will Need
- Purple and black candles with *Success* and *Justice* engraved into the side of each candle respectively
- An Astral candle to represent you
- Candle holders
- Legal papers
- Cinnamon Incense
- Crushed buckthorn
- Geranium oil for anointing the candles
- Timing for the waning to new moon

Method
- Face your altar east irrespective of the hemisphere you are in.
- Set the candles up in a triangular fashion on the altar.
- Carve *Success* and *Justice* into each candle respectively.
- Massage in geranium oil to the candles and roll them in crushed buckthorn.
- Light the purple candle. Focus your will and intent on the purple candle and chant, "Success be mine from Justice fair. Let me be empowered by the Air."
- Lay the legal papers between the candles.
- Light the black candle and focus your will and intent on it and chant, "Remove the walls and barriers be, powers of Air to set me free. Let justice come, so mote it be."
- Meditate on success in the legal matter.

Now we will look at the element of Fire. Fire purifies. It transforms most objects by either its light or its heat. The characteristics of Fire are as follows:
- **Direction**: South in the northern hemisphere and north in the southern hemisphere
- **Color:** Red or orange
- **Time:** Noon or summer

- **Plane:** Spirit
- **Sense:** Sight
- **Zodiac:** Aries, Leo, Sagittarius
- **Magickal Tools:** Candles, incense, burned paper petitions
- **Ritual Work:** Power, physical freedom, change, sexuality, energy, authority, confidence, success, destruction of negative energies.

The spell-work example we will use here is the destruction of negative energies.

What You Need
- Red and black candles
- An astral candle for you
- Small bowl of salt
- Small fireproof bowl
- Two pieces of red paper big enough to fit under candle holders
- Black pen
- Patchouli incense and oil
- Timing on a waning moon to new moon

Method
- Face your altar south in the northern hemisphere and north in the southern hemisphere.
- Trace the red candle bottom on the red paper.
- Draw an arrow on the other paper pointing to the black candle.
- Massage oil into the candles.
- Place the red candle on the right side of the altar and the black candle on the left side of the altar.
- Position the salt and the fireproof bowl between the two candles.
- Hold your palms over the red candle and visualize the positive energy flowing into this candle.
- Hold your palms over the black candle and visualize the negative energy being destroyed.
- Hold the bowl of salt in your hands and say, "Bowl of salt, draw all negatives into thee."

- Walk around your house with the bowl of salt in your hands and repeat the above.
- Return to the altar.
- Place your left palm over the black candle and your right one over the red candle.
- Visualize the place cleansed of negative energy.
- Clap your hands sharply and say, "This place is now clean and free, only goodness come to me."
- Light the red paper from under the black candle in the fireproof bowl and visualize the negative energy being burned. Do the same for the paper under the red candle but visualize positive energy coming forward.
- Put out both the candles.
- Take the salt and pour it down the sink under running water.

Now we will discuss the element of water. Water represents anything liquid, therefore anything relating to emotion. The characteristics of water are as follows:

- **Direction:** West
- **Color:** Blue or gray
- **Time:** Sunset or autumn
- **Plane:** Astral
- **Sense:** Taste
- **Zodiac:** Cancer, Scorpio, Pisces
- **Magickal tools:** Water chalice, mirrors, cauldron
- **Ritual Work:** Change, divination, love, medicine, emotions, intuition, communication, clairvoyance

For magick of this kind, we will look a spell to enhance divination.

What You Need
- Blue candles
- Astral candle to represent you
- Tools of divination, such as a deck of tarot cards or a pendulum

- Chalice of water
- Camphor oil
- Myrrh incense

Method
- Face your altar west.
- Rub your blue candles with camphor oil and light them.
- Place your candles on opposite sides of the altar.
- Between them place the chalice of water and the tools of divination.
- Light the myrrh incense.
- Place your hand into the chalice of water and swirl it around chanting, "Water spirits come to me that I may divine, so mote it be."
- Pick up your divination tools and pass them through the smoke of the incense and over the flame of the candles.
- Visualize power coming into the tools.
- Look into the chalice and visualize seeing the past, present and future.
- Chant, "All will be revealed to me, past, present, and future, so mote it be."
- Snuff out your candles and discard your water.

The next section discusses traditional necromancy and the magick associated with it.

Necromancy

Necromancy is another form of magick that is commonly utilized. This is divination by means of the spirits of the dead. From the Greek word *nekro*, meaning "dead," and *manteria*, meaning "divination." This practice is very old and involves invocation of the spirits from the "other" realm into this one for the purposes of divination, telling the future, and seeking hidden knowledge. I will not discuss necromancy at length here, nor will I show people how to perform it. Rather, we will discuss necromancy and what it is and what it requires in order to be successful.

Necromancy is not worship of the dead, just to be clear. Also, necromancy is not clairvoyance, trance mediumship, or channeling, nor is it having séances. It requires a different mindset to those aforementioned skills. Clairvoyants and those of a similar ilk tend to be passive personalities who will allow a spirit to take them over to deliver a message. They can move from one location to another to do this. Necromancers must be the doyens of self-mastery in every area of life. They must me tough and cunning. Necromancers require a stable fixed location from which to work as they work with housed oracular and operative spirits. These spirits cannot be moved from house to house.

Necromancers enter into a contract with a spirit for the mutual benefit of both parties involved. This can be to perform magickal practices or divination or to influence the thought processes of others using spirit. As there are trickster spirits, the necromancer must test the spirits against their claims and never accept what a spirit says at face value.

Necromancers use two tools, the Oboth and the Yiddeonim. An Oboth is an oracular head stuffed with herbs and correspondences. This is a skull and first two vertebra of a deceased person, used with their permission, that speaks to the necromancer and passes on messages of wisdom. It is used for communication and not magick. Note that the oracular head is still used today in many cultures. Also take note that dead people are not wiser once dead than they were when alive.

The Yiddeonim is housing for an operative spirit. It can be a pot, jar, doll, or any item that is capable of housing a spirit. Operative spirits are used to carry out magickal purposes. Another tool necromancers use is automatic writing, where you communicate with the dead and write the messages down on paper.

There are rules as to which spirits to approach; narrow-minded bigoted spirits and religiously fanatical spirits are to be avoided. Necromancy does not require religion to work within its framework. Approachable spirits are those that seek to learn from the necromancer, who will train them to perform their functions.

Not everyone can speak to or see spirits. Some can see but can't speak, and yet others can speak to but can't see. To be a necromancer, you first have to examine yourself to see if you meet with certain criteria such as the following:

- Can you learn and accept your own limitations?
- Do you find the Ouija board easy to use, and do you obtain accurate information from it?
- Can you see or speak to spirits of the dead?
- Do you feel comfortable around death and dying, and are you accepting of death?
- Have you been closely exposed to death?
- Can you stick to a path in life and master it?
- Are you skilled at discernment?

What has been discussed is traditional necromancy. Now, we will discuss necromancy from the point of view of the demonolater. This is a slightly different method of communing with the dead, and it involves ritual and spell work.

One of the most important tools of a demonolatry necromancer is discernment and the ability to test the spirits. Like other forms of necromancy, the necromancer is cautioned not to worship the spirits but rather to leave them offerings of grains, wines, and fruits as payment for services rendered. It is recommended not to venerate them as they draw the life out of living things. They are not without their faults, as we have seen in the previous discussions on necromancy. If they are venerated, then feeders will come, and these are often followed with feelings of hatred and sorrow. It is urged that house cleaning become a regular practice with the necromancer.

Necromancers are urged to shield, clear, cleanse, and were necessary, exorcise as a last resort. Cleansing can be as simple as using sage, sea salt, and water and being firm with stubborn spirits.

Unlike conventional necromancy, demonolatry necromancy does not necessarily advocate "channeling," whereby the practitioner allows the spirit to speak through them, as opposed to "horsing" where the practitioner allows the spirit to completely take them over—this is a much more dangerous practice as you are not in control as you are with channeling.

The initiate necromancer is either connected to the death current and Demonic death current, or they are not. Some have a knack for it while others don't. Being that it is demonolatry driving this style of necromancy, there are a few Demons that you work with to accomplish necromancy successfully. These are the following:

- Erynomous
- Baalberith
- Babael
- Gamigin

The demonolatry necromancer uses a specific set of tools such as bones, athame, wands, offering bowls, staves, candle holders, prayer chords, patens for bloodletting, black mirrors, spirit pots, and warding crystals. Each item, including any sigils you use, are cleansed with saltwater and dried off or rubbed with sage oil. The items are also charged using a pillar ritual to the death current and stored in black fabric until used.

This has been a brief overview of necromancy from the point of view of the traditional necromancer and the demonolatry necromancer. The next section will discuss sex magick.

Sex Magick

Sex magick is where the practitioner utilizes orgasm to achieve a magickal purpose. It is a major energy generating source and can be used to create servitors and other magickal outcomes. It can be achieved alone or in unison with another. There are three stages in sex-magick initiation:

- Alphism, where there is abstinence from sex in the mind and body for a period of time.
- Dianism, where there is sexual congress but not to climax. The parties or party will envisage the other as their Demon lover. There will be no climax and sexual congress is slowed right down to the minimum movement. At this time, visions may appear.
- Quodosch, where the act of sexual congress is charged with will and intent. Where physical ecstasy is transmuted via an alchemical process into spiritual ecstasy. You also use sexual fluids for consecration and blessing of items in order to spike their potency.

Sex magick is an ancient Western tradition that differs in its purpose and methodology to Tantra, which is the Eastern equivalent. The two should not be confused. This section is about sex magick and not tantra. Sex magick and its performance comes with a lot of responsibility not to entrap another into a game with a view to promising sex magick, and to be careful of disease. The sex does not have to be between heterosexual couples either; it is not limited to that. It can happen between same-sex partners and, indeed, alone.

Some of the things you can use sex magick for are as follows:

- Raising energy for the creation of a servitor
- General spell work
- Consecration of tools
- Empowerment of talismans
- Empowerment of tools and divination tools
- Sexual meditation
- Yoga.
- Trance work
- Work with some Demons that cause sexual arousal and require the expansion of the mind through sexual pleasure. It strengthens the connection to the spirits and creates a pathway by which communication is facilitated.

I have my sigil cards that I have used for divination. Each card has a drop of blood and a drop of sexual fluid on it and is covered in laminate. This is to increase the divinatory power of the sigils. I have found this works rather well and is better than a sigil card without the consecration by blood and by sexual fluids.

Black, Gray and White Magick

Next, I address the question of black, gray, and white magick. You will hear a lot about black, gray and white magick. The basic delineation between the three is that black magick is baneful, gray magick can be baneful but isn't necessarily, and white magick harms no one. There is no such thing as a white magick curse, for instance. In appendix F—Examples of Loosing and Binding Spells, there are examples of binding and loosing spells that you would use to bind the behaviors of person/s who are causing you problems—this is gray magic. Black magick is also called execration magick or baneful magick. I will provide a few examples of baneful spells here. Before you endeavor to lay in a curse on someone, make sure you protect yourself. Make an amulet or talisman using herbs and sigils.

Protection Amulet

What You Need

- An amulet of Jupiter (see the figure below)
- A small black bag you can affix to a chain
- An acorn
- Dried African violet
- Dried ague
- Aloe
- Amber

Figure 20—Amulet of Jupiter

Method
On a full moon combine all of the ingredients into a small black bag. Focus your intent and will. Affix the bag to a chain and wear it around your neck.

Witch Jars

What You Need
- A tag lock from your target. I use photos.
- A mason jars
- Rusty nails
- Broken glass
- Urine
- Vinegar
- Jezebel root
- Peppercorns
- Chili flakes
- Black candle

Method
Place all the ingredients in the mason jar focusing on your intent and will. Also focus your hate and distain. Burn the candle on top of the jar; bury the jar on the property of your target. Let the jar go undisturbed. In time, terrible things will happen to the target of your curse. They will have a succession of bad luck.

Curse to Inflict Disease

What You Need
- Sock of your enemy
- Black and white candles
- Needle and thread
- Scissors
- Musk incense
- Sliced, dried Jezebel root

Method
- Lay the sock flat.
- Visualizing the person, cut the shape of a doll from the sock.
- Sew the sides together.
- Turn it inside out.
- Stuff it with sliced, dried Jezebel Root
- Finish the sewing.
- Breathe life into the doll and charge it by naming it.
- Light the white candle and say, "This is your health [person's name]."
- Light the black candle and say, "Darkness begins to fill your life, always coming with disease and strife."
- Light the incense.
- Hold the doll over the incense and say, "Your light grows dim, as ill you'll be. I curse you with sickness, so mote it be."
- Blow out the white candle and break it, all the while focusing your anger.
- When your anger is at its height, stick a pin in the doll and say, "By baneful blow, your health is low. Of sickness, you are not free, so mote it be!"
- Every night for as long as the candle lasts, light the black candle and visualize the person's health diminishing.

Blood Magick

Next, we will discuss blood magic as a special form of sympathetic magick. Blood is the life and embodies the will and intent of the magickian. It is a type of sympathetic magick as well as being arcane. Blood is a powerful tool for offerings and empowerment just like sexual fluids. It represents a sacrifice of self. It is particularly potent in pacts and contracts with Demons. A few drops of blood extracted using a diabetic lancet is useful in empowering sigils and tools and in spell work. Generally speaking, you destroy the pact petition and contract by burning it after you have completed your work. It is a form of arcane magick, and it is one of the oldest forms of magick there is. While blood magick utilizing one's own blood is ok, the sacrifice of animals is taboo. If you are to use your blood to empower divinatory tools and other tools, be sure to never allow another to touch or use the tool, as it has become uniquely yours.

The blood oath is perhaps the most potent of all blood magick because it binds the magickian to the pactee, whether it be another magickian or a Demon. It is tantamount to saying that your blood and the blood of your ancestors is standing behind the pact and to break that oath or pact has serious ramifications. It also contains the intent and will of the magickian.

The aims of this type of magick is to avoid irreparable harm to oneself and to avoid infection. So bloodletting should always be carried out using a sterilized lancet and alcohol washes for the target area. It is said that there is a rush from letting blood for the purposes of magick. Always make sure your hands are clean and that you wash the affected area carefully afterward. Women can use menstrual blood for offerings, and again, this is to be obtained cleanly and with clean instruments.

Uses of Blood Magick
- Drawing sigils with ink made from the blood of the sorcerer mixed with dragon's blood powder in a carrier fluid such as water
- The empowerment of charms and talismans
- The empowerment of ritual tools
- Signing of petitions, oaths and contracts
- As a correspondence in spell work
- Drawing runes with it
- Consecrating blades with it
- Scrying
- Consuming in rituals

The Evil Eye Curse

What You Need
- Two black candles
- Frankincense incense

- A clean and sterile lancet
- Alcohol swabs to swab the affected area of the lancing
- An ink made out of your own blood and dragon's blood powder mixed with water
- A piece of parchment
- Will and intent of the sorcerer
- A photograph of the target
- A quill pen
- Glue
- Method
- Wash your hands first.
- Apply an alcohol swab to the area you intend to puncture (e.g., your finger typically).
- Prick your finger with the lancet.
- Squeeze your finger so that droplets of blood collect in a chalice or bowl.
- Add one-quarter teaspoon of dried dragons blood powder.
- Add one-half teaspoon of clean water and mix into a thick ink like consistency.
- Add to an inkwell.
- Place your quill pen into the inkwell.
- Wash your hands again.
- Light your candles at opposite ends of the altar.
- Light your incense
- Affix the photograph of your target with a small dab of glue.
- Focusing your intent and will and your hatred and malice into the drawing, draw the evil eye next to the photo in your ink you have made.
- Affix the evil eye picture to the photograph.
- Chant the following incantation: "Malice be born to thee that thou may suffer, so mote it be."
- Burn the parchment and the photo.

Figure 21—The Evil Eye

In the next section, we will discuss setting up an altar for use in magickal rituals. This is something I am often asked about, so I thought I would include this section in the book.

Setting Up an Altar

Generally, setting up an altar depends largely on what you are using it for. If it is a place of worship or invocation, you will need statues in addition to other things. If it is just for spell work, you only need the barest of minimum items such as a wand, an athame, chalices, a cauldron, and a boline. Generally, your altar will face north, but you may need to change its facing, depending on the working you are doing.

My altar is used for invocation and worship as well as spell work. My altar faces north and has an altar cloth on it, a Baphomet statue, a skull, some candle holders, a chalice, a scrying mirror, a box of precious stones, my pendulum, and some sigils. It also has an athame, a boline knife, a cauldron, and a wand made of yew. I have candles and my astral candle as well as crystals of various types and sizes.

An altar setup is a personal choice. You can have as many things on your altar as you wish or as few as you wish. At the end of the day it is you using the altar and therefore it has to be both practical and functional in its setup.

Consecrating Your Altar items

What You Need
- A bowl of black rock salt
- A bowl of water
- Lit white candles
- Hyssop soap
- White sage incense
- A sage stick

Some of the hardier metal items you would rub with rock salt and rinse with water, towel drying as you go. Run them through the incense smoke and over the top of the flame so they are cleansed by the elements. Visualize your items being spiritually cleansed. You also use hyssop soap to cleanse items. I also burn a sage stick in the area so as to cleanse the air around the altar space. Additionally, I will place sigils of Demons around my altar for protection.

This chapter has been about the types of magick that you will encounter in your studies of the left-hand path. I have included examples of spells with most types of magick for your perusal. The next chapter is about sigils and sigil making.

CHAPTER 9

Sigils and Sigil Making

The key to the subconscious mind is symbols or, in our case, sigils. Sigils or seals are pictures that are used to unlock the magick of the subconscious mind by causing a shift in our emotional state. The sigil represents your desire and also pushes forward your intent.

Sigil making has been around for a long time. However, Austin Osman Spare (1886–1956) developed a simple technique for creating them. There are two basic ways to make sigils. You can make one quite simply through a statement of your desire, or you can make them utilizing magick squares. There are also free-form sigils created purely out of the mind if the caster. Once you have made a sigil, you can then create a mantra from your statement of intent that basically allows you to access the symbol you have created for your subconscious mind.

There are two formalized ways to make a sigil. You can represent a picture or sigil as the culmination of a sentence that has been edited to remove doubled letters, or you can use the magick square. We shall discuss both types here.

The first thing you need to make a sigil is an idea of what you want. For example, you may want a new car or extra money. This is your desire, now it's time to create it into intent through a pictorial image that the subconscious mind will not forget. Secondly, you need to word your sigil spell, for example:

I WANT A CAT

This is just an example, but you would generally be more specific than this. Instead of "I want money," for example, you would say, "I want X amount of money," and verbalize that in a sentence. The verbalization is your desire. Thirdly, you need to pare down the sentence into its main components, striking out all double letters and sometimes removing vowels or leaving only consonants. Some people just take the first letters of each word to do this, others make it so it can be used as a mantra at some stage.

I W̶A̶N̶T̶ ̶A̶ CAT

You get left with the resulting letters:

I W N C A T

Then you draw these letters as such. Remembering that M, N, and W look the same and look like E when facing forward. This makes it easier to simplify:

I W C A T

Then you pictorialize the letters.

Figure 22—Pictorialization of a Sigil

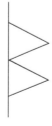

I and W

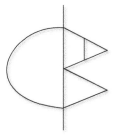

Now add the C and A.

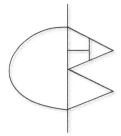

Now add the T.

The next thing you would do is stylize the drawing so that it is appealing to your subconscious mind. Keep it relatively simple, however.

Figure 23—Power Word Sigil

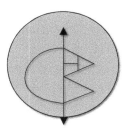

There you have a simple sigil. The next step is if you want to make a mantra that goes with this sigil to repeat over and over again once the sigil is charged. Mantras are another way the mind can implement your intent. Remember our pared down version of our desire? We take those letters and form a nonsensical word using a couple of methods:

The spinning mantra is where you place the emphasis on the second and fourth syllable of each line in your statement of intent. To create the mantra, you do the following:

- Have your statement of intent: **I WANT A CAT.**
- Spell the sentence phonetically: **I WUH-NT UH CAH-T**
- Delete repeated letters: **I WUHNT CA**
- Rearrange the letters: **WUN CHAIT** this becomes your spell mantra or words of power.
- When you chant your mantra, you put emphasis on **UN** and **AIT.**

The next thing you need to do is take a few days with meditation to meditate on your sigil. Once you have done this for, say, three to four days, you are ready to proceed to the next step which is whirling and chanting.

When you are ready for the next step, meditate on the sigil one more time. Light your candles and incense. Approach the altar and call the four quarters (earth, air, fire, and water).

The next step in the process is to chant your mantra with your sigil in front of you. You basically set up some rhythmic drumming in order to help you focus on the syllabic mechanisms described. This is done in your altar room, so set up your incense and candles, and you can whirl and chant, or you can just chant. It is up to you. However, you are vibrating the words for your mantra when you are doing this, which helps your subconscious mind remember the sigil as well as charges the sigil. The sigil will come to life for you. Begin whirling and chanting/vibrating the mantra with a picture of the sigil in your mind's eye.

Once you have gotten to the point where you are entranced from the whirling and vibrating of the sigil, then you have created a link between your conscious and subconscious mind. You get to a point where you have memorized the sigil. At this time, when you are confident, you will slowly stop spinning and chanting.

Close the circle and dismiss the quarters. Once you have done this, you then destroy the sigil and dispose of it. While it is destroyed, it is not really forgotten. It is buried deep within your subconscious mind. You will recall it when you think about your intention.

The second way of sigilization is Hermetic in origin and is much older than the Austin Osman Spare's simple method. This involves having columns and rows of numbers that all add up to the same number at the conclusion of the column or row. I will go through the math of the magick square here to try and demystify it as it is not a very difficult concept to follow.

First, you need your sentence of intent/desire. You must convert this into numbers.

Table 15—Simple Alpha-Numeric Conversion

1	2	3	4	5	6	7	8	9
A	B	C	D	E	F	G	H	I
J	K	L	M	N	O	P	Q	R
S	T	U	V	W	X	Y	Z	

The number of letters will signify the size of the square you use in terms of the numbers you go up too. In other languages this could be quite a high number so it's a good idea to condense by adding dual numbers like twenty-three, for example, together—2+3=5. There are differing numerologies for different languages. I will not go into that here, as it is quite complex.

Remember our example **I WANT A CAT**? Well we are going to use this to make a sigil with a magick square. You go through the same process of reducing letters as you did with word sigils. So, you end up with **I W C A T**. Numerically, this becomes 9, 5, 3, 1, 2.

We are going to make a 3x3 square. To make this square you need to know a few things to apply the principles of magick squares. Firstly, you need to calculate the magickal constant for the square. The formula we use is below:

Equation 1—The Magickal Constant

$$n[((n^2) +1)/2]$$

Now do not get stressed seeing this as it is quite simple to work out. Using a 3x3 square, we will work out its magickal constant. This is where n=3, as we are using a 3x3 square. It would be 6 if you were using a 6x6 square, and so on.

= 3 x [(9 +1)/2]
= 3 x [10/2]
= 3 x 5
= 15

This means all rows, columns, and diagonals must add up to 15, in this case. The sum of the whole square will be 45 but I will get to this.

Table 16—The Magick Square

	1	

So we start by putting the 1 in the center box of the top row. This is always where you begin your magick square when it has odd-numbered sides (in this case, 3 being the odd number). The next thing we want to do is place the number 2. Now before we place the number 2, there are a couple of rules to note:

- You use an up one row and across to the right one column unless the number you are placing is above the square.

- In this case, for example, 2 would be above the square, so the rule is to go across one column to the right and place the number in the bottom of that column.
- If the movement takes you to the boxes outside the square on the right, then you remain in that box's row but place the number in the furthest column.
- If the movement takes you to a box that is already filled in, then go back to the box that's filled in and place the number directly below it.

Figure 24—Following Magick Square Rules

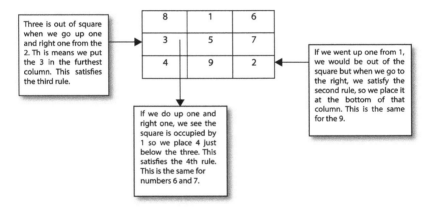

Three is out of square when we go up one and right one from the 2. Th is means we put the 3 in the furthest column. This satisfies the third rule.

If we went up one from 1, we would be out of the square but when we go to the right, we satisfy the second rule, so we place it at the bottom of that column. This is the same for the 9.

If we do up one and right one, we see the square is occupied by 1 so we place 4 just below the three. This satisfies the 4th rule. This is the same for numbers 6 and 7.

So now we have solved it for an odd-numbered square, what about even numbered squares? The rules are the same. The formula for the magickal square constant is the same. The rules that are additional are as follows:

- A square with even sides is divisible by 2 but not by 4.
- The smallest number of squares you can have is 6x6 as 2x2 and 4x4 are not practical.

With a 6x6 magick square, the magickal constant is 111 using the same formula we used for a 3x3 square. This means all columns, rows and diagonals must sum to 111. The difference in making the square, however, is this: you have to divide your square into four quadrants.

Table 17—6x6 Magick Square

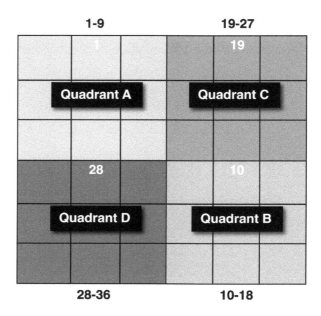

- Quadrant A gets the first numbers, quadrant B gets the second quarter, quadrant C gets the third quarter, and so on.
- You then place the first number of each quadrant into its box on the top middle row.
- Treat each quadrant as its own square and follow the same rules.
- If you try and add up each column, row, and diagonal, you will not get the magickal constant, so you have to do a swap with some numbers.

Table 18—Preswapped 6x6

8	1	6	26	19	24
3	5	7	21	23	25
4	9	2	22	27	20
35	28	33	17	10	15
30	32	34	12	14	16
31	39	29	13	18	11

- You create a swap between quadrant A and quadrant D. You mark all of the numbers in the top row of your square and find the median. In quadrant A, it is 8, and in quadrant D, it is 35. If this was a 10x10 square, you would mark off the first two boxes.
- In the row directly below the top highlight, skip the number in the first column, then mark off the second column square. See above.
- Then go back to the first column in the row below and mark off the first square. See above.
- Do exactly the same in quadrant D.
- Swap the boxes marked in A quadrant with those in D quadrant. See below.
- Do more swaps with quadrant B and C when you are dealing with a higher even square such as 14x14 square.

Table 19—A 6x6 with Swaps

35	1	6	26	19	24
3	32	7	21	23	25
31	9	2	22	27	20
8	28	33	17	10	15
30	5	34	12	14	16
4	39	29	13	18	11

Then there is the special case of a double-even square. This would be a 4x4 for instance. The magick constant for a 4x4 square is 34. The special case has special rules.

Table 20—4x4 Square

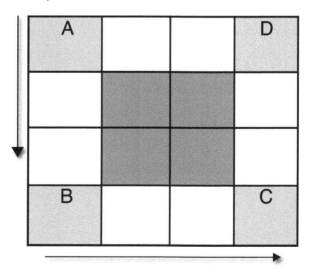

First, you draw your square and highlight the corners and mark them A, B, C and D respectively. Make sure you mark them in a counterclockwise manor. You need to know what these anchors are so leave them marked. If you are using an 8x8 or 12x12 square, you would mark two x two boxes in each corner and 3x3 boxes respectively.

- Second, you mark out the central focus, which is 2x2 squares in the center. See above. If you are working with an 8x8 square, you would make it a 4x4 central square. In a 12x12 it would be a 6x6 central square.

Table 21—Starting a 4x4 Square

1			4
	6	7	
	10	11	
13			16

- Fill out only the marked squares as above.
- Fill out the rest of the squares (see below) by counting backward. Begin with the largest number; avoid filled boxes.
- All the columns, rows, and diagonals will add up to your magick square constant.

Table 22—A Filled Out 4x4

1	15	14	4
12	6	7	9
8	10	11	5
13	3	2	16

Now that we have discussed how to draw magick squares, you need to draw your sigil, so we will go back to our first example, **I W C A T,** and our 3x3 square.

Table 23—3x3 Magick Square with Sigil

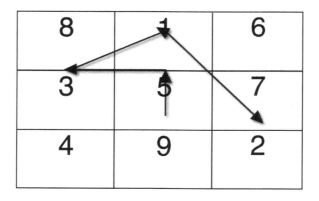

8	1	6
3	5	7
4	9	2

Now we assign our letters to numbers (refer to table 11), and we get:

I = 9

W = 5

C = 3

A = 1

T = 2

Then we transpose the sigil to paper. It looks fairly basic at this stage, but then you decorate it.

Figure 25—Transposed Sigil from a Magick Square

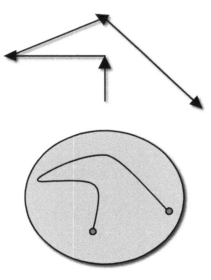

That concludes our discussion of sigil magic. With the sigil you have created using a magick square, you would charge it and dispense with it in the same way you do with a word sigil and using the mantra we created using our example. Below you can see some sigils made by an artist using free-form sigil work. The next chapter will discuss pacts and how to create them.

Figure 26—Mahazael

A Prince whose name means "Devourer"

Earth

Figure 27—Dominus Penarum

**Lord of Torment, but ironically used in love spells
to break the will of the opposite sex**

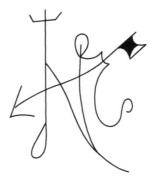

Jupiter

Figure 28—Pathophas

Can stave off decay, reversing or stopping it completely. He can also kill with a single word.

Mars/Fire

Figure 29—Arioch

Demon of Vengeance. His name literally means "Fierce Lion."

Moon/Air

Figure 30—Assaibi

His name inspires emotions of anger, sadness, and hatred.

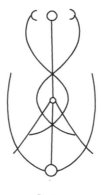

Saturn

Figure 31—Chatas

Summoned as part of the spell for crafting a ring of the Sun, a powerful astrological talisman used to bind an enemy's tongue.

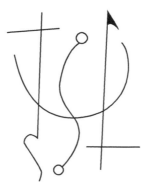

Sun

Figure 32—Chamoriel

Spirit of the air, but prefers in wetlands or swamps. Appears as a serpent with a human head.

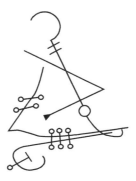

Water/Air

Figure 33—Sambas

Gathers good spirits for familiars, knows all manner of secret thoughts and deeds.

Mercury

Figure 34—Rubeus Pugnator

His name means "Red Fighter." Used to create the ring of Mars, which can be used to bring destruction to an enemy.

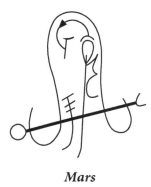

Mars

Figure 35—Cynassa

Appears as a shining star. Incites love and lust. Increases personal pleasure. He can also provide luxurious items, such as costly perfumes and fabrics.

Venus

Sigils used with permission and drawn by Brian Snelling © 2019

CHAPTER 10

Making Pacts

P acts are agreements between you and another being, whether it be a person or a Demon. Sometimes, making a pact is necessary to get what you want and to get things in motion for success. They can be short or long term and are generally time locked. Pacts should be specific and should include the usual who, what, where, when by.

Pacts are troublesome to most people because of the following:

A. They believe in engaging in a pact is putting their souls and minds on the line. This is not true. A pact is simply an agreement or contract. One does not sell one's soul or relinquish one's mind to the principal in the pact. You are in full control of all your faculties and your soul at the end of the day. What does a Demon want with your soul? Nothing whatsoever. They are Demonic divine intelligences that have no need of souls.

B. People fear that engaging in an agreement with the Demonic divine is considered a "devilish" act that is tantamount to spiritual suicide. Again, this assertion is incorrect. You merely enter a contract for services rendered, the consideration for which is determined by you alone. This act of entering into a pact with a Demon is in fact the oldest form of initiation known in history. Even in Christianity, you enter into a pact with God for your salvation. This is even a blood pact. Conjuring Demons and entering contracts with them is not so diabolical as it sounds. The Christian upbringing of many people make them balk at the notion of entering into a contract with a Demon, and this is ludicrous. This goes right back to the beginning of this book where I discuss evil versus good and light versus dark. It behooves us to break traditional programming that we have received in our previous lives by realizing that this was what we did all along and put faith into the new life we have chosen to live.

The first rule of making a pact is to know what you want. This should be specific and not general. In saying that, though, you must also work toward your pact objective yourself. Do not expect a Demon to drop $20,000 into your lap without work on your part to achieve that.

Secondly, you decide what you are willing to sacrifice of yourself to get the pact fulfilled. For example, some Demons like to be given wine or plants you have grown yourself. You may want to use art you have made yourself also.

Thirdly, you need to find a Demon who will work with you on the pact, and you need to work out what offering to give. For example, Belial likes plants. Then you need to decide what you want from the Demon. Then you will word your pact using your name and the Demon's name: write it on a piece of paper. Infuse it with your intent. Say the pact out loud to help this along. Sign your name and make your offering then burn the piece of paper along with drops of your blood. The Demon will provide you with the knowledge and opportunity, it is up to you to act on it.

Pacts are not the same as petitions. Petitions are done regularly during rituals and can include pacts. A petition is an appeal or request. It can even be a prayer. It is not a contract like a pact where there is consideration or *quid pro quo* involved.

So What Do You Need to Make a Good Pact?

1. You need a piece of paper—preferably parchment.
2. A pen to sign your name. If you have a nibbed pen, that is perfect.

3. A few drops of your own blood taken cleanly with a diabetic lancet. These are available from most pharmacies.
4. The gift you are giving to your Demon of choice. Choose a Demon per their purpose (See Correspondences).
   a. This could be a painting or a poem.
   b. This could be a plant or flowers for a period of days.
   c. This could be a glass of wine or some food.
   d. This could be a promise of some sort like to perform a service for them, to change for the better, and so on.
5. Your correspondence you are using to summon (See appendix C— Demon Correspondences).
6. Your incense for summoning according to your Demon's preference (See appendix C—Demon Correspondences).
7. Colored candles according to the choice of the Demon with whom you are making a pact (See appendix C).
8. A balanced elemental circle (See appendix B on circle development).
9. The sigil of the Demon you are working with (See appendix C— Demon Correspondences).

Pacts should be kept secret. They are between you and the entity you are entering the contract with and should not be spoken of outside of that. Some people are against this, but in my experience, it is essential to keep this a secret.

It pays to be specific in your pact. So, nominate the why, when by, and where of the pact before entering it. See the example of a pact below.

Example of A Pact to Lucifer for Creativity

1. Get a bell.
2. Salt
3. Water
4. Incense that your Demon prefers
5. Dagger

6. A fire-resistant bowl
7. Pen and paper
8. A diabetic lancet
9. Before the ritual begins, shower with hyssop soap or bathe with hyssop essential oil.
10. Draw a circle with salt.
11. From the east, call Amaymon using his enn: "Elan Reya Amaymon."
12. From the west you call to Goap using his enn: "Anana avac Goap."
13. Likewise, you call Corson from the south: "Ana tasa Corson nanay."
14. Ziminiar from the north using his enn: "Renin Ziminiar et élan."
15. This part is optional. However, you can also call Satan using his enn—"Tasa Reme Laris Satan"—to signify the fifth element of spirit. Connolly (2006) uses Eurynomous in addition to Satan as well, but again, I do not use him as he is not a Goetic spirit.
16. Write on a piece of paper:

I, Andhaku Amelatu, offer this poem to Lucifer in return for

creativity boost in writing this book. That I may complete it in

your name by the 30 of June 2019. I affix my seal below.

Note this is not an actual pact, just a demonstration of one.

1. Place a couple of drops of blood on the parchment that you have extracted using the diabetic lancet.
2. Meditate on your contract for about an hour
3. When you feel the Demons presence, burn the parchment in a fireproof bowl.
4. Close the circle and thank the Demon for coming.
5. Ring the bell to signal the close of the ritual.

In conclusion, making a pact is quite easy. It requires very little by way of resources and equipment. I think that everyone should at least try a pact once in order to see what it does. By way of a case study, a friend of mine entered a pact with Belial for a new job and ended up working for the exact company she wanted to. Pacts are accessible to everyone. I hope you have enjoyed this book!

Andhaku Amelatu

History and Anatomy
of the Baphomet

The image of the Baphomet is most familiar to us as Satanists and Occultists alike. It has a very long history and is representative of some very deep and profound ideas. Baphomet is a representation of Lucifer, and likewise, it represents the cosmic balance between all things as well as being a symbol of the becoming of mankind from the bestial to the enlightened. I wanted to know more about Baphomet and its origins, so I have been doing quite a bit of reading and meditating on the image of Baphomet, and hence, I am excited to present this to you, brothers and sisters, in the name of Satan!

Historical Viewpoint

Baphomet has been mentioned across several cultures from the ancient Egyptian (where it formally became known as the Ram of Mendes, later the Goat of Mendes) to Herodotus who discussed the Mendesian culture in Egypt, through to the Knights Templar and modern-day Occultists. Baphomet has therefore traversed many religious definitions from Egyptian through to Gnostic and finally the Occult and Satanism. There are also some highly refutable links with Freemasonry mentioned in the literature.

According to several sources Baphomet was first seen in literature around the twelfth century AD. It is thought to have been the Latinization (provincial French) of the name of Mohamed, and hence, it was later determined in the trials of the Templars to be one of the idols they are reputed to have worshipped. This could have been a grave misunderstanding because of the nature of the imagery associated with the talisman. If the Knights Templar did use it (and it was a representation of the name Mohamed), then it was because they were on a mission to eradicate Islam and felt that everything representative of Mohamed was evil and that Islam constituted a rebellion against the God of the Christians. This image was created to remind them of their objective but was taken by the Christian church to later represent the notion that the Knights Templar were secretly Islamic or even, worse still, secret practitioners of Gnostic magick—and hence, many were purportedly executed for these revelations that were given by those Templars who were tortured at the hands of King Philip IV of France. If the truth be known, it was because Phillip IV of France owed them large sums of money but had no intention of paying it back, so he concocted this as an excuse to kill off the Templars.

The ancient Greek historian Herodotus (circa 484–425 BC) had written histories of Egypt where he referred to the ram worshipping tribes of Mendes. Herodotus put his own spin on things and changed the idea of the ram to that of a goat in fitting with the Greek horned God Pan.[39] The image of the Egyptian God Banebdjed (or soul of Osiris) was the God of Mendes as later described by Levi. Essentially, the Goat of Mendes was represented as a man with a goat's head.

The most prominent work is that associated with Eliphas Levi (nineteenth century) who tied the notion of the Baphomet to Occultism via Gnosticism. He believed that the Baphomet was the true vision of mercy and justice. Levi was the first one to coin the term *Goat of Mendes*, and to date, he has provided a most illuminating understanding of the Baphomet—hence, the Baphomet became the "Sabbatic goat." Levi was also associated with the first depiction of the reverse pentagram as the personification of Satanic mysticism and the famous Cabalistic Tetragrammaton. In fact, it was Levi whose

---

[39]   See http://en.wikipedia.org/wiki/Eliphas_Levi sourced 23 February 2012.

imagery of the Baphomet found itself utilized in the original Rider-Waite Tarot deck—hence, the subsequent idea that the Baphomet was a Demon or, at the very least, a gargoyle.

Levi's work was passed via Crowley into Cabalistic magick where it was associated with sexuality and sex magick. The image of the Baphomet changed significantly during this time to include the Hermetic Caduceus and the Pythagorean pentagon. This was a far cry from the image of the man-goat with the flame emanating from its head that was seen in the earliest Pagan cultures. Crowley's definition of the Baphomet was one pertaining to the power of creation I will explain this symbolism later.

Etymological Understanding

In ancient Hebrew, Greek, Arabic and even Latin the name Baphomet translates into the following:

- Greek βαφ μήτεος—The Baptism of wisdom
- Arabic أبو فهمة—The Father of Understanding
- Hebrew איפוש—Wisdom
- Baptism of Fire (Gnostic) [40]
- Father of the Temple of Peace to All Men (Cabalistic) [41]

---

[40] Emile Littré (1801–1881) *Dictionnaire de la Langue Francaise*. This reference denotes also to the original provincial French corruption of the word Mohamed. Crowley went on further to describe the Cabbalistic meaning of the word Baphomet as the cube of nine which was reference to κηφας or rock of the church. Hence it was a reference to the cornerstone. See http://en.wikipedia.org/wiki/Baphomet (2012).
[41] "In a midrash (Genesis Rabbah 19) Samael, the lord of the satan, was a mighty prince of angels in heaven. Satan came into the world with woman, that is, with Eve (Midrash Yalkut, Genesis 1:23), so that he was created and is not eternal. Like all celestial beings, he flies through the air (Genesis Rabbah 19) and can assume any form, as of a bird (Talmud, Sanhedrin 107a), a stag (ibid, 95a), a woman (ibid, 81a), a beggar, or a young man (Midrash Tanchuma, Wayera, end); he is said to skip (Talmud Pesachim 112b and Megilla. 11b), in allusion to his appearance in the form of a goat." A direct quote from http://freemasonrywatch.org/baphomet.html accessed 23 February 2012.

So you can see how the Baphomet then became the representation of Lucifer, "the bearer of light." Despite earlier references in the Talmud and other books, which refer to Satan as capable of shapeshifting into many forms including that of the goat.

What Does the Symbolism Mean?

Androgyny

You will notice on inspection of the image that it is an image that is neither male nor female. One could say this is because the image is embodying the comfortable union of all duality in the cosmos—much like the Chinese yin and the yang. All things in creation are spawned out of the union between male and female. If you study the picture carefully it also has the duality of night and day, heaven and earth, up and down, Moon and Sun. This is an all-encompassing idea of all dualities and how they are unified in the one divine being. This notion comes directly from the Crowley interpretation of the Baphomet. Lucifer is therefore the union or balance between **ALL** dualities.

Cryptic Writing

The arms are symbolic of hermeticism. One is female and the other is androgynous. Down the left arm (that points downward) is written the word *congeal*, translated into English. This is meant to be the masculine element, according to Levi. This symbolism is representative of the condensation and consolidation of knowledge—for example, if you study a field of science you become intensely knowledgeable about that field the more you specialize. The right arm of the Baphomet (feminine aspect) has the word *dissolve* written on it and it points to the heavens. This is talking about the other end of the spectrum from consolidation where knowledge is so broad that its meaning is lost and it is mere information—a good example of this is where you hear of a topic via popular media, but you are not an expert in that knowledge—it is information in your head that has nothing more than a flimsy impact on your existence. You can also see this also representative of the dichotomy of spirit versus embodiment—Lucifer is in the middle as the eternal balance between the two.

Pythagorean Pentacle

You will notice the Pythagorean pentacle on the head of the Baphomet. This represents Lucifer's connection to the elements as of earth, wind, fire, air, water, and spirit (the "five sanctuaries"). This connectivity is housed in the oneness of knowledge. The placement can even be argued as significant as it rests in the position of the third eye. The Pythagorean pentacle was mathematical perfection, hence its use in the Cabalistic Tetragrammaton. In ancient Greek mythology the pentacle was also the symbol of the Goddess Hygieia, or the Goddess of health and well-being.

Breasts and Phallus

The word *breast* comes from the proto-Indo-European word *bhreus,* which means "to sprout or grow."[42] The breasts represent fecundity or fertility and motherhood and have throughout ancient culture for thousands of years as evidenced by the many thousands of differing statues and carvings of various pagan Gods and Goddesses from around the world. Here with the Baphomet, the symbolism refers to birth and origination. For Levi, it was representative of humanity and its frailty. It can be said that the Baphomet is the birthplace of knowledge and enlightenment (in the feminine aspect). Likewise, the phallus of the Baphomet is the Hermetic Caduceus (twin snakes)—which represents again health and vitality, but one can also see this as representing the double helix of the DNA molecule that makes up all

---

[42]   See http://en.wikipedia.org/wiki/Exact_trigonometric_constants#36. C2.B0__Pentagon on the Exact Trigonometric Constants.

life. Again, it symbolizes birth and creation but from the masculine point of view. Crowley associated this with sex magick and the life-giving power of sperm. Levi indicated it was a symbol of eternal life.

Goats Head and Man's Body

As I have explained earlier, the head of the goat on the body of a man represents the Goat of Mendes and his infernal union with humanity—the body of man of course being representative of humans. Some believe that Satan and Eve conceived Cain—another reason for the infernal union of Father Satan with humanity. Adam and Eve did not have sex (allegedly) until after Eve's encounter with the Serpent in the Garden of Eden. The Serpent was said to have opened Eve's eyes—some believe it was to sexuality. It was believed by some that when Eve conceived Cain and Able that Cain was Satan's child and Able was therefore the son of Adam—despite them being twins. This was said to lead to the notion of the sinner versus the sinless (the head of the goat representing sin). This could just be a fanciful notion, but it is interesting nonetheless.

The Eternal Flame

This is said to represent intellect and the dark flame of illumination. Levi said in his book *Dogme et Rituel de la Haute Magie:*

> *The flame of intelligence shining between his horns is the magick light of the universal balance, the image of the soul elevated above matter, as the flame, while being tied to matter, shines above it.*[43]

We can also see it as a representation of Lucifer the bearer of light, enlightenment and knowledge.

---

[43] See Levi, E. (2011). *Dogme et Rituel de la Haute Magie.* Cambridge: Cambridge Library Collection.

The World

The Baphomet sits firmly on the world, cloven hooves and all. The world could be thought of as a depiction of creation and mankind. The Baphomet therefore becomes the light of the world and the cornerstone for its spiritual growth.

The Wings

All celestial beings in ancient cultures are depicted as creatures of flight. This is because the concept of the celestial refers to the esoteric. This also represented true freedom to ancient many ancient people as many had aspired to flight in order to transcend the mundane world. For the ancient Greeks, wings also represented spirituality, love, and victory.

The Baphomet is often seen as a talisman worn by many of us of the goat's head within a pentagram. This is symbolic of the elements as well as all the aforementioned ideas. My talisman has the face of a goat, but the nose is an uncircumcised penis and the head of the goat between the horns (from whence springs the eternal flame) is a vagina. This is a common sexualization of the symbol and often associated with sexuality in magick and, indeed, sex magick itself. The head of the goat and the horns also depict the Satanic hand sign \m/ or even the sign of the cloven hoof (as do the hands of the Baphomet in the drawing).

APPENDIX B

Dedication Rite to a Patron/ Matron Demon

This rite is designed to help the practitioner reinforce the tie between the practitioner and their patron/matron Demon.

What You Need

1. A bell
2. Salt
3. Water
4. Incense (generally that preferred by your patron/matron)
5. Dagger
6. A fire-resistant bowl
7. Paper and pen

What to Avoid

- Fast for twenty-four hours from all food, tobacco, and drugs where possible.

- Avoid sex where possible for twenty-four hours prior to the dedication.
- Make sure you are somewhere where you won't be disturbed.

The Ritual Itself

This ritual should be performed on an even day after the full moon up to fourteen days into the moon itself.

1. Have a ritual bath with Hyssop and sea-salt water.
2. Draw a circle with salt, three meters round, with the names of the primary sources written around the outside.
3. From the east call to Amaymon using his enn: "Elan Reya Amaymon."
4. From the south you call to Goap using his enn: "Anana avac Goap."
5. Likewise, you call Corson from the west: "Ana tasa Corson nanay."
6. Ziminiar from the north using his enn: "Renin Ziminiar et élan."
7. This part is optional. However, you can also call Satan using his enn—"Tasa Reme Laris Satan"—to signify the fifth element of spirit.
8. Write on a piece of paper:
   a. "I, {your name}, offer my allegiance and dedication to {patron/matron name} by Satan herein after. I pledge to answer the call you give, to do as requested, to follow as you lead. I affix my seal below."
9. Sign your name on your petition.
10. Meditate on your petition for about an hour.
11. When you feel the Demon's presence, then burn the petition to release the intent and will to the universe.
12. Close the circle, thank the Demon for coming.

APPENDIX C

Demon Correspondences

These are the spirits of the Goetia. They are led by four cardinal spirits who are under Satan the Lord of Darkness. These four cardinal spirits are:

1. **Goap** (or Gaap) is also one of the four cardinal spirits, of the south in The Lesser Key of Solomon, the west in the Pseudomonarchia Daemonum.

2. **Amaymon** (also Amaimon, or Amoymon) is a Prince of Hell. According to Pseudomonarchia Daemonum, he is the King of the West, although for some translations of The Lesser Key of Solomon, he is King of the east.

3. **Corson** is the King of the west according to some translations of The Lesser Key of Solomon and king of the south according to Pseudomonarchia Daemonum.

4. **Ziminiar** (or Zymymar) is one of the four principal kings that have power over the north.

Some believe the four cardinal spirits are Belial, Beleth, Asmoday and Gaap. This depends largely on the translation of the Pseudomonarchia Daemonum and The Lesser Key of Solomon.

Duke Agares

Dates: Mar 31—Apr 10

Position: Day Demon

Direction: North

Planet: Venus

Metal: Copper

Element: Earth

Color: Green

Plant: Carnation

Incense: Sandalwood

Zodiac: Aries

Gems: Moss agate, antigorite, zoisite, ruby in fuchsite, emerald, seraphinite, hiddenite, jade and green quartz, green calcite, aventurine, tree agate, prasiolite peridot, malachite, green kyanite, green tourmaline, green fluorite, garnet, diopside, tsavorite, pyromorphite, pargasite, rainforest rhyolite, moldavite. wavellite, actinolite, epidote, fuchsite, green sphene, serpentine, vesuvianite, alexandrite. chlorite in quartz, apophyllite, prehnite

Enn: Rean ganen ayar da Agares.

Purpose: *Agares teaches languages, stops and retrieves runaway persons, causes earthquakes, and grants noble titles. He can aid with prosperity, jobs and travel.*

Duke Aim

Dates: Nov 4—Nov 12

Position: Solar Demon

Direction: South

Planet: Venus

Metal: Copper

Element: Fire

Colors: Green

Plant: Lemon

Incense: Sandalwood

Zodiac: Cancer

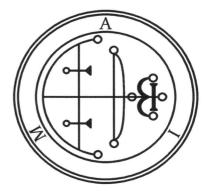

Gems: Amethyst, emerald, diamonds, alexandrite and tanzanite, rose quartz, malachite, red jasper

Enn: Ayer avage secore Aim.

Purpose: *Gives true answers to private matters.*

Duke Alloces

Dates: Aug 24—Sep 3

Position: Night Demon

Direction: South

Planet: Venus

Metal: Copper

Element: Fire

Color: Green

Plant: Sage

Incense: Sandalwood

Zodiac: Virgo

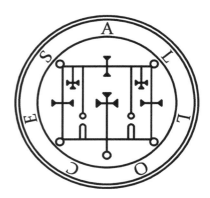

Gems: Moss agate, antigorite, zoisite, ruby in fuchsite, emerald, seraphinite, hiddenite, jade and green quartz, green calcite, aventurine, tree agate, prasiolite peridot, malachite, green kyanite, green tourmaline, green fluorite, garnet, diopside, tsavorite, pyromorphite, pargasite, rainforest rhyolite, moldavite, wavellite, actinolite, epidote, fuchsite, green sphene, serpentine, vesuvianite, alexandrite. chlorite in quartz, apophyllite, prehnite

Enn: Typan efna Alloces met tasa.

Duke Amducius/Amdusias/Amdukias

Dates: Jan 20—Jan 29

Position: Night Demon

Direction: East

Planet: Venus

Metal: Copper

Element: Air

Color: Green

Plant: Mimosa

Incense: Sandalwood

Zodiac: Aquarius

Gems: Moss agate, antigorite, zoisite, ruby in fuchsite, emerald, seraphinite, hiddenite, jade and green quartz, green calcite, aventurine, tree agate, prasiolite peridot, malachite, green kyanite, green tourmaline, green fluorite, garnet, diopside, tsavorite, pyromorphite, pargasite, rainforest rhyolite, moldavite. wavellite, actinolite, epidote, fuchsite, green sphene, serpentine, vesuvianite, alexandrite. chlorite in quartz, apophyllite, prehnite

Enn: Denyen Valocur Avage Secore Amducious.

Purpose: *He is said to provide good familiars and to teach astronomy and liberal arts.*

Marquis Amon

Dates: May 21—May 31

Position: Day Demon

Direction: North

Planet: Moon

Metal: Silver

Element: Water

Color: Violet

Plant: Nightshade

Incense: Jasmine

Zodiac: Gemini

Gems: Ametrine, amethyst, violet sapphire, amethyst cacoxenite, sugilite, lepidolite, covellite, manganese with sugilite, scapolite, charoite, vera cruz amethyst, chevron amethyst, botswana agate, rainbow fluorite, purple fluorite

Enn: Avage Secore Amon Ninan.

Purpose: *Amon helps with family matters. He is an entity many looked to reconcile friends and foes and procure love for those seeking it. He can assist in the manipulation of people.*

President Amy/Avnas

(Under Ziminiar)

Dates: Oct 23—Nov 1

Position: Night Demon

Direction: South

Planet: Mercury

Metal: Mercury

Element: Fire

Color: Orange

Plant: Vervain

Incense: Storax

Zodiac: Scorpio

Gems: Tangerine aura quartz, goldstone, amber, aragonite, orange aventurine, carnelian, citrine, orange calcite, scheelite, amber calcite, coral calcite, copal, wulfenite, orange kyanite, imperial topaz, smoky citrine, golden healer quartz

Enn: Tu Fubin Amy secore.

Purpose: *He helps to uncover the truth of a situation. He is claimed to teach astronomy and liberal arts, give familiars, incite positive reactions from rulers, and reveal treasures.*

Marquis Andras

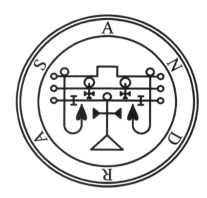

Dates: Dec 13—Dec 21

Position: Solar Demon

Direction: East

Planet: Pluto

Metal: Iron and silver

Element: Air

Colors: Violet

Plant: Violet

Incense: Jasmine

Zodiac: Aquarius

Gems: Fire agate, obsidian, black tourmaline, red goldstone, mookaite, red tiger eye, red jasper, red agate, garnet, red selenite, red aventurine, tiger eye, fire opal, fire agate

Enn: Entey ama Andras anay.

Purpose: *Helps to see the truth of a situation. He stirs up trouble and dissension and can also mollify situations as well by bringing peace, stability and resolution.*

Marquis Andrealphus

Dates: Dec 31—Jan 9

Position: Night Demon

Direction: East

Planet: Moon

Metal: Silver

Element: Air

Color: Violet

Plant: Lotus

Incense: Jasmine

Zodiac: Gemini

Gems: Ametrine, amethyst, violet sapphire, amethyst cacoxenite, sugilite, lepidolite, covellite, manganese with sugilite, scapolite, charoite, vera cruz amethyst, chevron amethyst, botswana agate, rainbow fluorite, purple fluorite

Enn: Mena Andrealphus tasa ramec ayer.

Purpose: *He teaches cunning in astronomy and. when in human form. also teaches geometry.*

Earl Andromalius

Dates: Mar 11—Mar 20

Position: Night Demon

Direction: South

Planet: Mars

Metal: Copper or silver

Element: Fire

Color: Red

Plant: Wormwood

Incense: Dragon's blood

Zodiac: Pisces

Gems: Red goldstone, mookaite, red tiger eye, red jasper, red agate, garnet, red selenite, red aventurine, tiger eye, fire opal, fire agate

Enn: Tasa fubin Andromalius on ca.

Purpose: *He can bring back both a thief and the stolen goods, punishes all thieves and other wicked people, and discovers hidden treasures, all evilness, and all dishonest dealing.*

King Asmoday

(Under Ziminiar)

Dates: Jan 30—Feb 8

Position: Day Demon

Direction: East

Planet: Sun

Metal: Gold

Element: Air

Color: Yellow

Plant: Mint

Incense: Frankincense

Zodiac: Aquarius

Gems: Yellow jasper, amber calcite, chrysoberyl, gold apatite, yellow aventurine, imperial topaz, lemon quartz, heliodor, sulphur, yellow calcite, yellow sphene, golden healer quartz

Enn: Ayer Avage Aloren Asmodeus Aken.

Purpose: *Asmodeus helps with love and lust. He can also assist with creativity.*

Duchess Astaroth

Dates: Dec 31–Jan 9

Position: Day Demon

Direction: South

Planet: Venus

Metal: Copper

Element: Earth

Color: Green

Plant: Laurel

Incense: Sandalwood

Zodiac: Capricorn

Gems: Moss agate, antigorite, zoisite, ruby in fuchsite, emerald, seraphinite, hiddenite, jade and green quartz, green calcite, aventurine, tree agate, prasiolite peridot, malachite, green kyanite, green tourmaline, green fluorite, garnet, diopside, tsavorite, pyromorphite, pargasite, rainforest rhyolite, moldavite. wavellite, actinolite, epidote, fuchsite, green sphene, serpentine, vesuvianite, alexandrite. chlorite in quartz, apophyllite, prehnite

Enn: seerena Alora Astaroth Aken.

Purpose: *She teaches mathematical sciences and handicrafts, can make men invisible and lead them to hidden treasures, and answers every question formulated to him. She was also said to give to mortal beings the power over serpents. She helps in matters of love and also friendship. She also helps with divination.*

King Bael

Dates: Mar 21–Mar 30

Position: Day Demon

Direction: South

Planet: Sun

Metal: Gold

Element: Fire

Color: Yellow

Plant: Fern

Incense: Frankincense

Zodiac: Aries

Gems: Yellow jasper, amber calcite, chrysoberyl, gold apatite, yellow aventurine, imperial topaz, lemon quartz, heliodor, sulphur, yellow calcite, yellow sphene, golden healer quartz, black tourmaline, onyx, tektite, black agate, black jasper, black opal, zebra jasper, stibnite, tourmalated quartz, hematite, black onyx, jet, galena, meteorite, apache tears, snowflake obsidian, azurite-galena, molybdenite, magnetite, lodestone, rainbow obsidian, granite, black kyanite, zircon, sphalerite

Enn: Ayer Secore On Ca Bael.

Purpose: *Bael has the power to make men invisible. He assists with matters of friendship and success.*

King Balam

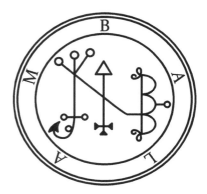

Dates: Aug 12—Aug 22

Position: Night Demon

Direction: West

Planet: Sun

Metal: Gold

Element: Earth

Color: Yellow

Plant: Oak

Incense: Frankincense

Zodiac: Leo

Gems: Yellow jasper, amber calcite, chrysoberyl, gold apatite, yellow aventurine, imperial topaz, lemon quartz, heliodor, sulphur, yellow calcite, yellow sphene, golden healer quartz

Enn: Lirach tasa vefa wehlc Balam.

Purpose: *He helps with family matters. He gives perfect answers on things past, present, and to come, and can also make men invisible and witty.*

Duke Barbatos

(Under Ziminiar)

Dates: Jun 1—Jun 10

Position: Day Demon

Direction: South

Planet: Venus

Metal: Copper

Element: Fire

Color: Green

Plant: Ivy

Incense: Sandalwood

Zodiac: Gemini

Gems: Moss agate, antigorite, zoisite, ruby in fuchsite, emerald, seraphinite, hiddenite, jade and green quartz, green calcite, aventurine, tree agate, prasiolite peridot, malachite, green kyanite, green tourmaline, green fluorite, garnet, diopside, tsavorite, pyromorphite, pargasite, rainforest rhyolite, moldavite. wavellite, actinolite, epidote, fuchsite, green sphene, serpentine, vesuvianite, alexandrite. chlorite in quartz, apophyllite, prehnite

Enn: Eveta fubin Barbatos.

Purpose: *He bestows psychic abilities. He can speak to animals, can tell the future, conciliates friends and rulers, and can lead men to treasure hidden by the enchantment.*

Duke Bathin

(Under Amaymon)

Dates: Sep 12—Sep 22

Position: Day Demon

Direction: West

Planet: Venus

Metal: Copper

Element: Earth

Color: Green

Plant: Mistletoe

Incense: Sandalwood

Zodiac: Virgo

Gems: Moss agate, antigorite, zoisite, ruby in fuchsite, emerald, seraphinite, hiddenite, jade and green quartz, green calcite, aventurine, tree agate, prasiolite peridot, malachite, green kyanite, green tourmaline, green fluorite, garnet, diopside, tsavorite, pyromorphite, pargasite, rainforest rhyolite, moldavite. wavellite, actinolite, epidote, fuchsite, green sphene, serpentine, vesuvianite, alexandrite. chlorite in quartz, apophyllite, prehnite

Enn: Dyen Pretore on ca Bathin.

Purpose: *He knows the virtues of precious stones and herbs and can bring men suddenly from one country to another. He helps one attain astral projection and takes one wherever one wants to go. He can help with prosperity.*

Lord Beelzebub

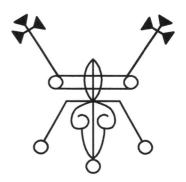

Dates: Mar 21–Mar 25

Direction: North

Planet: Jupiter

Metal: Titanium

Element: Earth

Color: Red, black, gray, silvers and blues

Plant: Fern

Incense: Myrrh

Zodiac: Aries

Gems: Moldavite, dendritic opal, smoky quartz and obsidian, black tourmaline, onyx, tektite, black agate, black jasper, black opal, zebra jasper, stibnite, tourmaline quartz, hematite, black onyx, jet, galena, meteorite, apache tears, snowflake obsidian, azurite-galena, molybdenite, magnetite, lodestone, rainbow obsidian, granite, black kyanite, zircon, sphalerite

Enn: Adey Vocar Avage Beelzebuth.

Purpose: *He is known for flying. Can bring all manner of pestilence and can remove all manner of pestilence.*

King Beleth

Dates: Jul 23—Aug 1

Position: Day Demon

Direction: North/West

Planet: Sun

Metal: Gold

Element: Earth

Color: Yellow

Plant: Dill

Incense: Frankincense

Zodiac: Leo

Gems: Yellow jasper, amber calcite, chrysoberyl, gold apatite, yellow aventurine, imperial topaz, lemon quartz, heliodor, sulphur, yellow calcite, yellow sphene, golden healer quartz

Enn: Lirach tasa vefa wehlc Beleth.

Purpose: *He helps with love and lust.*

King Belial

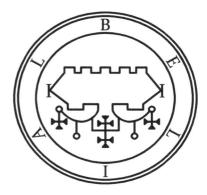

(Under Corson)

Dates: Jan 30—Feb 8

Position: Night Demon

Direction: North/South

Planet: Sun

Metal: Gold

Element: Fire

Color: Yellow

Plant: Mullein

Incense: Frankincense

Zodiac: Aquarius

Gems: Yellow jasper, amber calcite, chrysoberyl, gold apatite, yellow aventurine, imperial topaz, lemon quartz, heliodor, sulphur, yellow calcite, yellow sphene, golden healer quartz

Enn: Lirach Tasa Vefa Wehlc Belial.

Purpose: *He provides health and stability. He provides good familiars. He also incites lawlessness and instability.*

Duke Berith

(Under Goap)

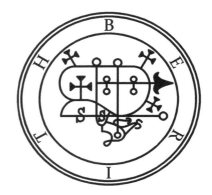

Dates: Dec 22—Dec 30

Position: Day Demon

Direction: South

Planet: Venus

Metal: Copper

Element: Fire

Color: Green

Plant: Heliotrope

Incense: Sandalwood

Zodiac: Capricorn

Gems: Moss agate, antigorite, zoisite, ruby in fuchsite, emerald, seraphinite, hiddenite, jade and green quartz, green calcite, aventurine, tree agate, prasiolite peridot, malachite, green kyanite, green tourmaline, green fluorite, garnet, diopside, tsavorite, pyromorphite, pargasite, rainforest rhyolite, moldavite. wavellite, actinolite, epidote, fuchsite, green sphene, serpentine, vesuvianite, alexandrite. chlorite in quartz, apophyllite, prehnite

Enn: Hoath Redar Ganabal Berith.

Purpose: *Berith answers truly of things present, past, and to come. Berith also has the power to transmute all base metals into gold. He imparts knowledge of sorcery.*

Earl Bifrons

(Under Corson)

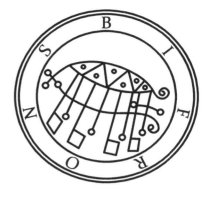

Dates: Jun 21—Jul 1

Position: Night Demon

Direction: North

Planet: Mars

Metal: Copper or silver

Element: Earth

Color: Red

Plant: Basil

Incense: Dragon's blood

Zodiac: Cancer

Gems: Red goldstone, mookaite, red tiger eye, red jasper, red agate, garnet, red selenite, red aventurine, tiger eye, fire opal, fire agate

Enn: Avage secore Bifrons remie tasa.

Purpose: *He teaches sciences and arts, the virtues of the gems and woods, herbs, and changes corpses from their original grave into other places, sometimes putting magick lights on the graves that appear like candles.*

President Botis

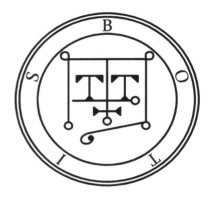

(Under Amaymon)

Dates: Sep 2—Sep 11

Position: Day Demon

Direction: North

Planet: Mercury

Metal: Mercury

Element: Water

Color: Orange

Plant: Lily

Incense: Storax

Zodiac: Virgo

Gems: Tangerine aura quartz, goldstone, amber, aragonite, orange aventurine, carnelian, citrine, orange calcite, scheelite, amber calcite, coral calcite, copal, wulfenite, orange kyanite, imperial topaz, smoky citrine, golden healer quartz

Enn: Jedan hoesta noc ra Botis.

Purpose: *He tells of all things past and future and reconciles friends and foes. He can aid in matters of love and reconciliation.*

President Buer

(Under Ziminiar)

Dates: Jun 21—Jul 1

Direction: South

Planet: Mercury

Metal: Mercury

Element: Fire

Color: Orange

Plant: Aloe

Incense: Storax

Zodiac: Cancer

Gems: Tangerine aura quartz, goldstone, amber, aragonite, orange aventurine, carnelian, citrine, orange calcite, scheelite, amber calcite, coral calcite, copal, wulfenite, orange kyanite, imperial topaz, smoky citrine, golden healer quartz

Enn: Erato on ca Buer anon.

Purpose: *He teaches natural and moral philosophy, logic, and the virtues of all herbs and plants (through the use of reversals) and is also capable of healing all infirmities. According to some accounts, he also bestows familiars.*

Duchess Bune/Bime

(Under Goap)

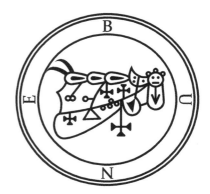

Dates: Dec 3—Dec 12

Position: Day Demon

Direction: West

Planet: Venus

Metal: Copper

Element: Earth

Color: Green

Plant: Orange

Incense: Sandalwood

Zodiac: Sagittarius

Gems: Moss agate, antigorite, zoisite, ruby in fuchsite, emerald, seraphinite, hiddenite, jade and green quartz, green calcite, aventurine, tree agate, prasiolite peridot, malachite, green kyanite, green tourmaline, green fluorite, garnet, diopside, tsavorite, pyromorphite, pargasite, rainforest rhyolite, moldavite. wavellite, actinolite, epidote, fuchsite, green sphene, serpentine, vesuvianite, alexandrite. chlorite in quartz, apophyllite, prehnite

Enn: Wehlc melan avage Bune Tasa.

Purpose: *Bune makes men eloquent and wise and gives true answers to their demands and also richness.*

President Camio/Caim

(Under Goap)

Dates: Sep 2—Sep 11

Position: Night Demon

Direction: East

Planet: Mercury

Metal: Mercury

Element: Air

Color: Orange

Plant: Centaurea

Incense: Storax

Zodiac: Virgo

Gems: Tangerine aura quartz, goldstone, amber, aragonite, orange aventurine, carnelian, citrine, orange calcite, scheelite, amber calcite, coral calcite, copal, wulfenite, orange kyanite, imperial topaz, smoky citrine, golden healer quartz

Enn: Tasa on ca Caim Renich

Purpose: *He is a good disputer, gives men the understanding of the voices of birds, bullocks, dogs, and other creatures, and of the noise of the waters too, and gives true answers concerning things to come.*

Marquis Cimejes/Cimeies/Kimaris

Dates: Jan 11—Jan 19

Position: Night Demon

Direction: West

Planet: Moon

Metal: Silver

Element: Earth

Color: Violet

Plant: Pine

Incense: Jasmine

Zodiac: Capricorn

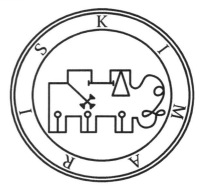

Gems: Ametrine, amethyst, violet sapphire, amethyst cacoxenite, sugilite, lepidolite, covellite, manganese with sugilite, scapolite, charoite, vera cruz amethyst, chevron amethyst, botswana agate, rainbow fluorite, purple fluorite

Enn: Ayer avage secore Cimejes.

Purpose: *He can cause a person to cross seas and rivers quickly. He is useful in the manipulation of people.*

Duke Crocell

(Under Goap)

Dates: Jul 22—Aug 1

Position: Night Demon

Direction: North/West

Planet: Venus

Metal: Copper

Element: Water

Color: Green

Plant: Wood betony

Incense: Sandalwood

Zodiac: Leo

Gems: Moss agate, antigorite, zoisite, ruby in fuchsite, emerald, seraphinite, hiddenite, jade and green quartz, green calcite, aventurine, tree agate, prasiolite peridot, malachite, green kyanite, green tourmaline, green fluorite, garnet, diopside, tsavorite, pyromorphite, pargasite, rainforest rhyolite, moldavite. wavellite, actinolite, epidote, fuchsite, green sphene, serpentine, vesuvianite, alexandrite. chlorite in quartz, apophyllite, prehnite

Enn: Jedan tasa Crocell on ca.

Purpose: *He can teach geometry and other liberal sciences. He can also warm bodies of water, create the illusion of the sound of rushing waters, and reveal the location of natural baths. He is associated with water.*

Duke Dantalion

(Under Corson)

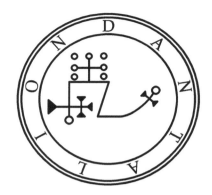

Dates: Mar 11—Mar 15

Position: Night Demon

Direction: North

Planet: Venus

Metal: Copper

Element: Water

Color: Green

Plant: Honeysuckle

Incense: Sandalwood

Zodiac: Pisces

Gems: Moss agate, antigorite, zoisite, ruby in fuchsite, emerald, seraphinite, hiddenite, jade and green quartz, garnet, diopside, tsavorite, pyromorphite, pargasite, rainforest rhyolite, moldavite. wavellite, actinolite, epidote, fuchsite, green sphene, serpentine, vesuvianite, alexandrite. chlorite in quartz, apophyllite, prehnite.

Enn: Avage ayer Dantalion on ca.

Purpose: *He knows the thoughts of all men and can change them at will. He can cause love and give visions.*

Marquis Decarabia

(Under Corson)

Dates: Feb 9—Feb 18

Position: Night Demon

Direction: East

Planet: Moon

Metal: Silver

Element: Air

Color: Violet

Plant: Lunaria

Incense: Jasmine

Zodiac: Aquarius

Gems: Ametrine, amethyst, violet sapphire, amethyst cacoxenite, sugilite, lepidolite, covellite, manganese with sugilite, scapolite, charoite, vera cruz amethyst, chevron amethyst, botswana agate, rainbow fluorite, purple fluorite

Enn: Hoesta noc ra Decarabia secore.

Purpose: *Decarabia knows the virtues of all herbs and precious stones and can change into all birds and sing and fly like them. He helps with creativity and truth.*

Duke Eligos

Dates: Aug 13—Aug 22

Position: Day Demon

Direction: North

Planet: Venus

Metal: Copper

Element: Water

Color: Green

Plant: Thyme

Incense: Sandalwood

Zodiac: Leo

Gems: Moss agate, antigorite, zoisite, ruby in fuchsite, emerald, seraphinite, hiddenite, jade and green quartz, green calcite, aventurine, tree agate, prasiolite peridot, malachite, green kyanite, green tourmaline, green fluorite, garnet, diopside, tsavorite, pyromorphite, pargasite, rainforest rhyolite, moldavite. wavellite, actinolite, epidote, fuchsite, green sphene, serpentine, vesuvianite, alexandrite. chlorite in quartz, apophyllite, prehnite

Enn: Jedan on ca Eligos inan.

Purpose: *He discovers hidden things and knows the future of wars and how soldiers should meet. He also attracts the favor of lords, knights and other important persons.*

Duke Focalor

(Under Amaymon)

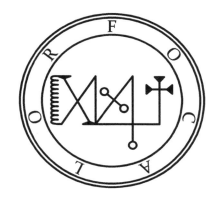

Dates: May 1—May 10

Position: Night Demon

Direction: North

Planet: Venus

Metal: Copper

Element: Water

Color: Green

Plant: Wild rose

Incense: Sandalwood

Zodiac: Taurus

Gems: Moss agate, antigorite, zoisite, ruby in fuchsite, emerald, seraphinite, hiddenite, jade and green quartz, green calcite, aventurine, tree agate, prasiolite peridot, malachite, green kyanite, green tourmaline, green fluorite, garnet, diopside, tsavorite, pyromorphite, pargasite, rainforest rhyolite, moldavite. wavellite, actinolite, epidote, fuchsite, green sphene, serpentine, vesuvianite, alexandrite. chlorite in quartz, apophyllite, prehnite

Enn: En Jedan on ca Focalor.

Purpose: *He discovers hidden things and knows the future of wars and how soldiers should meet. He also attracts the favor of lords, knights and other important persons.*

President Foras

(Under Ziminiar)

Dates: Jan 20—Jan 29

Position: Day Demon

Direction: West

Planet: Mercury

Metal: Mercury

Element: Earth

Color: Orange

Plant: Century

Incense: Storax

Zodiac: Aquarius

Gems: Tangerine aura quartz, goldstone, amber, aragonite, orange aventurine, carnelian, citrine, orange calcite, scheelite, amber calcite, coral calcite, copal, wulfenite, orange kyanite, imperial topaz, smoky citrine, golden healer quartz

Enn: Kaymen vefa Foras.

Purpose: *He teaches logic and ethics in all their branches, the virtues of all herbs and precious stones, can make a man witty, eloquent, invisible, and live long, and can discover treasures and recover lost things.*

Marquis Forneus

(Under Goap)

Dates: Jan 10—Jan 19

Position: Day Demon

Direction: North

Planet: Moon

Metal: Silver

Element: Water

Color: Violet

Plant: Sunflower

Incense: Jasmine

Zodiac: Capricorn

Gems: Ametrine, amethyst, violet sapphire, amethyst cacoxenite, sugilite, lepidolite, covellite, manganese with sugilite, scapolite, charoite, vera cruz amethyst, chevron amethyst, botswana agate, rainbow fluorite, purple fluorite

Enn: Senan okat ena Forneus ayer.

Purpose: *He causes men to have a good name and to have the knowledge and understanding of tongues. He makes one beloved by his foes as well as of his friends.*

Knight Furcas

(Under Goap)

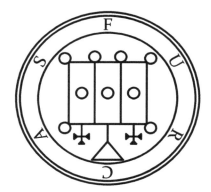

Dates: Aug 2—Aug 11

Position: Night Demon

Direction: East

Planet: Saturn

Metal: Lead

Element: Air

Color: Black

Plant: Cinquefoil

Incense: Myrrh

Zodiac: Leo

Gems: Black tourmaline, onyx, tektite, black agate, black jasper, black opal, zebra jasper, stibnite, tourmalated quartz, hematite, black onyx, jet, galena, meteorite, apache tears, snowflake obsidian, azurite-galena, molybdenite, magnetite, lodestone, rainbow obsidian, granite, black kyanite, zircon, sphalerite

Enn: Secore on ca Furcas remie.

Purpose: *He teaches philosophy, rhetoric, logic, astronomy, chiromancy, pyromancy. He can aid with legal matters.*

Earl Furfur

(Under Ziminiar)

Dates: Feb 19—Feb 28

Position: Day Demon

Direction: South

Planet: Mars

Metal: Copper or silver

Element: Fire

Color: Red

Plant: Cypress

Incense: Dragon's blood

Zodiac: Pisces

Gems: Red goldstone, mookaite, red tiger eye, red jasper, red agate, garnet, red selenite, red aventurine, tiger eye, fire opal, fire agate

Enn: Ganen menach tasa Furfur.

Purpose: *He gives true answers to every question.*

President Gaap

(Under Ziminiar)

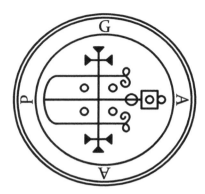

Dates: Feb 9—Feb 18

Position: Day Demon

Direction: East

Planet: Mercury

Metal: Mercury

Element: Air

Color: Orange

Plant: Moss

Incense: Storax

Zodiac: Aquarius

Gems: Tangerine aura quartz, goldstone, amber, aragonite, orange aventurine, carnelian, citrine, orange calcite, scheelite, amber calcite, coral calcite, copal, wulfenite, orange kyanite, imperial topaz, smoky citrine, golden healer quartz

Enn: Deyan Anay Tasa Gaap.

Purpose: *Prince in human form who incites love. Provides medical care for women.*

Marquis Gamigin/Samgina

Dates: Apr 20—Apr 29

Position: Day Demon

Direction: North

Planet: Moon

Metal: Silver

Element: Water

Color: Violet

Plant: Juniper

Incense: Jasmine

Zodiac: Taurus

Gems: Ametrine, amethyst, violet sapphire, amethyst cacoxenite, sugilite, lepidolite, covellite, manganese with sugilite, scapolite, charoite, vera cruz amethyst, chevron amethyst, botswana agate, rainbow fluorite, purple fluorite.

Enn: Esta ta et tasa Gamigin.

Purpose: *Helps with creativity and all manner of things concerning death. He teaches liberal arts and gives accounts of souls that died in sin.*

President Glasya-Labolas

(Under Goap)

Dates: Nov 23—2 Dec

Position: Day Demon

Direction: South

Planet: Mercury

Metal: Mercury

Element: Fire

Color: Orange

Plant: Rosemary

Incense: Storax

Zodiac: Sagittarius

Gems: Tangerine aura quartz, goldstone, amber, aragonite, orange aventurine, carnelian, citrine, orange calcite, scheelite, amber calcite, coral calcite, copal, wulfenite, orange kyanite, imperial topaz, smoky citrine, golden healer quartz

Enn: Elan tepar secore on ca Glasya-Lobolas.

Purpose: *He teaches all arts and sciences, in an instant, tells all things past and to come, and is the author and captain of manslaughter and bloodshed. He causes the love of both friends and foes, if desired, and can make a man invisible.*

Duchess Gremory/Gemory/Gamori

(Under Ziminiar)

Dates: Oct 3—Oct 12

Position: Night Demon

Direction: North/West

Planet: Venus

Metal: Copper

Element: Water

Color: Green

Plant: Fenugreek

Incense: Sandalwood

Zodiac: Libra

Gems: Moss agate, antigorite, zoisite, ruby in fuchsite, emerald, seraphinite, hiddenite, jade and green quartz, green calcite, aventurine, tree agate, prasiolite peridot, malachite, green kyanite, green tourmaline, green fluorite, garnet, diopside, tsavorite, pyromorphite, pargasite, rainforest rhyolite, moldavite. wavellite, actinolite, epidote, fuchsite, green sphene, serpentine, vesuvianite, alexandrite. chlorite in quartz, apophyllite, prehnite

Enn: An tasa shi Gremory on ca.

Purpose: *She tells all things past, present and future, about hidden treasures, and procures the love of women.*

Duke Gusion

Dates: Jul 2—Jul 12

Position: Day Demon

Direction: North

Planet: Venus

Metal: Copper

Element: Water

Color: Green

Plant: Aloe

Incense: Sandalwood

Zodiac: Cancer

Gems: Moss agate, antigorite, zoisite, ruby in fuchsite, emerald, seraphinite, hiddenite, jade and green quartz, green calcite, aventurine, tree agate, prasiolite peridot, malachite, green kyanite, green tourmaline, green fluorite, garnet, diopside, tsavorite, pyromorphite, pargasite, rainforest rhyolite, moldavite. wavellite, actinolite, epidote, fuchsite, green sphene, serpentine, vesuvianite, alexandrite. chlorite in quartz, apophyllite, prehnite

Enn: Secore vesa anet Gusion.

Purpose: *He tells all past, present and future things, shows the meaning of all questions that are asked to him, reconciles friends, and gives honor and dignity.*

President Haagenti

(Under Corson)

Dates: Jul 12—Jul 21

Position: Night Demon

Direction: West

Planet: Mercury

Metal: Mercury

Element: Earth

Color: Orange

Plant: Witch Hazel

Incense: Storax

Zodiac: Cancer

Gems: Tangerine aura quartz, goldstone, amber, aragonite, orange aventurine, carnelian, citrine, orange calcite, scheelite, amber calcite, coral calcite, copal, wulfenite, orange kyanite, imperial topaz, smoky citrine, golden healer quartz

Enn: Haagenti on ca Lirach.

Purpose: *He makes men wise by instructing them in every subject, transmutes all metals into gold, and changes wine into water and water into wine.*

Earl Halphas

Dates: Mar 30—Apr 8

Position: Night Demon

Direction: South

Planet: Mars

Metal: Copper or silver

Element: Air

Color: Red

Plant: Marjoram

Incense: Dragon's blood

Zodiac: Aries

Gems: Red goldstone, mookaite, red tiger eye, red jasper, red agate, garnet, red selenite, red aventurine, tiger eye, fire opal, fire agate

Enn: Erato Halphas on ca secore.

Purpose: *Sends men to war and provides ammunition. He also aids with stability.*

Duke Haures/Flauros/Haurus/Havres

(Under Amaymon)

Dates: Dec 22—Dec 30

Position: Night Demon

Direction: South

Planet: Venus

Metal: Copper

Element: Fire

Color: Green

Plant: Skullcap

Incense: Sandalwood

Zodiac: Capricorn

Gems: Moss agate, antigorite, zoisite, ruby in fuchsite, emerald, seraphinite, hiddenite, jade and green quartz, green calcite, aventurine, tree agate, prasiolite peridot, malachite, green kyanite, green tourmaline, green fluorite, garnet, diopside, tsavorite, pyromorphite, pargasite, rainforest rhyolite, moldavite. wavellite, actinolite, epidote, fuchsite, green sphene, serpentine, vesuvianite, alexandrite. chlorite in quartz, apophyllite, prehnite

Enn: Ganic tasa fubin Haures.

Purpose: *He gives true answers of all things past, present, and future.*

Prince Ipos

(Under Corson)

Dates: Oct 23—Nov 1

Position: Day Demon

Direction: North

Planet: Jupiter

Metal: Tin

Element: Water

Color: Blue

Plant: Sandalwood or cedar

Incense: Cedar

Zodiac: Scorpio

Gems: Angelite, cavansite, shattuckite, aqua aura quartz, larimar, lapis lazuli, chalcopyrite, chrysoprase, sodalite, blue lace agate, opal, azurite, sapphire, indigo aura quartz, iolite, tanzanite, blue quartz, chrysocolla, hemimorphite, blue goldstone, variscite, rosasite, dioptase, abalone

Enn: Desa an Ipos Ayer.

Purpose: *He knows and can reveal all things, past, present, and future and can make men witty and valiant.*

Marquis Leraje/Leraikha

(Under Goap)

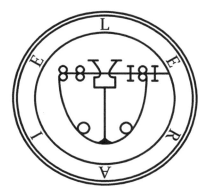

Dates: Aug 2—Aug 11

Position: Day Demon

Direction: South

Planet: Moon

Metal: Silver

Element: Fire

Color: Violet

Plant: Plantain

Incense: Jasmine

Zodiac: Leo

Gems: Ametrine, amethyst, violet sapphire, amethyst cacoxenite, sugilite, lepidolite, covellite, manganese with sugilite, scapolite, charoite, vera cruz amethyst, chevron amethyst, botswana agate, rainbow fluorite, purple fluorite

Enn: Kaymen vefa Leraje.

Purpose: *He causes great battles and disputes and makes gangrene wounds caused by arrows.*

Emperor Leviathan

Dates: All days

Direction: West

Planet: Neptune

Metal: Platinum

Color: Blue

Plant: Calamus

Element: Water

Color: Blue, teal, turquoise, silver, black and emerald green

Incense: Sandalwood and Eucalyptus

Gems: Aquamarine, kyanite, sapphire, pearl, moonstone, tanzanite, black tourmaline, clear quartz

Enn: Jaden Tasa Hoet Naca Leviathan.

Purpose: *Known for teaching all manner of divination.*

Dark Lord Lucifer

Dates: All days

Direction: East

Planet: Venus

Metal: Gold

Element: Air

Color: Blue, teal, white, yellow, gold, silver, black, and gray

Incense: Lemongrass

Plant: Lemon

Gems: Quartz, celestite, black tourmaline, apophyllite, tanzanite, herkimer diamond

Enn: Renich Tasa Uberaca Biasa Icar Lucifer.

Purpose: *Teacher of all knowledge and illumination. Helps with new beginnings, healing and wisdom.*

President Malphas

(Under Amaymon)

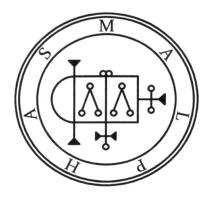

Dates: Apr 11—Apr 20

Position: Night Demon

Direction: East

Planet: Mercury

Metal: Mercury

Element: Air

Color: Orange

Plant: Marigold

Incense: Storax

Zodiac: Aries

Gems: Tangerine aura quartz, goldstone, amber, aragonite, orange aven-turine, carnelian, citrine, orange calcite, scheelite, amber calcite, coral calcite, copal, wulfenite, orange kyanite, imperial topaz, smoky citrine, golden healer quartz

Enn: Lirach tasa Malphas ayer.

Purpose: *Malphas is said to build houses, high towers, and strongholds, throw down the buildings of the enemies, destroy the enemies' desires or thoughts and all what they have done, give good familiars.*

President Marax/Narax

Dates: Oct 13—Oct 22

Position: Day Demon

Direction: West

Planet: Mercury

Metal: Mercury

Element: Earth

Color: Orange

Plant: Elder

Incense: Storax

Zodiac: Libra

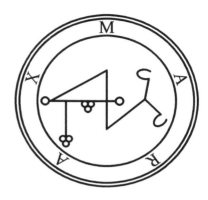

Gems: Red goldstone, mookaite, red tiger eye, red jasper, red agate, garnet, red selenite, red aventurine, tiger eye, fire opal, fire agate

Enn: Kaymen Vefa Marax.

Purpose: *He teaches Astronomy and all other liberal sciences and gives good and wise familiars that know the virtues of all herbs and precious stones.*

President Marbas

Dates: May 1—May 10

Position: Solar Demon

Direction: East

Planet: Mercury

Metal: Mercury

Element: Air

Colors: Orange

Plant: Chicory

Incense: Storax

Zodiac: Aries

Gems: Sardonyx, nephrite jade, bloodstone and hoplite, tangerine aura quartz, goldstone, amber, aragonite, orange aventurine, carnelian, citrine, orange calcite, scheelite, amber calcite, coral calcite, copal, wulfenite, orange kyanite, imperial topaz, smoky citrine, golden healer quartz, black tourmaline, onyx, tektite, black agate, black jasper, black opal, zebra jasper, stibnite, tourmalated quartz, hematite, black onyx, jet, galena, meteorite, apache tears, snowflake obsidian, azurite-galena, molybdenite, magnetite, lodestone, rainbow obsidian, granite, black kyanite, zircon, sphalerite

Enn: Renich tasa Uberaca Biasa Icar Marbas.

Purpose: *He answers truly on hidden or secret things, causes and heals diseases, gives wisdom and knowledge in mechanical arts, and can change men into other shapes.*

Marquess Marchosias

Dates: Mar 1—Mar 10

Position: Solar Demon

Direction: South

Planet: Moon

Metal: Silver

Element: Fire

Colors: Violet

Plant: Pennyroyal

Incense: Jasmine

Zodiac: Virgo

Gems: Golden sheen obsidian, carnelian, citrine and fire quartz, tangerine aura quartz, goldstone, amber, aragonite, orange aventurine, carnelian, citrine, orange calcite, scheelite, amber calcite, coral calcite, copal, wulfenite, orange kyanite, imperial topaz, smoky citrine, golden healer quartz

Enn: Es na ayer Marchosias Secore.

Purpose: *He gives true answers to all questions and is very faithful to the magician in following his commands.*

Duke Murmur/Murmus

Dates: Sep 13—Sep 22

Position: Night Demon

Direction: North

Planet: Venus

Metal: Copper

Element: Fire

Color: Green

Plant: Parsley

Incense: Sandalwood

Zodiac: Virgo

Gems: Moss agate, antigorite, zoisite, ruby in fuchsite, emerald, seraphinite, hiddenite, jade and green quartz, green calcite, aventurine, tree agate, prasiolite peridot, malachite, green kyanite, green tourmaline, green fluorite, garnet, diopside, tsavorite, pyromorphite, pargasite, rainforest rhyolite, moldavite. wavellite, actinolite, epidote, fuchsite, green sphene, serpentine, vesuvianite, alexandrite. chlorite in quartz, apophyllite, prehnite

Enn: Vefa mena Murmur ayer.

Purpose: *He teaches Philosophy and can oblige the souls of the deceased to appear before the conjurer to answer every desired question.*

Marquis Naberius

(Under Corson)

Dates: Nov 13—Nov 22

Position: Day Demon

Direction: East

Planet: Moon

Metal: Silver

Element: Fire

Color: Violet

Plant: Ash

Incense: Jasmine

Zodiac: Scorpio

Gems: Ametrine, amethyst, violet sapphire, amethyst cacoxenite, sugilite, lepidolite, covellite, manganese with sugilite, scapolite, charoite, vera cruz amethyst, chevron amethyst, botswana agate, rainbow fluorite, purple fluorite

Enn: Eyan tasa volocur Naberius.

Purpose: *He makes a man amiable and cunning in all arts and specializes in rhetoric.*

Marquis Orias/Oriax

(Under Ziminiar)

Dates: Nov 2—Nov 12

Position: Night Demon

Direction: East

Planet: Moon

Metal: Silver

Element: Air

Color: Purple

Plant: Seal wort

Incense: Jasmine

Zodiac: Scorpio

Gems: Ametrine, amethyst, violet sapphire, amethyst cacoxenite, sugilite, lepidolite, covellite, manganese with sugilite, scapolite, charoite, vera cruz amethyst, chevron amethyst, botswana agate, rainbow fluorite, purple fluorite

Enn: Lirach mena Orias Anay na.

Purpose: *His Office is to teach the Virtues of the Stars, and to know the Mansions of the Planets, and how to understand their Virtues.*

Prince Orobas

(Under Ziminiar)

Dates: Sep 23—Oct 2

Position: Night Demon

Direction: North/West

Planet: Jupiter

Metal: Tin

Element: Water

Color: Blue

Plant: Broom

Incense: Cedar

Zodiac: Libra

Gems: Angelite, cavansite, shattuckite, blue sapphire, blue topaz, blue kyanite, blue calcite, aqua aura quartz, larimar, blue tiger eye, lapis lazuli, chalcopyrite, chrysoprase, sodalite, blue lace agate, blue opal, azurite, blue apatite, blue fluorite, blue star sapphire, blue turquoise, indigo aura quartz, iolite, tanzanite, blue quartz, chrysocolla, hemimorphite, blue aventurine, blue goldstone, blue hackmanite, blue jade, blue spinel, blue zircon, variscite, rosasite, dioptase, abalone

Enn: Jedan tasa Hoet Naca Orobas.

Purpose: *He gives true answers of things past, present and to come, divinity, and the creation of the world; he also confers dignities and prelacies, and the favor of friends and foes. Orobas is faithful to the conjurer, does not permit that any spirit tempts him.*

President Ose/Voso/Oso

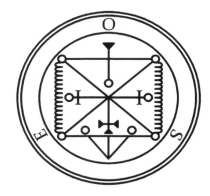

Dates: Oct 13—Oct 22

Position: Night Demon

Direction: East

Planet: Mercury

Metal: Mercury

Element: Air

Color: Orange

Plant: Horsetail

Incense: Storax

Zodiac: Libra

Gems: Tangerine aura quartz, goldstone, amber, aragonite, orange aventurine, carnelian, citrine, orange calcite, scheelite, amber calcite, coral calcite, copal, wulfenite, orange kyanite, imperial topaz, smoky citrine, golden healer quartz

Enn: Ayer Serpente Ose.

Purpose: *He makes men wise in all liberal sciences and gives true answers concerning divine and secret things; he also brings insanity to any person the conjurer wishes.*

King Paimon/Paymon

Dates: Jun 11—Jun 21

Position: Day Demon

Direction: West

Planet: Sun

Metal: Gold

Element: Water

Color: Yellow

Plant: Bindweed

Incense: Frankincense

Zodiac: Gemini

Gems: Yellow jasper, amber calcite, chrysoberyl, gold apatite, yellow aventurine, imperial topaz, lemon quartz, heliodor, sulphur, yellow calcite, yellow sphene, golden healer quartz

Enn: Linan tasa jedan Paimon.

Purpose: *He provides knowledge of past and future events, clearing up doubts, making spirits appear, creating visions, acquiring and dismissing servant spirits, reanimating the dead for several years, flight, remaining underwater indefinitely, and general abilities to "make all kinds of things" (and) "all sorts of people and armour appear" at the behest of the magician.*

Marquis Phenex/Pheynix

(Under Amaymon)

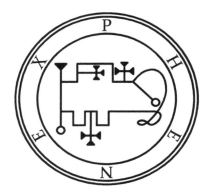

Dates: Mar 21—Mar 30

Position: Night Demon

Direction: East

Planet: Moon

Metal: Silver

Element: Air/fire

Color: Violet

Plant: Rose

Incense: Jasmine

Zodiac: Aries

Gems: Ametrine, amethyst, violet sapphire, amethyst cacoxenite, sugilite, lepidolite, covellite, manganese with sugilite, scapolite, charoite, vera cruz amethyst, chevron amethyst, botswana agate, rainbow fluorite, purple fluorite

Enn: Ef anay Phenex ayer.

Purpose: *He teaches all wonderful sciences, is an excellent poet, and is very obedient.*

King Purson

(Under Corson)

Dates: Oct 3—Oct 12

Position: Day Demon

Direction: West

Planet: Sun

Metal: Gold

Element: Earth

Color: Yellow

Plant: Orchid

Incense: Frankincense

Zodiac: Libra

Gems: Yellow jasper, amber calcite, chrysoberyl, gold apatite, yellow aventurine, imperial topaz, lemon quartz, heliodor, sulphur, yellow calcite, yellow sphene, golden healer quartz

Enn: Ana secore on ca Purson.

Purpose: *He knows of hidden things, can find treasures, and tells past, present, and future. Taking a human or aerial body he answers truly of all secret and divine things of Earth and the creation of the world. He also brings good familiars.*

Earl Raum

(Under Amaymon)

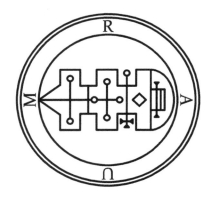

Dates: Apr 21–Apr 30

Position: Night Demon

Direction: East

Planet: Mars

Metal: Copper or Silver

Element: Air

Color: Red

Plant: Thistle

Incense: Dragon's blood

Zodiac: Taurus

Gems: Red goldstone, mookaite, red tiger eye, red jasper, red agate, garnet, red selenite, red aventurine, tiger eye, fire opal, fire agate

Enn: Furca na alle laris Raum.

Purpose: *He steals wonderfully out of the king's house and carries it where he is assigned. he destroys cities, and has shown great dislike for dignities. He knows things present, past, and to come and reconciles friends and enemies.*

Marquis Ronove/Ronwe

(Under Goap)

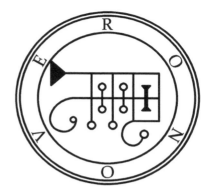

Dates: Dec 13—Dec 21

Position: Day Demon

Direction: East

Planet: Moon

Metal: Silver

Element: Air

Color: Violet

Plant: Cinnamon

Incense: Jasmine

Zodiac: Sagittarius

Gems: Ametrine, amethyst, violet sapphire, amethyst cacoxenite, sugilite, lepidolite, covellite, manganese with sugilite, scapolite, charoite, vera cruz amethyst, chevron amethyst, botswana agate, rainbow fluorite, purple fluorite

Enn: Kaymen Vefa Ronove.

Purpose: *He teaches art, rhetoric, languages, and gives good and loyal servants and the favor of friends and foes.*

Marquis Sabnock

(Under Corson)

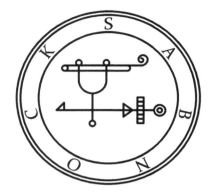

Dates: May 21—May 31

Position: Night Demon

Direction: South

Planet: Moon

Metal: Silver

Element: Fire

Color: Violet

Plant: Allspice

Incense: Jasmine

Zodiac: Gemini

Gems: Ametrine, amethyst, violet sapphire, amethyst cacoxenite, sugilite, lepidolite, covellite, manganese with sugilite, scapolite, charoite, vera cruz amethyst, chevron amethyst, botswana agate, rainbow fluorite, purple fluorite

Enn: Tasa Sabnock on ca Lirach.

Purpose: *He builds high towers, castles and cities, furnishing them with weapons, ammunition, and the like, gives good familiars and can afflict men for several days making their wounds and sores gangrenous or filling them with worms.*

Duke Sallos/Saleos

Dates: Sep 23—Oct 2

Position: Day Demon

Direction: West

Planet: Venus

Metal: Copper

Element: Earth

Color: Green

Plant: Aster

Incense: Sandalwood

Zodiac: Libra

Gems: Moss agate, antigorite, zoisite, ruby in fuchsite, emerald, seraphinite, hiddenite, jade and green quartz, green calcite, aventurine, tree agate, prasiolite peridot, malachite, green kyanite, green tourmaline, green fluorite, garnet, diopside, tsavorite, pyromorphite, pargasite, rainforest rhyolite, moldavite. wavellite, actinolite, epidote, fuchsite, green sphene, serpentine, vesuvianite, alexandrite. chlorite in quartz, apophyllite, prehnite

Enn: Serena Alora Sallos Aken.

Purpose: *He is of a pacifist nature and causes men to love women and women to love men.*

Lord Satan

Dates: All days

Direction: Center

Planet: Sun

Metal: Titanium

Element: Ether

Color: Blue, golds, blood red, death cold black

Plant: Any

Incense: Frankincense, myrrh, patchouli, sandalwood

Gems: Smoky quartz, quartz, obsidian, geodes, sodalite, jet, sapphires and rubies, black tourmaline, onyx, tektite, black agate, black jasper, black opal, zebra jasper, stibnite, tourmalated quartz, hematite, black onyx, jet, galena, meteorite, apache tears, snowflake obsidian, azurite-galena, molybdenite, magnetite, lodestone, rainbow obsidian, granite, black kyanite, zircon, sphalerite, angelite, cavansite, shattuckite, blue sapphire, blue topaz, blue kyanite, blue calcite, aqua aura quartz, larimar, blue tiger eye, lapis lazuli, chalcopyrite, chrysoprase, sodalite, blue lace agate, blue opal, azurite, blue apatite, blue fluorite, blue star sapphire, blue turquoise, indigo aura quartz, iolite, tanzanite, blue quartz, chrysocolla, hemimorphite, blue aventurine, blue goldstone, blue hackmanite, blue jade, blue spinel, blue zircon, variscite, rosasite, dioptase, abalone

Enn: Tasa Reme Laris Satan.

Purpose: *Lord and originator of all magick, witchcraft, and sorcery. Lord of All. Good for protection and cursings.*

Prince Seere/Sear/Seir

Dates: Feb 19—Feb 29

Position: Night Demon

Direction: East

Planet: Jupiter

Metal: Tin

Element: Fire

Color: Blue

Plant: Willow

Incense: Cedar

Zodiac: Pisces

Gems: Angelite, cavansite, shattuckite, blue sapphire, blue topaz, blue kyanite, blue calcite, aqua aura quartz, larimar, blue tiger eye, lapis lazuli, chalcopyrite, chrysoprase, sodalite, blue lace agate, blue opal, azurite, blue apatite, blue fluorite, blue star sapphire, blue turquoise, indigo aura quartz, iolite, tanzanite, blue quartz, chrysocolla, hemimorphite, blue aventurine, blue goldstone, blue hackmanite, blue jade, blue spinel, blue zircon, variscite, rosasite, dioptase, abalone

Enn: Jedan et Renich Seere tu tasa.

Purpose: *He can go to any place on earth in a matter of seconds to accomplish the will of the conjurer, bring abundance, help in finding hidden treasures or in robbery, and is not a demon of evil but good nature, being mostly indifferent to evilness.*

Marquis Shax

(Under Corson)

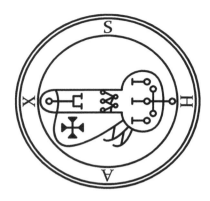

Dates: Jun 1—Jun 10

Position: Night Demon

Direction: East

Planet: Moon

Metal: Silver

Element: Air

Color: Violet

Plant: Purslane

Incense: Jasmine

Zodiac: Gemini

Gems: Ametrine, amethyst, violet sapphire, amethyst cacoxenite, sugilite, lepidolite, covellite, manganese with sugilite, scapolite, charoite, vera cruz amethyst, chevron amethyst, botswana agate, rainbow fluorite, purple fluorite

Enn: Ayer Avage Shax Aken.

Purpose: *He takes away the sight, hearing, and understanding of any person under the conjurer's request, and steals money out of kings' houses, carrying it back to the people. He also steals horses and everything the conjurer asks. Shax can also discover hidden things if they are not kept by evil spirits, and sometimes gives good familiars, but sometimes those familiars deceive the conjurer.*

Prince Sitri

(Under Ziminiar)

Dates: Jul 12—Jul 21

Position: Day Demon

Direction: West

Planet: Jupiter

Metal: Tin

Element: Earth

Color: Blue

Plant: Hyacinth

Incense: Cedar

Zodiac: Cancer

Gems: Angelite, cavansite, shattuckite, blue sapphire, blue topaz, blue kyanite, blue calcite, aqua aura quartz, larimar, blue tiger eye, lapis lazuli, chalcopyrite, chrysoprase, sodalite, blue lace agate, blue opal, azurite, blue apatite, blue fluorite, blue star sapphire, blue turquoise, indigo aura quartz, iolite, tanzanite, blue quartz, chrysocolla, hemimorphite, blue aventurine, blue goldstone, blue hackmanite, blue jade, blue spinel, blue zircon, variscite, rosasite, dioptase, abalone

Enn: Lirach Alora vefa Sitri.

Purpose: *He causes men to love women and vice versa and can make people bare themselves naked if desired.*

Prince Stolas/Stolos

(Under Goap)

Dates: Mar 11—Mar 20

Position: Day Demon

Direction: East

Planet: Jupiter

Metal: Tin

Element: Air

Color: Blue

Plant: Flax

Incense: Cedar

Zodiac: Pisces

Gems: Angelite, cavansite, shattuckite, blue sapphire, blue topaz, blue kyanite, blue calcite, aqua aura quartz, larimar, blue tiger eye, lapis lazuli, chalcopyrite, chrysoprase, sodalite, blue lace agate, blue opal, azurite, blue apatite, blue fluorite, blue star sapphire, blue turquoise, indigo aura quartz, iolite, tanzanite, blue quartz, chrysocolla, hemimorphite, blue aventurine, blue goldstone, blue hackmanite, blue jade, blue spinel, blue zircon, variscite, rosasite, dioptase, abalone

Enn: Stolas Ramec biasa on ca.

Purpose: *He teaches astronomy and the knowledge of poisonous plants, herbs and precious stones.*

Duke Uvall/Vual/Voval

(Under Corson)

Dates: Jul 2—Jul 11

Position: Night Demon

Direction: North

Planet: Venus

Metal: Copper

Element: Water

Color: Green

Plant: Myrrh

Incense: Sandalwood

Zodiac: Cancer

Gems: Moss agate, antigorite, zoisite, ruby in fuchsite, emerald, seraphinite, hiddenite, jade and green quartz, green calcite, aventurine, tree agate, prasiolite peridot, malachite, green kyanite, green tourmaline, green fluorite, garnet, diopside, tsavorite, pyromorphite, pargasite, rainforest rhyolite, moldavite. wavellite, actinolite, epidote, fuchsite, green sphene, serpentine, vesuvianite, alexandrite. chlorite in quartz, apophyllite, prehnite

Enn: As ana nany on ca Uvall.

Purpose: *He gives the love of women, causes friendship between friends and foes, and tells things past, present, and to come.*

Duke Valefor/Valfar

(Under Goap)

Dates: May 11—May 20

Position: Day Demon

Direction: North

Planet: Venus

Metal: Copper

Element: Earth

Color: Green

Plant: Dandelion

Incense: Sandalwood

Zodiac: Taurus

Gems: Moss agate, antigorite, zoisite, ruby in fuchsite, emerald, seraphinite, hiddenite, jade and green quartz, green calcite, aventurine, tree agate, prasiolite peridot, malachite, garnet, diopside, tsavorite, pyromorphite, pargasite, rainforest rhyolite, moldavite. wavellite, actinolite, epidote, fuchsite, green sphene, serpentine, vesuvianite, alexandrite. chlorite in quartz, apophyllite, prehnite

Enn: Keyman vefa tasa Valefor.

Purpose: *He teaches the subtle art of thievery but without a sense of self-preservation, so consequently, he left them at the gallows.*

Duke Vapula/Naphula

Dates: Nov 13—Nov 22

Position: Night Demon

Direction: East

Planet: Venus

Metal: Copper

Element: Air

Color: Green

Plant: Papyrus

Incense: Sandalwood

Zodiac: Scorpio

Gems: Moss agate, antigorite, zoisite, ruby in fuchsite, emerald, seraphinite, hiddenite, jade and green quartz, green calcite, aventurine, tree agate, prasiolite peridot, malachite, green kyanite, green tourmaline, green fluorite, garnet, diopside, tsavorite, pyromorphite, pargasite, rainforest rhyolite, moldavite. wavellite, actinolite, epidote, fuchsite, green sphene, serpentine, vesuvianite, alexandrite. chlorite in quartz, apophyllite, prehnite

Enn: Renich secore Vapula Typan.

Purpose: *He teaches philosophy, mechanics, and sciences.*

Prince Vassago

(Under Goap)

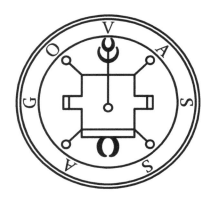

Dates: Apr 11—Apr 20

Position: Day Demon

Direction: North/West

Planet: Jupiter

Metal: Tin

Element: Water

Color: Blue

Plant: Leek

Incense: Cedar

Zodiac: Aries

Gems: Angelite, cavansite, shattuckite, blue sapphire, blue topaz, blue kyanite, blue calcite, aqua aura quartz, larimar, blue tiger eye, lapis lazuli, chalcopyrite, chrysoprase, sodalite, blue lace agate, blue opal, azurite, blue apatite, blue fluorite, blue star sapphire, blue turquoise, indigo aura quartz, iolite, tanzanite, blue quartz, chrysocolla, hemimorphite, blue aventurine, blue goldstone, blue hackmanite, blue jade, blue spinel, blue zircon, variscite, rosasite, dioptase, abalone

Enn: Keyman vefa jedan tasa Vassago.

Purpose: *He can be persuaded to tell the magician of events past and future, can discover hidden and lost things, and has a "good" nature.*

Duchess Vepar

(Under Amaymon)

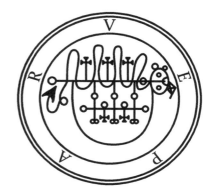

Dates: May 11—May 20

Position: Night Demon

Direction: North

Planet: Venus

Metal: Copper

Element: Water

Color: Green

Plant: Mugwort

Incense: Sandalwood

Zodiac: Taurus

Gems: Moss agate, antigorite, zoisite, ruby in fuchsite, emerald, seraphinite, hiddenite, jade and green quartz, green calcite, aventurine, tree agate, prasiolite peridot, malachite, green kyanite, green tourmaline, green fluorite, garnet, diopside, tsavorite, pyromorphite, pargasite, rainforest rhyolite, moldavite. wavellite, actinolite, epidote, fuchsite, green sphene, serpentine, vesuvianite, alexandrite. chlorite in quartz, apophyllite, prehnite

Enn: On ca Vepar Ag Na.

Purpose: *She governs the waters and guides armoured ships laden with ammunition and weapons; she can also make, if requested, the sea rough and stormy, and to appear full of ships. Vepar can make men die in three days by putrefying sores and wounds, causing worms to breed in them, but if requested by the conjurer, she can heal them immediately.*

King Vine

(Under Corson)

Dates: Jun 11—Jun 20

Position: Night Demon

Direction: North

Planet: Sun

Metal: Gold

Element: Water

Color: Yellow

Plant: Mallow

Incense: Frankincense

Zodiac: Gemini

Gems: Yellow jasper, amber calcite, chrysoberyl, gold apatite, yellow aventurine, imperial topaz, lemon quartz, heliodor, sulphur, yellow calcite, yellow sphene, golden healer quartz

Enn: Eyesta nas Vine ca laris.

Purpose: *They have the power to take one's soul without permission. Though according to spiritual teachings, one demon must ask permission from Satan before taking a soul, and Satan must get permission from God. They can tell present, past, and future, discover witches and hidden things, create storms and make the water rough by means of these storms, bring down walls and build towers.*

President Volac/Valac/Valu/Valak

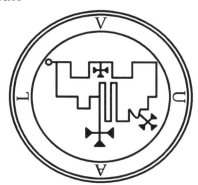

Dates: Dec 3—Dec 11

Position: Night Demon

Direction: West

Planet: Mercury

Metal: Mercury

Element: Earth

Color: Orange

Plant: Sesame

Incense: Storax

Zodiac: Sagittarius

Gems: Tangerine aura quartz, goldstone, amber, aragonite, orange aventurine, carnelian, citrine, orange calcite, scheelite, amber calcite, coral calcite, copal, wulfenite, orange kyanite, imperial topaz, smoky citrine, golden healer quartz

Enn: Avage Secore on ca Volac.

Purpose: *He has the power of finding treasures.*

King Zagan

(Under Amaymon)

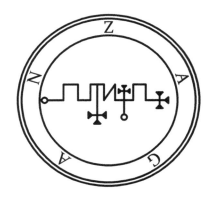

Dates: Nov 23—Dec 2

Position: Night Demon

Direction: North/West

Planet: Sun

Metal: Gold

Element: Earth

Color: Yellow

Plant: Hyssop

Incense: Frankincense

Zodiac: Sagittarius

Gems: Tangerine aura quartz, goldstone, amber, aragonite, orange aventurine, carnelian, citrine, orange calcite, scheelite, amber calcite, coral calcite, copal, wulfenite, orange kyanite, imperial topaz, smoky citrine, golden healer quartz

Enn: Anay on ca secore Zagan tasa.

Purpose: *He makes men witty; he can also turn wine into water, water into wine, and blood into wine, blood into oil, oil into blood, and a fool into a wise man. Other of his powers is that of turning metals into coins that are made with that metal.*

Duke Zepar

(Under Amaymon)

Dates: Aug 23—Sep 1

Position: Day Demon

Direction: West

Planet: Venus

Metal: Copper

Element: Earth

Color: Green

Plant: Mandrake

Incense: Sandalwood

Zodiac: Virgo

Gems: Moss agate, antigorite, zoisite, ruby in fuchsite, emerald, seraphinite, hiddenite, jade and green quartz, green calcite, aventurine, tree agate, prasiolite peridot, malachite, green kyanite, green tourmaline, green fluorite, garnet, diopside, tsavorite, pyromorphite, pargasite, rainforest rhyolite, moldavite. wavellite, actinolite, epidote, fuchsite, green sphene, serpentine, vesuvianite, alexandrite. chlorite in quartz, apophyllite, prehnite

Enn: Lyan Ramec Catya Zepar.

Purpose: *His office is to cause women to love men and bring them together in love. He makes women barren.*

APPENDIX D

Demons, Chakras, and Cardinal Points

Everything in the universe is tied together. This appendix could easily evolve into a crossover work discussing the principles of gestalt, entropy, thermodynamics, and the cosmic mapping of the energy that makes up the human soul. Sir Isaac Newton was not only a formidable scientific mind but also a great alchemist as well. In his quest to understand existence, he brought to the table the simple eloquence of thermodynamic theory.

There are four laws of thermodynamics. I do not see the need to discuss the nature of the zeroth law since it is related to thermal theory and therefore not relevant to this appendix directly, but I will simply illustrate the other three laws at a very cursory level in order to portray a point I am making about the nature of matter, universe, energy and the human soul.

The first law is that the amount of energy in the universe is finite.[44] This means no new energy is created and no old energy is destroyed, it just changes to a different form of energy—or changes hands, so to speak. For instance, wood will burn during a fire, and from its solid state of wood, using heat energy it will transform into smoke and heat as well as carbon dioxide and, later, into a stored form of chemical energy called charcoal. All these transformations that take place are simply one form of energy morphing into another form, kinetic energy, chemical energy, and so on.

---

[44] See Charles Kittel and Herbert Kroemer, *Thermal Physics*, Second Edition (San Francisco: W. H. Freeman, 1980).

The significance of this law to our subject matter is that the human soul is pure energy constructed like any other form of energy, as a resonating mass of infinitesimally small strings of vibrating sound that work together to make our corporeal bodies function and exist, think and learn. I argue that as there is a finite amount of energy in the universe, there are also a finite number of souls, and instead of a process of creating a new soul out of nothing, we have a process of cosmic recycling occurring that filters our soul selves back into the subatomic structure of the universe to be reborn as another living creature at some later point.

The second law is that disorder in the universe (or chaos) is constantly increasing—this is a principle called entropy.[45] This means for instance that if you do your dishes, they are bound to get dirty again, no matter what. This is a simplistic view, but it in its simplicity lays an astounding yet beautiful truth about the universe and how all things behave. In other words, everything is moving constantly toward a state of entropy (decay) no matter what we do. However, this entropy drives us toward re-creation, reutilization and rebirth through this decay. Death becomes the quintessence of life, as the alchemists would say. When old cells die, new ones are created elsewhere. This is a cycle we see in life constantly and not just in terms of physics but in terms of life in general at the most practical and mundane of levels.

With law number three, there is a point at which molecular structures cease to have chaos—it is frozen literally in time. This is the point of perfection. For scientists, this is denoted by a temperature of absolute zero expressed as a function of "degrees Kelvin" [–237 degrees Celsius, or bloody freezing].[46] This is absolute zero, and at this point, crystals have no chaos for a brief point in time or entropy exists at its minimum level.[47] However, this state of crystal perfection cannot last long as a function of the universe forever changing and creating and destroying using preexisting subatomic

[45] See E. A. Guggenheim, *Thermodynamics An Advanced Treatment for Chemists and Physicists*, Seventh Edition (Amsterdam: North-Holland, 1985).
[46] See Barry N. Taylor, *Guide for the Use of the International System of Units (SI)*, Special Publication 811 (National Institute of Standards and Technology, 2008).
[47] See "Primum Frigidum,"*Encyclopaedia of Human Thermodynamics, Human Chemistry and Human Physics*, August 1, 2011.

material.[48] This means that theoretically there is a point at which a soul can exist in perfection and in a state of nonentropic decay. I believe that point is reached through meditation and at the point at which death has brought the component aspects of the soul to the precipice of new life again through some form of cosmic recycling. With ourselves, we are both: pure energies made corporeal—we are flesh and blood and spirit in other words. Utilizing the energy, we have is simple once we understand the focus of that energy, where it comes from, and what it is akin to. This is where will is trained to excel over flesh. Flesh must submit to will and through will we have power in magick. Next we will discuss kundalini.

There is an ideology in yoga known as the Kundalini serpent, which is a primal energy that lives at the base of the spine. It is awakened during yoga. In Qigong, there is chi or qi, which is also a primal energy source. The term literally means "breath" in Chinese dialects. In Hinduism, there is the concept of shakti, which is very similar to kundalini.

Kundalini

So what is Kundalini, and why is it so important? Kundalini is Sanskrit for "coiled" or "wound." It refers to energy curled up like a snake waiting to be released at the base of our spine, and it lays dormant until we can entice it into ascension using the power of meditation. This is called the ascension of the human soul to a state sometimes referred to as nirvana or heaven,[49] or as aptly put by the Joy of Satan workshop on Kundalini meditation, "raising of the Devil."[50] The Kundalini consists of energy channels called nadis, psychic centers called chakras, subtle energies called prana, and the drops of essence called bindu. This is a complex system, but it is essentially a map of the human soul. Interestingly, it is not dissimilar to the Kabbalistic Sephirot tree idea.

---

[48] See Charles Kittel and Herbert Kroemer, *Thermal Physics*, Second Edition (San Francisco: W. H. Freeman, 1980).
[49] See Swami Vivekananda, *The Complete Works of Swami Vivekananda*, 1915), 185.
[50] See Joy of Satan, Exposing Spiritual Corruption: Spiritual Alchemy and The Bible, http://see_the_truth.webs.com/Exposing_Corruption.htm/.

While these systems were thought to develop in tandem, they actually are almost identical concepts. This is not new, as it was something the Egyptians did as well as the Sumerians before them. The Kundalini serpent is coiled three and a half times within the base of the spine. These coils are called guna or strands. Each strand is representative of creation, preservation, and destruction within our spiritual selves.[51]

Figure 36—Map of the Human Soul

Everyone has heard of the caduceus, which is a famous symbol once associated with trade communications and now medicine. It is a symbol that depicts two intertwined snakes around a staff.

This same imagery was discussed in ancient Mesopotamian literature. This notion was thought to have been in existence some four thousand years before Christ existed and was later adopted by the Greeks who made it the

---

[51] See Bernard Theos, *Hindu Philosophy* (Motilal Banarsidass Publishing, 1999).

left-hand-wielded staff of their God Hermes.[52] Either way, it's an iconic symbol that has been used throughout the ages to represent all sorts of things, the basis of which is a Kundalini-styled pair of snakes with three and a half coils. This is a commonly recurring theme in history, it seems, with origination of many ideas in religious philosophy from all over the world coming from a single point of origin.

In addition to Kundalini and the relationship with the caduceus, you may also have heard me speak of how it is also representative of the double-helix structure of DNA. All of this is true. However, I digress. The relevance of Kundalini is that it is a vehicle for obtaining what we want spiritually. Learning to drive the Kundalini upward into ascension and managing chakra power centers using Kundalini is pivotal to gaining access to other planes of existence, in exercising will over flesh, and in generally empowering self. It is also used as a fertile communication system whereby you can communicate with entities of all types in the spirit world.

Figure 37—The Caduceus

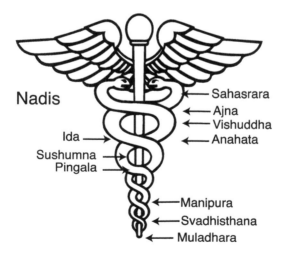

---

[52] See William Hayes Ward, *The Seal Cylinders of Western Asia* (Washington, 1910).

The term *chakra* means "disk," and it refers to the spinning, disk-like energy centers in the body. There are literally hundreds of these energy centers but only a few key ones that we focus on in our meditation. It's interesting to note that each of these chakras corresponds to a bundle of nerves at each point, called a *ganglion*. These branch off the spinal column and serve as major transit stations for sensory information. In terms of the chakras themselves, however, these refer to levels of consciousness within the psyche.[53] For the purposes of this discussion, we will only be dealing with seven chakras. Each chakra not only denotes a level of consciousness, but it is also thought to control major organs in their area. This is where we can see our own will overcoming flesh, as an example. It is important to note that chakras when active will spin until we will them to do otherwise.

Figure 38—The Chakras

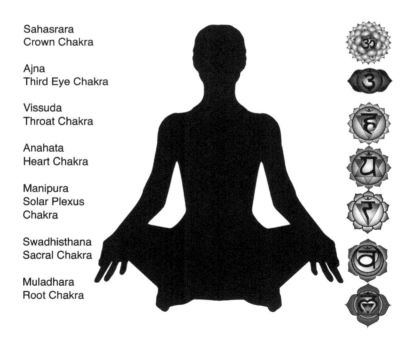

Sahasrara
Crown Chakra

Ajna
Third Eye Chakra

Vissuda
Throat Chakra

Anahata
Heart Chakra

Manipura
Solar Plexus
Chakra

Swadhisthana
Sacral Chakra

Muladhara
Root Chakra

---

53   See K. Ravenmoon, *Imder La Lune Noire* (2010).

One could say the seven chakras are like the seven seals mentioned in the Bible. In other words, they are seven lamps that burn before the throne of God, God being an allegory for our higher-level consciousness. In this case, the term *God* is therefore used to refer to one's self. It is very important that in enabling our serpentine ascension that we keep our chakras always clean, using meditation. There are only a few specific examples where they become closed. Blockages can be caused from many things in life such as worry, illness (which also is from blockages as well), imbalance in our food intake, use of substances, and so on. It can also be a result of your own will to close these chakras.

The next element of this chart I am about to give you is that of cardinal direction. It is commonly believed that the body (and, therefore, the soul) is ruled by elements as well as cardinality. The front of the soul is northern, and it is ruled by the earth element. The back of the soul is of course facing south and therefore ruled by the fire element. The left side or negative pole is the side we draw in energy, and it is ruled by water facing the direction west. The right side or positive pole is the side we direct energy, and it is ruled by air and faces east. The center of this is the quintessence of self. This is where we expend energy, and if you now think of all of this when thinking of the sigil of infernal union, you will start to see where I am heading with this. In terms of energies, fire and air are electrical in nature, and water and earth are magnetic in nature, so we have two polar opposites ruling us—the push (electric) and the pull (magnetic) between the two is balance, and that is where we reside.

Cardinal Points

On that note, I will raise the issue of using cardinal and intercardinal directionality in ritual and altar preparation. Assigning cardinal directions to Demonic entities is something we tend to do more in modern Western society, and you will see it in works written by LaVey, for example, and a few other contemporaries.

The sun sets in the west and moves toward darkness throughout the day. The sun also rises in the east bringing with it illumination and dispelling the darkness. Therefore, we have west-facing altars in Satanism. We are concerned with the sinister (in the magickal sense), and we step in to meet the darkness as the darkness steps forward to meet us. In doing so, the light will enter to illuminate and bring wisdom, and it will dispel the hidden and the unknown. If we were looking to invoke Lucifer, we would face east. If we are looking to invoke Satan, we face west.

On the Sigils and the Quinary

Figure 39—Sigil of Infernal Union

The pentagram is depicted in a circle without end. This represents the ALL, or Satan, as the all-encompassing energies. Some would depict it as encircled by the Leviathan. Each of the points on the sigil of infernal union correspond with several cardinal and intercardinal points (cardinal points being N, S, E, W and intercardinal points being NE, SE, NW, SW). In the case of the sigil of infernal union, we are concerned with S, SE, NW, SW, and Center. We have what is called a quinary. The Christians have the trinity, the Wiccans have their quadrants, and we have a quinary. [54] These are where

---

[54]   See Father Leved, Church of Lucifer, Five Faces of Satan, http://slickaz. tripod.com/play/fiveface.html, accessed June 2, 2012.

the crown princes of hell are aligned to a cardinal or intercardinal point or where the Hebraic Demons are aligned to a cardinal or intercardinal point. They also in turn align with a corresponding chakra, color correspondence, and day and hour of power. You will see a neat summary of this listed in the table below.

The Pentagram in Satanism as depicted by LaVey has a dual circle around it. This is a Pythagorean symbol that denotes the presence of a void or abyss. Some replace this with the Leviathan and prefer to think of it as the Leviathan of the deep encircling the energies of the infernally united Demonic archetypes of Lilith, Samael, Lucifer, Satan, Belial, Leviathan, and so on. This symbology truly unifies Goetic thinking with Judaeo-Christian thinking in many ways. Many will also know this dual circle phenomenon to be a symbol used by those of the Abrahamic faiths to denote a place with the absence of life where the deposed angels were tossed down to Earth and into Hell. The pentagram also has three downward facing points, which are a mockery of the holy trinity of Christianity.[55] Hence, we have a quinary.

Just a note of historical correction here, LaVey was not the first to evolve the sigil we have come to know of as the sigil of infernal union. This sigil was depicted in the earlier works of Marice Bessey (1961) in his Encyclopaedia of the Occult called "Histoire en de la Magie." It was much later in that era that LaVey decided to use the symbol but removed Lilith and Samael, so it became the Sigil of the Baphomet.[56] Together, these keys unlock within us the refracting light of Lucifer and symbolize the awakening of self into undefiled wisdom.

I want to stress here that there are several Demonic systems and combinations out there. Each culture has their own list of Demons, and it's important not to confuse them. For instance, Lilith and Samael are Jewish in origin. They are not listed as Goetic (Demons of Solomon) whereas Belial and Asmodeus are. Likewise, the Egyptians had their own list as well. These days there is more of a move toward combining all lists of Demons as just

---

[55] See The 600 Club Dictionary—http://www.the600club.com/encyclopedia/ Pentagram accessed June 10, 2012.
[56] See K. Ravenmoon, Under La Lune Noire: Traditional Orthodox Satanism, Natural Satanic Witchcraft, 2012 http://orthodoxsatanism.webs.com/, accessed June 5, 2012.

Demons and not really paying much heed to the intracultural nature of the lists. However, some do cross over with archetypes for Satan. For instance, you will see Satan as a Judeo-Christian God, and with the Egyptians, he is Set, for example. This convergence is because more and more information is being uncovered that shows the similarities between the stories. As we delve deeper into the history of man, as it predates Judaeo-Christian mythos, we see where these points all converge in tales that have more originality than those of the Judaeo-Christian mythos.

The Demonic Judaeo-Christian inverse pentagram features the following:
- West—Leviathan (Abrahamic)—(Water) also LaVeyan
- South—Samael (Abrahamic)—also Satan (Fire) [LaVeyan]
- East—Lucifer (Abrahamic)—(Air) also LaVeyan
- North—Lilith (Abrahamic)—also Belial (Earth) [LaVeyan][57]

---

[57]   See Anton LaVey, *The Satanic Bible* (New York: Avon Books, 1969).

APPENDIX E

Examples of Loosing and Binding Spells

L oosing and binding spells are incredibly powerful yet simple to use. Effectively, you use loosing spells when you want to release a particular energy into a situation—the energy can be negative or positive depending on the cause. A simple yet effective example of a good loosing spell is one where you loose healing energy onto a target supplicant. Binding spells allow you to work against energy—to contain it magickally so that it will stop its work in a situation. It is advisable to use binding work prior to exacting a curse as it can make a curse much more powerful. You do not need to use correspondences to affect this kind of working, but it helps to strengthen the work you are doing. It is critical when you are exacting this kind of spell work that you are precise—for example, there is no use in loosing chaos into the Abrahamic faiths on its own. You need to be specific (e.g., I loose Asmodeus into the Church of St XYZ on ABC Rd on the twenty-third day of the third month of the 2012 year to create travesty and Demonic havoc among the religious teachers of X and Y effective immediately).

Please note this is only a guide. It is not in-depth, and I will not give personal advice on how to do things, as the level to which you use this kind of work will very much depend on how much research you do. Research is critical, and doing things verbatim per a book is not advisable because you do not know the exact situation the working is used for. These are just basic guidelines.

Rules of Loosing and Binding

- Always work with your Demon guardians on this and in consultation with Father Satan. Your work with your Demons should always be respectful. Your rituals should start and end with respectful adoration of your Demons and Father Satan always.
- Once you have completed *any* binding or loosing spell work, you must put it out of your mind. Do not revisit it. This is like saying you do not believe in the power of the Dark Flame to absolve you.
- Always ensure you clean your ritual space magickally before and after you have exacted the ritual.
- Always clean your Chakras after you complete these workings to short out any reflective energy, stop any negativity creeping in on you.
- Put out of your mind all rules relating to Karmic justice, threefold laws, and that crap. *You* are your magickal powerhouse. So long as you clean up afterward and do your Chakra cleansing, there will be no issue.
- *Always* visualize the working you are doing; focus on it and the supplicants you are doing this work on.
- Be very specific with what you are binding and when it is to be bound by and for how long. General spells with no time limits and no specificity will not necessarily work when you need them to.
- You may work within a magickal circle or triangle it is up to you. It depends for me on the working. For more complex workings, I rely on sigil magick along with binding and loosing so I use chalk to draw out my sigils on the ground. This draws particular Demons and energies into the work. This is very complex but not necessary. I find the power of the will is enough sometimes in creating an effective binding or loosing. *Always* know and have no doubt at all that what you bind is bound and what you loose will indeed be loosed. These spells *do* work. I have used them many times.
- Binding must always be done on a waning moon and all movements are widdershins (counterclockwise). If you want to use

correspondences, I suggest black candles, animal totems used, as correspondence would be images of the serpent. Herbs I recommend are apple, wormwood, black pepper, rowan, and pine. You will need to research all correspondence use before you use it. Do not just rely on what is said here verbatim as each situation is different. You need to *know* what you are doing. I personally do not use them in binding unless I am doing something really big. Ensure all correspondences are magickally cleaned and blessed.

- Loosing must always be done on a waxing moon and all movements are doesil (clockwise). For loosing the candle, sigil, and herbal correspondences will again depend on the type of loosing it is. You will need to research this.

An Example of a Simple Binding Spell—Binding Using a Witch's Spiral

This is obviously one of my favorites as it is so multipurpose. I use it when I am binding the energies of bad people, and it is also useful to do prior to a curse. I used this to teach my daughter when she was young how to combat bullies at school. She found it fun to do as well, and in doing so, I introduced her to simple magickal forms through this spell.

1. Follow all the rules mentioned in the last paragraph.
2. To do this it is quite simple, put the person's name on a piece of paper. You can also do this with poppets (my favorite also), but for this work you may need a photo, hair, or nails from the person directly.
3. Wrap the paper into a tight cylinder.
4. Seal it with black-candle wax if you wish or even wax mixed with your own blood (use this at your own risk, however, as blood magick is extremely powerful).
5. Tie a string around the paper slowly in a counterclockwise fashion and while walking widdershins (counterclockwise).
6. Chant, "I bind thee [name of the person and their obsession] from doing me harm. I bind your lies, and I replace it with calm. You shall no more hinder me. I am untied from you. So mote it be." It is preferred that you write your own spell as well because again each

situation, need and ritual is for a different cause. Do this the entire time you are wrapping the string around the paper.

7. You can tie off the string or seal it with more black wax.
8. Thank father Satan.
9. Bury the paper wound in string in the dirt. Forget it—do not revisit it.
10. When you do the ritual, ensure you are focused, and you are using the full force of your will.

A More Complicated Binding Spell-Work Success Story

A young man came to me several years ago. He was a student of mine at the university. He was exceedingly bright but very troubled because he had gotten himself into a relationship with a girl whom he now could not get rid of—she was like a psychic vampire and was holding him back from a brilliant career.

He could not get rid of her no matter what he did, so after two years of putting up with this, he came to me for help. He knew what I was at the time and proclaimed himself boldly as a nonbeliever, but he said he was so desperate he would give it a try. He came to my house around 9:00 p.m. where I had prepared a ritual working area. I already had collected hair from each of the target supplicants (himself and this girl), and I made poppets for this work as I felt this was appropriate for the kind of work this was.

Each poppet was created and empowered with the life of each subject, and it was a living representation of its living subject. Each one had the hair corresponding to its living person, and there were certain herbs and various other elements within the wax I used. I placed the poppets together with red ribbons connecting the two individuals on each Chakra they were connecting on.

We sat in a magickal circle that had been blessed and we did the Lesser Banishing Ritual of the Pentagram/Dark Lord/Demonic/Demon Lord before we started. We called upon the dark energies to protect us in the working, and we made an offering of honey mead and bread to the spiritual entities I had called upon. I made sure all of the elemental representations present, and I had meditated and fasted to ensure the work would be complete (a sacrifice of self to my guardians to ensure powerful support). I started by binding the girl's emotional neediness (note it was very specific wording and I did not bind the girl herself) effective immediately and binding his need to feel love and weakness that drove him to love out of pity, effective immediately. Note that using time and date specificity is a requirement.

I used my ritual knife to cut the ties one by one on the poppets. Each time I cut a tie, we loosed healing energies into those areas to stop up the gaps left and to ensure there was not a releeching that occurred (for both parties). Anyway, the ritual took three hours to exact with two days of preparation. I did it very carefully. I asked him to verbally respond to questions such as (A) Are you absolutely certain you want to be rid of this girl from your life? (B) Are you absolutely certain this is the best thing for both of you, and so on? To each question he had responded yes. This was to establish his will and intent for the spiritual energies that I was working with. We gave thanks, closed the circle, and then shared some libations. He went home that night, but before he went, he said he was not sure it would work. I told him that it would most definitely work and to go home and put it out of his mind. He got home, and within an hour, he called me. He said disbelievingly that she was gone! He went on to build at business at the age of nineteen and has had a successful and ongoing relationship with multiple girls at the same time!

APPENDIX F

Herbs and Their Magickal Use

Herb	Magickal Use
Acacia	Protection, psychic and spiritual enhancement, money, platonic love, and friendship
Aconite	Use aconite as a magickal wash for ritual tools and space. **Poisonous, do not consume.**
Acorn	Good luck, protection, wisdom, and personal power
Adam and Eve Root	Principally used by lovers; one lover carries the Eve Root and the other lover carries the Adam Root.
Adder's Tongue	Stops gossip and slander, promotes healing. Used in divination, healing magick, lunar magick, and dream magick.
African Violet	Spirituality, protection, and healing
Agar	Promote joy and success, attract opportunities, and blessings to the household
Agrimony	Overcoming fear and inner blockages; dispelling negative emotions. Also used for reversing spells.
Ague	Protection and hex breaking
Alder	Associated with divination, music, poetry, wind magick, weather magick, teaching, and decision making
Alfalfa	Money, prosperity

Herb	Magickal Use
Alkanet	Purification, prosperity. Burned as an incense to replace negativity with positive influence.
Allspice	Money, luck, healing, obtaining treasure. Provides added determination and energy to any spells and charms. Burn crushed allspice to attract luck and money. Use in herbal baths for healing.
Almond	Wisdom, money, fruitfulness and prosperity. Invokes healing energy. Provides magickal help for overcoming dependencies and addiction.
Aloe	Protection and luck
Althea Root	Protection and to calm an angry person and aid psychic powers
Alyssum	Protection and moderating anger, protection
Amaranth	Healing, summoning spirits, healing broken hearts, protection from bullets, and invisibility
Amber	Protection from harm, outside influences and psychic attacks. Mental clarity and focus. Transforming negative energy to positive energy.
Ambergris	Enhancing dreams and psychic ventures, attracting men
Anemone	Healing and protection
Angelica	Protection. Use in healing and exorcism incenses; scatter for purification, protection and uncrossing. Add to incense to promote healing or to the bath to remove curses, hexes, or spells.
Anise	Used to help ward off the evil eye, find happiness and stimulate psychic ability. Use in purification baths with bay leaves.
Apple	Love, garden magick, immortality, friendship, healing
Apricot	Love. Add leaves and flowers to love sachets or carry apricot pits to attract love.
Arabic Gum	Protection, psychic and spiritual enhancement, money, platonic love and friendship. Use in incense to promote a meditative state.
Arnica Flowers	Increases psychic powers

Herb	Magickal Use
Arrow Root	Purification and healing; can be used as a substitute for graveyard dust.
Ash	Sea spells/magick/rituals, image magick, invincibility, protection from drowning, general protection and luck.
Asafoetida	Protection and banishing negativity
Asparagus	Male sex magick
Aspen	Eloquence, clairvoyance, healing and antitheft.
Aster	Love
Astragalus Root	Protection and energy
Avocado	Love, lust and beauty. Also used for sex magick.
Azalea	Happiness, gaiety and light spirits, first love. **Note: Poisonous, do not consume.**
Bachelor Buttons	Love
Bakuli Pods	Difficult to find magick item also used in sachets and potpourri.
Balm of Gilead Tears	Love, manifestations, protection, healing, de-stressing and assisting in healing.
Balmony	Steadfastness, patience and perseverance. Associated with the tortoise or turtle.
Balsam Fir	Strength and breaking up negativity; insight, progress against goals and bringing about change.
Bamboo	Hex breaking, wishes, luck, and protection.
Banana	Fertility, potency, and prosperity
Banyan	Happiness, luck
Barberry	Cleansing, sorcery, atonement, freeing oneself from the power or control of another
Barley	Love, healing and protection, harvests
Basil	Love, exorcism, wealth, sympathy, and protection
Bat's Head Root	Use in spell work, rituals, gris gris bags, etc., to obtain wishes.
Bay Laurel	Purification, house and business blessing and clearing confusion. Attracts romance.
Bay Leaf	Protection, good fortune, success, purification, strength, healing, and psychic powers

Herb	Magickal Use
Bayberry	Good fortune, luck, healing, and stress relief.
Bedstraw	Love and lust
Bee Pollen	Friendship, attraction, love, strength, happiness, and overcoming depression
Beech	Wishes, happiness and divination. Improves literary skills.
Beet	Love. Beet juice can be used as ink for love magick or as a substitute for blood in spells and rituals.
Belladonna	Healing and forgetting past loves. Provides protection. **Note: Deadly poison, do not ingest.**
Benzoin	Purification, prosperity, soothing tension, dispelling anger, diminishing irritability, relieving stress and anxiety, and overcoming depression
Bergamot	Money, prosperity, protection from evil and illness, improving memory, stopping interference, and promoting restful sleep
Betel Nut	Protection and banishing
Bilberry Bark	Used for protection
Birch	Protection, exorcism, and purification
Bistort	Fertility, divination, clairvoyance, psychic powers
Black Cohosh	Love, courage, protection, and potency
Black Haw	Protection, gambling, luck, power, and employment
Black Pepper	Banishing negativity, exorcism, and protection from evil
Black Walnut	Access to divine energy, bringing the blessing of the Gods, wishes
Blackberry	Healing, protection and money. Leaves and berries said to attract wealth and healing.
Bladderwrack	Protection, sea spells, wind spells, money, psychic powers and attracting customers.
Blessed Thistle	Purification, protection against negativity and evil, hex breaking. Carry for strength and protection.

Herb	Magickal Use
Bloodroot	Love, protection and purification. Steep in red wine for a full cycle of the moon to use as a "blood offering" for spells that call for this. **Note this is poisonous.**
Blowball	Love and wishes
Blue Cohosh	Empowerment, purification, money drawing, love breaking, and driving away evil.
Blue Violet	Love, inspiration, good fortune, and protection from all evil
Bluebell	Luck, truth, and friendship
Blueberry	Protection. Causes confusion and strife when tossed in the doorway or path of an enemy.
Boneset	Protection, exorcism, and warding off evil spirits
Borage	Courage and psychic powers
Brazil Nut	Good luck in love affairs
Brimstone	Dispels or prevents a hex on you; destroys an enemy's power over you.
Broom	Purification, divination, and protection. Sprinkle an infusion of broom tops around the home to clear away all evil.
Buchu	Divination, wind spells, psychic powers, and prophetic dreams.
Buckeye	Divination, good luck, and attracting money and wealth
Buckthorn	Used as a luck generator in legal matters and for winning in court
Buckwheat	Money, protection, and fasting. Use in charms and spells to obtain treasure, riches, and wealth.
Burdock	Used for cleansing magick when feeling highly negative about oneself or others. Use in protection incenses and spells.
Burnet	Used for protection, consecration of ritual tools, and counter magick; also used to magickally treat depression and despondency.
Butchers Broom	Wind spells, divination, protection, psychic powers

Herb	Magickal Use
Butterbur	Used for love divination and to raise one's spirits by increasing sense of hope and faith.
Cabbage	Fertility, profit, good luck, lunar magick, money magick
Cactus	Chastity, banishing, and protection.
Calamint	Soothes sorrows and helps in recovery from emotional pain.
Calamus	Luck, money, healing and protection. Note: **Use with caution, can be poisonous.**
Calendula Flowers	Protection, legal matters, and psychic/spiritual powers.
Camellia	Riches
Camphor	Dreams, psychic awareness, and divination
Caper	Potency, lust, and love
Caraway	Health, love, protection, mental powers, memory, passion, and antitheft
Cardamom	Lust, love, and fidelity
Carnation	Protection, strength, healing, enhancing magickal powers, and achieving balance
Carob	Health and protection
Carrot	Lust, fertility
Cascara Sagrada	Legal matters, money spells, and protection against hexes
Cashew	Money
Catnip	Sacred to Bast; should be used in any ritual involving cats or cat deities. Use with rose petals in love sachets.
Cat's Claw	Vision quests, shamanic journeys, and money drawing
Cat-tail	Lust
Cayenne	Dealing with separations or divorce; cleansing and purification; repels negativity; speeds up the effect of any mixture to which it is added.
Cedar	Confidence, strength, power, money, protection, healing, and purification.
Cedar Berries	Antitheft

Herb	Magickal Use
Celandine	Cures depression, brings victory and joy, assists in legal matters. **Note: Deadly poison, use with caution**
Celery	Mental powers, psychic powers, lust, fertility, and male potency
Celery Seed	Mental and psychic powers, concentration. Burn with orris root to increase psychic powers.
Centaury	Adds power to any magickal workings. Used to repel anger and hurtful energy.
Chamomile	Love, luck, healing, and reducing stress
Cherry	Love, divination, gaiety, and happiness
Cherry Bark	Lust, direction, frugality, favors, invisibility, and magickal potency
Chervil	Brings a sense of the higher self, placing you in touch with your divine, immortal spirit. Helps in contacting a deceased loved one.
Chestnut	Love
Chia	Protection and health
Chickweed	Fertility and love
Chicory	Frigidity, favors, removing obstacles, and invisibility. Promotes a positive outlook and improves sense of humour.
Chili Pepper	Fidelity, love, and hex breaking
China Berry	Luck
Chives	Protection and weight loss
Chrysanthemum	Protection. Grow in the garden to ward off evil spirits.
Cilantro	Protection of gardeners; brings peace to the home and helps to attune one with their soul.
Cinnamon	Spirituality, success, healing, protection, power, love, luck, strength, and prosperity
Cinquefoil	An all-purpose magickal herb. The five points of the leaf represent love, money, health, power, and wisdom. Stimulates memory, eloquence and self-confidence.

Herb	Magickal Use
Citronella	Draws friends to the home, customers to the business. Promotes eloquence, persuasiveness, and prosperity. Protects and cleanses the aura.
Clove	Exorcism, love, money, and protection
Clover	Fidelity, protection, money, love, and success
Clover, Red	Put in baths to aid in financial arrangements. Also used in potions for lust.
Cloves	Protection, banishing hostile/negative forces, and gaining what is sought.
Club Moss	Protection and power
Coconut	Chastity, protection and purification
Coffee	Helps to dispel nightmares and negative thoughts and to overcome internal blockages. Provides peace of mind and grounding.
Coltsfoot	Wealth, prosperity, and love
Columbine	Love and courage
Comfrey	Money, safety during travel, real estate
Copal Resin	Love, purification. Use a piece of copal to represent the heart in poppets.
Coriander	Love, health, immortality, and protection
Corn	Protection, divination, good luck
Cornflower	Alleviates discord and strife.
Cotton	Fishing magick, rain, protection, luck, and healing.
Cowslip	Treasure finding, youth, concentration, focus, and house and business blessing.
Coxcomb	Protection
Cramp Bark	Used for protection and female energy
Crowfoot	Love
Cubeb Berries	Love, lust and adding fire to spells. Use in sachets for love and sex.
Cucumber	Chastity, fertility, and healing
Culvers Root	Purification
Cumin	Fidelity, protection, and exorcism
Curry	Protection

Herb	Magickal Use
Cyclamen	Fertility, happiness, lust, and protection
Cypress	Associated with death and mourning; stimulates healing and helps overcome the pain of loss. Calmness and tranquillity.
Daffodil	Love, luck, and fertility
Daisy	Love, luck, and innocence
Damiana	Lust, sex magick and attracting love. Useful for any love or sex spells. Used by solitary practitioners to open the chakras and increase psychic abilities. Note: Internal use of this herb can be toxic to the liver.
Dandelion Leaf	Summoning spirits, healing, purification, and defeating negativity
Dandelion Root	Divination as well as wishes and calling spirits
Deer's Tongue	Aid in increasing psychic powers
Devil Bone Root	Cut into small pieces and carry in a red flannel bag to ward off arthritis.
Devil's Bit	Exorcism, love, protection. and lust
Devil's Bone Root	Sexual attractiveness, warding off negative energies
Devil's Claw	Protection and dispelling unwanted company
Devil's Shoestring	Protection, luck, attracting a new raise or job, giving control over opposite sex, and invisibility.
Dill	Money, protection, luck and lust. Used in love and protection charms. Effective at keeping away dark forces, useful for house blessing.
Dogwood	Wishes, protection, and good health
Dragon's Blood	Protection, energy, and purification
Dulse	Lust, harmony in the home, sea rituals, and pacifying sea winds
Earth Smoke	Associated with the underworld. Financial gain.
Ebony	Protection, power
Echinacea	Adds powerful strength to charms, sachets, and herb mixes. Useful for money drawing magick.

Herb	Magickal Use
Elder	Sleep, releasing enchantments, protection against negativity, wisdom, house blessing, and business blessing. **Note: Elder leaves, bark, roots and raw berries are poisonous. Use with caution.**
Elecampane	Banishing and to dispel angry or violent vibrations
Elm	Love, protection from lightning
Endive	Love spells, sex magick
Eucalyptus	Attracts healing vibrations, great for protection and healing sachets. Use to purify any space.
Evening Primrose	Love
Eyebright	Increase psychic ability, improve memory, encourage rationality, and increase positive outlook.
False Unicorn Root	Lust spells and protection for mother and baby
Fennel Seed	Imparts strength, vitality, sexual virility; prevents curses, possession and negative problems. Use in spells for protection, healing and purification.
Fenugreek	Used for money drawing and fertility magick
Fern	Mental clarity, cleansing, purification and dispelling negativity
Feverfew	Protection against accidents and cold/flu
Fig	Divination, fertility, and love
Figwort	Magickal balms, house and business blessing, protection for the home. Protection against the evil eye.
Flax Seed	Used for money spells and healing rituals. Burn for divinatory powers.
Fleabane	Exorcism, protection, chastity.
Foxglove	Protection of home and garden, vision, and immortality. Used to commune with those of the Underworld.
Frangipani	Promoting openness in those around you; attracting love, trust and admiration.
Frankincense Resin	Successful ventures, cleansing, purification. Burn for protective work, consecration and meditation.
Fumitory	Associated with the underworld

Herb	Magickal Use
Galangal Root	Winning in court, doubling money, hex breaking, and sex magick
Gardenia	Promoting peace/repelling strife, protection from outside influences.
Garlic	Healing, protection, exorcism, purification of spaces and objects. Used to invoke Hecate. Guards against negative magic, spirits, and the envy of others.
Gentian	Power and strength
Geranium	Overcoming negative thoughts and attitudes, lifting spirits, promoting protection and happiness. Repels insects. Balances mind and body.
Ginger	Draws adventure and new experiences. Promotes sensuality, sexuality, personal confidence, prosperity, and success. Adds to the strength and speed of any mixture of which it is a part.
Ginkgo Biloba	Aphrodisiac associated with fertility. Useful in ritual healing. Useful in all creative work.
Ginseng	Love, beauty, protection, healing, and lust
Goldenrod	Money, divination
Goldenseal	Healing rituals, money spells, success. Beneficial in business dealings and matters of finance.
Goosegrass	Wisdom, tenacity, luck in love, and pleasant dreams.
Gorse	Associated with love, protection, romance, and weddings. Protects against negativity and dark magick.
Gotu Kola	Burn prior to (but not during) meditation.
Grape	Fertility, money, mental powers, and garden magick
Grape Seed	Used for garden magick and fertility
Grapefruit	Cleansing and purification
Gravel Root	Used to increase the chances of getting a job. Aids one during times of distress.
Guinea Peppers	Hexing and cursing
Gum Arabic	Protection, psychic and spiritual enhancement, money, platonic love, and friendship

Herb	Magickal Use
Hawthorn	Chastity, fertility, used for success in matters related to career, work, and employment
Hay	Pregnancy and fertility
Heal All	All-purpose healing and successful gambling
Heather	Protection, luck, and immortality
Heliotrope	Cheerfulness, gaiety, prosperity, and protection
Hemlock	Use to paralyse a situation. **Note: Highly poisonous, do not consume.**
Henbane	Dried leaves are used in the consecration of ceremonial vessels.
Henna	Attracts love, wards off the evil eye, and provides protection from illnesses
Hibiscus	Attracting love and lust, divination, and dreams
Hickory	Legal matters, love, lust, and protection
High John	An "all-purpose" herb, the uses of High John include strength, confidence, conquering any situation, obtaining success, winning at gambling, luck, money, love, health, and protection.
Holly	Marriage, dream magick, luck, and love
Hollyhock	Increase success in the material world, increase flow of money, or acquire new possessions
Honey	For attraction and solar magick
Honeysuckle	Draws money, success and quick abundance; Aids persuasiveness and confidence, sharpens intuition.
Hops	Relaxing and sleep producing
Horehound	Protection and helps with mental clarity during ritual; stimulates creativity/inspiration; balances personal energies.
Horseshoe Chestnut	Money and healing
Hyacinth	Promotes peace of mind and peaceful sleep. Attracts love, luck and good fortune.
Hydrangea	Hex breaking, love drawing, bringing back a lover, fidelity, and binding.

Herb	Magickal Use
Hyssop	The most widely used purification herb in magick. Lightens vibrations and promotes spiritual opening; used for cleansing and purification. Said to protect property against burglars and trespassers.
Indigo Weed	Protection
Iris	Attracts wisdom, courage, and faith
Irish Moss	An excellent luck herb
Iron Weed	Control over others
Ivy	Protection, healing, fertility, and love
Jamaican Ginger	Gambling luck
Jasmine	Divination; good for charging quartz crystals.
Jezebel Root	Used for spells and castings for money and achievement. Also used to place curses and hexes.
Job's Tears	Luck in finding employment, wishes, and blessing
Juniper	Banishes all things injurious to good health; attracts good, healthy energies and love.
Kava Kava	Aphrodisiac; potent sacramental drink; potions; induces visions; astral work; travel protection.
Knotweed	Binding spells, health, and cursing
Kola Nut	Peace, removing depression, and calming
Lady Slipper	Used for protection against hexes, curses, and the evil eye
Lady's Mantle	Aphrodisiac, transmutation
Larch	Protection and antitheft
Larkspur	Health and protection
Laurel	Love and protection
Lavender	Love, protection, healing, sleep, purification, and peace. Promotes healing from depression.
Leek	Love, protection, exorcism, and strengthening existing love
Lemon	Cleansing, spiritual opening, purification, and removal of blockages
Lemon Balm	Love, success, healing, and psychic/spiritual development. Good for mental health.
Lemon Grass	Psychic cleansing and opening, lust potions.

Herb	Magickal Use
Lemon Verbena	Attractiveness, to prevent dreams.
Lettuce	Divination, lunar magick, sleep, protection, love spells and male sex magick.
Liquorice	Love, lust and fidelity. Carry to attract a lover.
Lilac	Wisdom, memory, good luck and spiritual aid.
Lily	Fertility, renewal, rebirth, marriage, happiness and prosperity.
Lily of the Valley	Soothing, calming, draws peace and tranquillity and repels negativity. Assists in empowering happiness and mental powers. **Note: Poisonous, use with caution.**
Lime	Purification and protection, promoting calmness and tranquillity and strengthening love.
Linden Flowers	Used in love spells/mixtures and protection spells and incenses.
Little John	Place in holy water to bring good luck in everything you attempt.
Lo John	Money, success and luck
Lobelia	Used for attracting love and preventing storms.
Lotus	Love, protection, psychic opening and spiritual growth.
Lotus Root	Carry to keep thoughts pleasant and clear.
Lovage	Prophetic dreams, energy and purification.
Lucky Hand Root	Good luck, protecting owner from all harm, travel safety and gaining employment. Great for use in mojo and charm bags.
Lungwort	Blessing while traveling by air
Mace	Promotes concentration, focus and self-discipline; great for study and meditation. Used in reuniting rituals.
Magnolia Flowers	Health, beauty, love, loyalty, peace, calming anxieties, marital harmony, and overcoming addictions and obsessive behavior.
Magnolia Bark	Magickal uses include fidelity, love, and hair growth.
Maidenhair Fern	Brings beauty and love into your life

Herb	Magickal Use
M and rake	Protection, prosperity, fertility, and exorcising evil
Maple	Love, money, wealth, longevity, and good luck
Maple Syrup	Longevity, money, and love
Marigold	Attracts respect and admiration, provides good luck in court and other legal matters.
Marjoram	Cleansing, purification, and dispelling negativity
Marshmallow Root	Protection and psychic powers
May Flowers	Attract adventure and chaos to your life
Meadowsweet	Used to increase the chances of getting a job. Aids one during times of distress. Useful as an altar offering, especially during love magick.
Mesquite	Healing
Milk Thistle	Strength, perseverance, wisdom, aid in decision making
Mimosa	Protection, purification, love, dream magick.
Mint	Promotes energy, communication and vitality. Draws customers to a business.
Mistletoe	Used for fertility, creativity, prevention of illness/misfortune and protection from negative spells and magick. **Note: Poisonous, use with caution.**
Monkshood	Invisibility and protection from evil. **Note: Poisonous, use with caution and do not consume.**
Morning Glory	Used for binding, banishing and promoting attraction to someone or something. **Note: Poisonous, use with caution.**
Motherwort	Bolstering ego, building confidence, success, and counter magick
Mugwort	Carried to increase lust and fertility, prevent backache and cure disease and madness. Place around divination and scrying tools to increase their power or near the bed to enable astral travel.
Mullein	Protection from nightmares and sorcery, courage, cursing, and invoking spirits
Musk	Encourages self-esteem and desirability. Can assist in transmuting sexual love into spiritual connection. Stimulates the root chakra.

Herb	Magickal Use
Mustard Seed	Courage, faith, and endurance
Myrrh	Spiritual opening, meditation and healing. This herb has high psychic vibrations that will enhance any magickal working.
Myrtle	Love, fertility, youth, peace, and money
Narcissus	Calms vibrations and promotes harmony, tranquillity, and peace of mind
Neroli	Joy, happiness, confidence, and overcoming emotional blockages
Nettle	Dispelling darkness and fear, strengthening the will and aiding in the ability to hand le emergencies.
Nutmeg	Attracting money/prosperity, bringing luck, protection, and breaking hexes
Oak	Making of magickal tools
Oak Moss	Luck, money, protection, and strength
Oat straw	Draw in money and prosperity
Olive	Fidelity, marriage, peace, money
Olive Leaf	Peace, potency, fertility, healing, protection, and lust
Onion	Prosperity, stability, endurance, and protection
Orange	Attracts abundance and happiness through love and marriage. Concentrate on a yes/no question while eating an orange, then count the seeds—an even number of seeds means the answer is no, an odd number of seeds means yes.
Orange Bergamot	Money drawing
Orange Blossoms	Attracts prosperity and stability; brings harmony, peace, emotional openness, and love.
Orange Peel	Love, divination, luck, money, and house and business blessing
Orchid	Concentration, strengthening memory, focus, and will power
Oregano	Joy, strength, vitality and added energy

Herb	Magickal Use
Orris Root Cut	Promotes popularity, persuasiveness and personal success. Aids communication and helps to open dialogs.
Orris Root Powder	Love, romance, companionship, and a loving mate
Osha Root	Protection against evil spirits
Palm	Fertility, focus, potency, and divination
Palo Santo	If you feel you have been cursed, rub this herb on your body and then bathe.
Pansy	Love, divination related to love and relationships, rain magick
Papaya	Keep out evil. Intensify your love.
Paprika	Use to add energy to any spell or mixture.
Papyrus	Protection
Parsley	Calms and protects the home; draws prosperity, financial increase and luck. Restores a sense of well-being.
Parsnip	Male sex magick
Passion Flower	Attracting friendship and prosperity and heightening libido
Patchouli	Used in spells for money and love
Pau d'Arco	Magickal use is for the ritual healing of severe diseases.
Peach	Fertility, love, and wisdom.
Pear	Lust and love. Eating pears induces love.
Pearl Moss	Encourages good spirits
Peas	Money and love
Peat Moss	Protection
Pecan	Associated with employment, success, job security, and career matters
Pennyroyal	Magickal uses include peace and tranquillity.
Peony	Protection from hexes and jinxes. Good luck, good fortune, prosperity, and business success.
Pepper, Black	Courage, banishing negative vibrations.
Peppermint	Use to increase the vibrations of a space or in spells and incense for healing and purification.

Herb	Magickal Use
Periwinkle	Love within marriage, mental powers, and money. **Note: Can be poisonous, use with caution.**
Persimmon	Changing sex, healing, and luck
Petitgrain	Protection
Pikaki	Draws comfort, prosperity, success, and well-being
Pimento	Love
Pimpernel	Protection and health
Pine	Promotes clean breaks, new beginnings, prosperity, success, strength, grounding and growth; also used for cleansing, purification and repelling negativity.
Pineapple	Luck, money and chastity. Add an infusion of pineapple to the bath to attract luck.
Pink Root	Healing
Pink Rose Buds	Divine, emotional and thinking love; start with these to build a long-lasting relationship.
Pistachio	Breaking love spells.
Plantain	Protection from evil spirits, removing weariness, healing headaches; house and business blessing.
Pleurisy Root	Healing
Plum	Healing, peace, and love
Plumeria	Promotes persuasiveness, eloquence and success in dealing with people; attracts the notice of others.
Poke Root	Finding lost objects and breaking hexes and curses. Increases courage.
Pomegranate	Divination, wishes, wealth, and fertility
Poppy	Fertility, prosperity, love, and abundance.
Poppy Seeds	Pleasure, heightened awareness, love, luck, invisibility.
Potato	Image magick, money, luck, and healing
Prickly Ash Bark	Safe travel, fertility, removing spells, and breaking hexes.

Herb	Magickal Use
Primrose	Promotes the disclosure of secrets, resolution of mysteries and revelation of truth; breaks down dishonesty and secrecy.
Pumpkin	Lunar magick
Pumpkin Seed	Health
Quassia	Love
Quince	Love, happiness, luck, and protection from evil
Radish	Protection and lust
Ragwort	Courage. Used in charms to ward off evil spirits.
Raspberry Leaf	Used for healing, protection, love.
Red Clover	Fidelity, love, money, protection, and the blessing of domestic animals
Red Willow Bark	Meditation and clearing
Rhubarb	Fidelity and protection
Rice	Rain, fertility, money, and protection
Rose	Divine love, close friendships, domestic peace/happiness, and lasting relationships.
Rose Geranium	Averts negativity, especially in the form of gossip or false accusations
Rose Hips	Used in healing spells and mixtures, brings good luck, calls in good spirits
Rosemary	Carried and used in healing poppets for good health
Rowan	Protection, magickal power, success, antihaunting
Rue	Healing, health, mental powers, freedom and protection against the evil eye. **Note: Can be poisonous, use with caution.**
Rye	Love, fidelity, and self-control
Safflower	Mix with jinx incense to cause destruction to an enemy
Saffron	Aphrodisiac, love, healing, happiness, lust, and strength.
Sage	Used for self-purification and dealing with grief and loss

Herb	Magickal Use
Salt Peter	For women who do not want their partners to have outside relationships. Stops sexual tension.
Sandalwood	Clears negativity. Protection, healing, and exorcism spells.
Sanicle	Used for safety in travel
Sarsaparilla	Sexual vitality, health, love, and money
Sassafras	Health, money, and overcoming addictions
Savoury	Sensuality, sexuality and passion; great for sex magick!
Saw Palmetto Berries	Magickal uses include healing protection, exorcism, passion, and spiritual openings.
Skullcap	To keep husband s faithful. Relaxation and peace. Used to bind oaths and consecrate vows and commitments.
Sea Salt	Cleansing crystals, purification, grounding, protection magick, and ritual
Senna	Lust and love. Enhances tact and diplomacy.
Sesame	Money, lust, and passion
Shallots	Luck
Shave Grass	Fertility
Sheep Sorrel	Heart disease. Recuperation from illnesses and wounds.
Shepherd's Purse	Healing
Skunk Cabbage	Legal matters
Slippery Elm	Protection and halting gossip
Snapdragon	Protection, exorcism, and purification
Snowdrop	Passing of sorrow
Solomon's Seal Root	Protection and cleansing. Used in offertory incense.
Sow Thistle	Increases strength and stamina, repels witches, and provides invisibility from enemies.
Spanish Moss	Protection, opening blockages, and dispelling negativity
Spearmint	Healing, love, and protection while sleeping.
Spiderwort	Love

Herb	Magickal Use
Spikenard	Luck and ward off illness
Squaw Vine	Fertility and childbirth
Squill Root	To draw money
St. John's Wort	Prevent colds and fevers. Placed under pillow to induce prophetic, romantic dreams. Protects against all forms of black witchcraft.
Star Anise	Psychic awareness and abilities.
Straw	Image magick and luck
Straw Flower	Luck, longevity, and protection. **Note: Poisonous, use with caution.**
Strawberry	Attracts success, good fortune, and favorable circumstances.
Sugar	Love spells, sex magick
Sugar Cane	Love, lust, and sympathy
Sulphur Powder	Dispels or prevents a hex on you; destroys an enemy's power over you.
Sunflower	Energy, protection, power, wisdom, and wishes.
Sweet Bugle	Crush and place under the mattress to attract love and marriage prospects.
Sweet Pea	Attracts friends and allies; draws the loyalty and affection of others.
Sweet Potato	Image magick
Sweetgrass	Peace, unity, and calling spirits
Tamarind	Love
Tangerine	Promotes energy, strength, and vitality. Awakens joy and dissolves negativity.
Tansy	Health, invisibility, immortality, longevity; keeps evil out of the home.
Tarragon	Healing in abuse situations, compassion magick for others. Use for consecrating chalices.
Tea Leaves	Courage or strength
Tea Tree	Eliminating confusion and increasing harmony
Thistle	Healing, protection. Speedy recovery from illness.
Thyme	Attracts loyalty, affection and the good opinion of others.

Herb	Magickal Use
Toadflax	Protection and hex breaking
Toadstool	Rain magick
Tobacco	Promotes peace, confidence, and personal strength. Also used for banishing.
Tomato	Love spells
Tonka Bean	Love; wishes and courage.
True Unicorn Root	Hex breaking, uncrossing, and protection against evil and malevolent magick.
Tuberose	Sensuality, serenity, and calming nerves. Brings peace to the mind and heart, enhances the capacity for emotional depth.
Turnip	Ending relationships
Uva Ursi	Increasing intuitive and psychic powers. **Note: Can be poisonous, use with caution.**
Valerian	Dream magick, reconciliation, love, and harmony
Vanilla Bean	Love, lust, passion, and restoring lost energy
Venus Flytrap	Love and protection
Vertivert	Draws money and prosperity, love and attraction; Overcomes obstacles, breaks hexes and repels negativity.
Vervain	Protection, purification, money, youth, peace, healing, and sleep
Vetch	Fidelity
Vinegar	Banishing, binding, averting evil
Violet	Calms the nerves, draws prophetic dreams and visions, stimulates creativity, and promotes peace and tranquillity
Walnut	Access to divine energy, bringing the blessing of the Gods, wishes
Watercress	For lunar magick and sex magick
Wheat	Inducing fertility and conception, attracting money
White Sage	Use as an incense, for smudging, or for purification

Herb	Magickal Use
White Willow Bark	Brings blessings of the moon into one's life and guards against negativity and evil forces. Used in healing spells.
Willow	Lunar magick, drawing or strengthening love, healing, and overcoming sadness.
Wintergreen	Good fortune and luck. Purification.
Wisteria	Raises vibrations, promotes psychic opening, overcomes obstacles, and draws prosperity
Witch Hazel	Chastity and protection
Witches Burr	Adds great power to spells and rituals
Witches Grass	Happiness, lust, love, and exorcism
Wood Aloe	Protection, consecration, success, and prosperity
Wood Betony	Purification, protection, and the expulsion of evil spirits, nightmares, and despair.
Woodruff	Victory, protection, and money
Wormwood	Removes anger, stop war, inhibit violent acts, and for protection from the evil eye.
Xanthan Gum	Incense bonding agent
Yarrow Flower	Healing and divination. Draws love.
Yellow Dock	Fertility, healing, and money
Yerba Mate	Fidelity, love, and lust
Yerba Santa	Beauty, healing, psychic powers, and protection.
Yew	Raising the dead, protection against evil, immortality, and breaking hexes
Ylang-Ylang	Increases sexual attraction and persuasiveness
Yohimbe Bark	Love, lust, virility and fertility. Curing impotency. Cursing.
Yucca	Transmutation, protection, and purification

Index

Recommended Reading

Abdu'l-Bahá. *The Nonexistence of Evil—Some Answered Questions.* Retrieved January 23, 2014, from https://www.bahai.org/beliefs/life-spirit/human-soul/articles-resources/non-existence-evil.

Admin, H. R. *Zohar.* Retrieved January 23, 2014, from My Jewish Learning: https://www.myjewishlearning.com/article/the-zohar/.

Aleph. *Luciferian Black Flame.* Retrieved January 10, 2019, from My Thoughts Born From Fire. https://mythoughtsbornfromfire.wordpress.com/2015/06/20/the-luciferian-black-flame/.

Aleph. *The Black Flame, The Fire Within.* Retrieved January 10, 2019, from My Thoughts Born From Fire: https://mythoughtsbornfromfire.wordpress.com/2015/05/09/the-black-flame-the-fire-within/

Alexander, S. *The Everything Tarot Book.* Avon: Adams Media, 2006.

Apiryon, H. A. *The Invisible Basilica: The Creed of the Gnostic Catholic Church: An Examination.* Retrieved January 23, 2014, from Ordo Templi Orientis. https://hermetic.com/sabazius/creed_egc.

Arbel, D. I. "Chapter 7: Flora and Fauna in Encyclopedia Mythica." In *Witchcraft.* Retrieved February 23, 2009, from Pantheon. http://www.pantheon.org/areas/featured/witchcraft/chapter-7.html.

Asatryan, G. S., & Arakelova, V. *The Religion of the Peacock Angel: The Yezidis and Their Spirit World.* London: Routledge, Taylor & Francis Group, 2004.

Belanger, M. *Vampires in Their Own Words: An Anthology of Vampire Voices.* Woodbury: Llewellyn Worldwide, 2007.

Beyer, C. *Exploring the Different Types of Satanic Beliefs.* Retrieved December 29, 2018, from ThoughtCo. https://www.thoughtco.com/laveyan-satanism-theistic-satanism-and-luciferianism-95715.

Beyer, C. *How Luciferians Differ from Satanists.* Retrieved December 26, 2018, from ThoughtCo. https://www.thoughtco.com/how-luciferians-differ-from-satanists-95678.

Black Tower Publishing. *Lilith: Goddess of the Sitra Ahra.* USA: Black Tower Publishing, 2015.

Blackwood. *Origins of Satanism? Why Sumeria?* Retrieved January 6, 2019, from The Voice of Satanism. http://voiceofsatanism.com/2010/09/21/origins-of-satanism-why-sumeria/.

Blavatsky, H. P. *Occultism of the Secret Doctrine.* Montana: Kessinger Publishing, 1897.

Breese, C. *Astral Projection.* USA: University of Metaphysical Sciences, 2005.

Briar, W. *Daemonic Dreams.* Edmonton: Brassvessel Books, 2018.

Brown, D. R. *Astral Travel: Travelling the Astral Planes and Out of Body Experience.* USA: New Breed Publishing, 2017.

Bruce, R. *Treatise on Astral Projection.* USA: Robert Bruce, 1994.

Budge, E. A. *A History of Egypt from the End of the Neolithic Period to the Death of Cleopatra VII B.C. 30.* New York: Oxford University Press, 1908.

Budge, E. A. *The Gods of the Egyptians Volume 1 of 2.* New York: Dover Publications, 1969.

Budge, E. W. *The Gods of the Egyptians. Vol. 1.* New York: Dover Publications, 2003.

Budge, S. E. *The Gods of the Egyptians (Volume II).* London: Methuen & Co., 1904.

Burman, E. *Supremely Abominable Crimes : The Trial of the Knights Templar.* London: Allison and Busby, 1994.

Car, N. V. *Practical Magic: A Beginners Guide to Crystals, Horoscopes, Psychics & Spells.* Philadelphia: Running Press, 2017.

Church of Satan. Retrieved January 23, 2014, from http://en.wikipedia.org/wiki/Church_of_Satan.

Cirlot, J. E. *A Dictionary of Symbols.* New York: Dover Editions, 1971.

Connolly, S. *Modern Demonolatry.* Arvada: DB Publishing, 1997.

Connolly, S. *The Complete Book of Demonolatry.* USA: DB Publishing, 2006.

Connolly, S. *The Daemonolater's Guide to Daemonic Magick.* USA: DB Publishing, 2009.

Connolly, S. *Modern Demonolatry.* USA: DB Publishing, 2010.

Connolly, S. *Sigillum Diaboli: A Complete Guide To Divining With Daemonic Sigils.* USA: DB Publishing, 2012.

Cooper, P. *Basic Sigil Magic.* York Beach: Weiser Books, 2001.

Crabb, G. *English Synonyms Explained, New York.* New York: Thomas Y. Crowell Co., 1927.

Crowley, A. *The Confessions of Aleister Crowley.* London: Mandrake Press, 1929.

Cunningham, S. *Divination for Beginners: Reading the Past, Present and Future.* Woodbury: Llewellyn Publishers, 2003.

Daraul, A. *A History of Secret Societies.* New York: Citadel Press, 1984.

Darling, J. L. *How To Spot A Fraud In The Occult.* Retrieved January 2, 2019, from Wordpress. https://jymiedarling. wordpress.com/2016/16/04/how-to-spot-a-fraud-i n-the-occult-by-jymie-darling/.

Davidson, G. "Samael." In *A Dictionary of Angels, including the fallen angels,* 255. New York: Simon and Schuster, 1924.

Dean, L. *The Ultimate Guide To Tarot.* Beverly: Fair Winds Press, 2015.

Dee, J. *Liber Mysteriorum, Sextus et Sanctus.* Retrieved January 23, 2014, from Esoteric Archives. http://www.esotericarchives.com/dee/ sl3189.htm.

Dickason, C. F. *Angels: Elect & Evil, Revised.* Chicago: Moody Publishers, 1995.

Dominguez, I. *Practical Astrology for Witches and Pagans.* San Francisco: Red Wheel/Weiser, 2016.

Dunstan, P. *The Dark Powers That Bind.* Tamarac: Llumina Press, 2005.

Dyrendal, A. "Devilish Consumption: Popular Culture in Satanic Socialization." *Numen 55.1,* 68–98, 2008.

Eason, C. *The Art of the Pendulum.* Boston: Red Wheel/Weiser, 2005.

Eds A. Crowley, H. B. *The Goetia: The Lesser Key of Solomon the King: Lemegeton—Clavicula Salomonis Regis, Book 1*. New York: Red Wheel, 1995.

Encyclopædia Britannica. Islam: Satan, Sin, and Repentance. In Various, *Encyclopædia Britannica*. Encyclopædia Britannica, 2010.

Encyclopaedia Britannica. *Lucifer*. Retrieved December 29, 2018, from Encyclopaedia Britannica. https://www.britannica.com/topic/Lucifer-classical-mythology.

Etymonline. *Demon*. Retrieved December 30, 2018, from Etymonline. https://www.etymonline.com/word/demon.

Evans, D. *The History of British Magick after Crowley*. London: Hidden Publishing, 2007.

Evans, D. *The History of British Magick After Crowley*. London: Hidden Publishing, 2007.

Evelyn-White, H. G. *Hesiod*. London: Harvard University Press; London, William Heinemann, 1914.

Ford, M. W. *The Bible of the Adversary*. Houston: Succubus Productions Publishing, 2007.

Ford, M. W. *The First Book of Luciferian Tarot*. Houston: Succubus Publishing, 2007.

Ford, M. W. *Scales of the Black Serpent*. USA: Michael W. Ford, 2009.

Ford, M. W. *Maskim Hul: Babylonian Magick*. Houston: Succubus Productions, 2010.

Ford, M. W. *The Order of Phosphorus*. Retrieved January 23, 2014, from http://www.theorderofphosphorus.com/.

Ford, M. W. *Luciferianism: an Introduction*. Retrieved December 28, 2018, from Luciferian Apotheca. https://www.luciferianapotheca.com/pages/luciferianism-an-introduction

Frater Acher. *On the Nature of the Qlippoth*. Retrieved January 13, 2019, from Theomagica: https://theomagica.com/on-the-nature-of-the-qlippoth/

Frater Acher. A Course in Dream Magic. USA, January 26, 2019.

FVF. *Occult Study*. Retrieved December 31, 2018, from Basics of Demonolatry. https://occult-study.org/basics-of-demonolatry/

Gardner, L. *Genesis of the Grail Kings.* New York: Bantam Press, 1999.

Giuseppe Furlani, J. U. *The Religion of the Yezidis: Religious Texts of the Yezidis.* Bombay: J.M. Unvala, 1940.

Granholm, K. "Post-Satanism, Left-Hand Paths and Beyond." *The Devil's Party: Satanism in Modernity*, 207, 2012.

Gray, W. *Exorcising The Tree of Evil: How To Use The Symbolism Of The Qabalistic Tree of Life To Recognise And Reverse Negative Energy.* New York: Helios, 1974.

Hakl, H. T. "Fraternitas Saturni" In W. H. (ed), *Dictionary of Gnosis & Western Esotericism*, 381. Leiden: Brill Academic Publishers, 2006.

Hamill Nassau, R. *Fetichism In West Africa.* Philadelphia: Charles Scribners Son, 1904.

Hamilton-Parker, C. *Pyromancy: How to Perform Fire Divination.* Retrieved February 10, 2019. from Psychics UK. https://psychics.co.uk/blog/pyromancy/.

Hammer, J. *Lilith, Lady Flying in Darkness.* Retrieved December 27, 2018, from My Jewish Learning. https://www.myjewishlearning.com/article/lilith-lady-flying-in-darkness/

Hammer-Purgstall, F. V. *Mysterium Baphometis Revelatum.* Retrieved from Archive. https://archive.org/stream/MysteriumBaphometisRevelatumENG/Mysterium%20Baphometis%20Revelatum%20%5BENG%5D_djvu.txt.

Hansen, W. *Classical Mythology: A Guide to the Mythical World of the Greeks and Romans.* London: Oxford University Press, 2005.

Heiser, J. D. *Prisci Theologi and the Hermetic Reformation in the Fifteenth Century.* Texas: Repristination Press, 2011.

Hendel, R. *Was The Snake In The Garden Of Eden Satan.* Retrieved from Huffington Post: http:// www.huffingtonpost.com/ronald-hendel/was-the-snake-in-the-garden-of-edensatan_b_1900973.html.

Henry George Liddell, R. S. *A Greek-English Lexicon, of Perseus.* Retrieved December 23, 2018, from Library University of Chicago. https://www.lib.uchicago.edu/efts/PERSEUS/Reference/lsj.html.

Hugh Schonfield. *The Essene Oddesey.* England: Longmead, 1984.

Hyatt, C. S. *Pacts With the Devil.* Temple: New Falcon Publications, 1993.

Jeffrey, S. *How to Find Your Centre*. Retrieved January 24, 2019, from Scott Jeffrey. https://scottjeffrey.com/center-yourself/.

Jensen, K. F. A Century with the Waite-Smith Tarot (and all the others...). *The Playing Card*, 217–222, 2010.

Johnson, E. D. *The Myth of Sacred Prostitution in Antiquity*. Retrieved January 9, 2019, from Rosetta: http://www.rosetta.bham.ac.uk.

Johnstone, M. *The Ultimate Encyclopedia of Fortune Telling*. London: Arcturus Publishing Limited, 2004.

Karlsson, T. *Qabalah, Qliphoth and Goetic Magic*. Jacksonville: Ouroborous Productions, 2004.

Kent, J. S. *Goetic Divination*. London: Hadrean Press, 2009.

Kreiter, J. *Create a Servitor: Harness the Power of Thought Forms*. USA: Amazon Kindle, 2014.

Krishnananda, S. *A Study of the Bhagavadgita; Sankhya—The Wisdom of Cosmic Existence*. Retrieved from Swami Krishnananda's official website: https://www.swami-krishnananda.org/index.html#.

LaVey, A. S. *Die Satanische Bible (Satanic Bible)* . Berlin: Second Sight Books, 1999.

Levi, E. *Dogme et Rituel de la Haute Magie*. Cambridge: Cambridge Library Collection, 2011.

Lewis, J. R. *Controversial New Religions*. London: Oxford University Press, 2004.

Lim, S. *Dagon, Baal, Astarte, and other Modern Idols*. Retrieved January 10, 2019, from Ichthus. http://www.harvardichthus.org/2013/11/dagon-baal-astarte-and-other-modern-idols/?fbclid=IwAR0DU WOWx-1Rl1A4Zsv9r9QbktrNh-3U8wqdb_P-yb6JFF2 XnCwc2dZAnNc.

Littleton, C. *Mythology. The illustrated anthology of world myth & storytelling*. London: Duncan Baird Publishers, 2002.

Live Journal. *Chaosophia*. Retrieved January 10, 2019, from Live Journal: https://chaosophia.livejournal.com/2611.html.

Luciferian Info. *Luciferian Info FAQ*. Retrieved December 24, 2018, from Luciferian Info: http://luciferian.info/faq/.

Lyon, A. Immutable Laws of Nature. *Proceedings of the Aristotelian Society.* 1976.

Mark, J. J. *Set.* Retrieved January 8, 2019, from Ancient History Encyclopedia. https://www.ancient.eu/Set_(Egyptian_God)/.

Mark, J. J. *The Mesopotamian Pantheon.* Retrieved January 6, 2019, from The Ancient History Encyclopedia. https://www.ancient.eu/article/221/the-mesopotamian-pantheon/?fbclid=IwAR1LQWqPIpR-FBg9QgXVYXRU6ZDacLg4xeWZFv0TA1waDAL3oGqkVi93Jd0.

Mason, A. *Lilith: Dark Feminine Archetype.* Temple of Ascending Flame. 2018.

Mattfeld, W. R. *Eden's Serpent: Its Mesopotamian Origins.* USA: Walter R. Mattfeld, 2010.

Mbpay, K. *The Question of Evil in Ancient Egypt.* London: Golden House Publications, 2010.

McManus, C. *Right Hand, Left Hand: The Origins of Asymmetry in Brains, Bodies, Atoms and Cultures.* New York: Harvard University Press, 2004.

McRobbie, L. R. *Smithsonian Mag.* Retrieved October 27, 2013, from The Strange and Mysterious History of the Ouija Board. https://www.smithsonianmag.com/history/the-strange-and-mysterious-history-of-the-ouija-board-5860627/.

Michaud, J. *The History of the Crusades (Vol III).* New York: Redfield, 1853.

Misanthropic Luciferian Order. *Misanthropic Luciferian Order.* Retrieved October 27, 2013, from Slayer Magazine. http://www.angelfire.com/extreme/slayermagazine/interview_mlo1.html

Mitchell, B., & Robinson, F. C. *A Guide to Old English. Glossary.* Blackwell Publishing, 2001.

Morris Jastrow, P. J. *Astronomy: Helel Son of Dawn.* Retrieved December 24, 2018, from Jewish Encyclopedia. http://www.jewishencyclopedia.com/articles/2052-astronomy.

Mortin, M. Q. *In the Heart of the Desert.* Hopper: Green Mountain Press, 2007.

NAA 218. *The Book of Sitra Achra.* USA: Ixaxaar Occult Literature, 2013.

Nacht, A. *Aleister Nacht.* Retrieved December 19, 2018, from Aleister Nacht: http://www.aleisternacht.com/.

NASA. *What Is Dark Energy.* Retrieved January 23, 2014, from http://science.nasa.gov/astrophysics/focus-areas/what-is-dark-energy/.

New World Encyclopedia. *Hermeticism.* Retrieved January 3, 2019, from New World Encyclopedia. http://www.newworldencyclopedia.org/entry/Hermeticism#cite_note-0

Nietzsche, F. *Friedrich Nietzsche.* Retrieved January 23, 2014, from Wikipedia. http://en.wikipedia.org/wiki/Friedrich_Nietzsche.

Noah Kramer, S. A. *Myths of Enki, the Crafty God.* New York: Oxford University Press, 1989.

Oracc Museum. *Dagan (god).* Retrieved January 10, 2019, from Ancient Mesopotamian Gods and Goddesses. http://oracc.museum.upenn.edu/amgg/listofdeities/dagan/index.html?fbclid=IwAR3LMDK7EniYVgEhBeVFRE1EzSpQRuwAqlBp3gyiGaQ7_hHbkW1ahr6Kq9o.

Oracle ThinkQuest. *The Physics of Light: What is Light?* Retrieved February 12, 2012, from Think Quest. http://library.thinkquest.org/27356/p_index.htm.

Order of Nine Angles. *Understanding Satanism.* Retrieved December 17, 2018, from Order of Nine Angles. https://lapisphilosophicus.wordpress.com/about-2/understanding-satanism/.

Parpola, S. "The Assyrian Tree of Life: Tracing the Origins of Jewish Monotheism and Greek Philosophy." *Journal of Near Eastern Studies,* 161–208, 1993.

Pertile, P. B. *The Cambridge History of Italian Literature.* London: Cambridge University Press, 1997.

Peterson, J. *Pseudomonarchia Daemonum (Liber officiorum spirituum).* Retrieved January 5, 2019, from Esoteric Archives. http://www.esotericarchives.com/solomon/weyer.htm.

Peterson, J. H. (Ed.). *Lemegeton Clavicula Salomonis: The Lesser Key of Solomon, Detailing the Ceremonial Art of Commanding Spirits Both Good and Evil.* Maine: Weisner Books, 2001.

Plawiuk, E. *Liber Capricornus : The Symbolism of the Goat in Presentations To The Norwood Lodge.* Retrieved September 3, 1991, from Masonic World: http://www.masonicworld.com/education/articles/LIBER-CAPRICORNUS-THE-SYMBOLISM-OF-THE-GOAT.htm.

Przylepa, A. *Encyclopedia Satanica.* Retrieved December 19, 2018, from Encyclopedia Satanica. http://encyclopediasatanica.wordpress.com/category/satanicdenominations/.

Quincey, T. D. Historico-Critical Inquiry into the Origin of The Rosicrucians and the Freemasons. *London Magazine,* 1824.

Reese, W. L. *Dictionary of Philosophy and Religion.* Sussex: Harvester Press, 1980.

Routledge, M. *The Troubadours: An Introduction.* London: Cambridge University Press, 1999.

Ryan, N. *Into a World of Hate.* New York: Routledge, 1994.

Sara E. Karesh, M. M. *Encyclopedia of Judaism.* USA: Infobase Publishing, 2005.

Satan & Sons. *Demons and Demonolatry.* Retrieved January 4, 2019, from Demons and Demonolatry: https://demonsanddemonolatry.com/.

Savedow, S. *Goetic Evocation: The Magicians Workbook Volume 2.* Chicago: Eschaton Books, 1996.

Senholt, J. Secret Identities in The Sinister Tradition: Political Esotericism and the Convergence of Radical Islam, Satanism and National Socialism in the Order of Nine Angles. (P. F. Petersen, Ed.) *The Devil's Party: Satanism in Modernity,* 260, 2012.

Sitchin, Z. *The 12th Planet.* New York: Avon Books, 1986.

Smith, D. D. Exploring the Electromagnetic Spectrum: The Herschel Experiment. *Space Telescope Science Institute,* 2007.

Smith, W. *Prometheus.* Retrieved December 28, 2018, from Perseus Tufts. http://www.perseus.tufts.edu/hopper/text?doc=Perseus%3Atext%3A1999.04.0104%3Aalphabetic+letter%3DP%3Aentry+group%3D47%3Aentry%3Dprometheus-bio-1.

Spence, L. *An Encyclopedia of Occultism.* New York: Carol Publishing Group, 1993.

Suster, G. *The Hell-Fire Friars*. London: Robson, 2000.

Sutcliffe, R. J. Left-Hand Path Ritual Magick: An Historical and Philosophical Overview. In G. H. Hardman, *Paganism Today* (pp. 109–137). London: Thorsons/HarperCollins, 1996.

Swatos, W. H. Adolescent Satanism: A Research Note on Exploratory Survey Data. *Review of Religious Research 34.2*, 1992, 161–69.

Temple of Ascending Flame. *Tree of Qliphoth*. USA: Temple of Ascending Flame, 2016.

Tenney, M. *The Zondervan Pictorial Encyclopedia of the Bible Vol 2*. New York: Zondervan Publishing House, 1976.

The Black Light Catechism. *Anti-Cosmic Satanism Part I: Why Anti-Cosmic Satanism is not Satanism, but Gnostic Fascism*. Retrieved December 17, 2018, from Medium. https://medium.com/@ blacklightcatechism/anti-cosmic-satanism-part-i-why-anti-cos mic-satanism-is-not-satanism-but-fascist-fan-fiction-bc6544ca0a60.

The Luciferian Next Door. *The Black Flame*. Retrieved January 10, 2019, from The Luciferian Next Door. https://theluciferiannextdoor. com/2014/09/26/the-black-flame/.

Thorp, J. *Divining and Speaking with Daemons: A Practical Guide*. USA: DB Publishing, 2005.

Thorp, J. *The Complete Book of Demonolatry Magic*. USA: DB Publishing, 2006.

U.D., F. *Practical Sigil Magic: Creating Personal Symbols for Success*. Minnesota: Llewellyn Publications, 2012.

University of Texas. *Indo-European Lexicon: Pokorny Master PIE Etyma. Utexas.edu*. Retrieved December 23, 2018, from University of Texas. http://www.utexas.edu/cola/centers/lrc/ielex/PokornyMaster-X.html.

Vera, D. *What Is Orthodox Satanism*. Retrieved January 23, 2014, from Theistic Satanism. http://theisticsatanism.com/bgoat/orthodox.html.

Waite, A. *The Pictorial Key to the Tarot*. Santa Cruz: Evinity Publishing, 1911.

Waite, A. E. *Sacred Texts*. Retrieved January 23, 2014, from Devil Worship In France: http://www.sacred-texts.com/evil/dwf/ dwf03.htm.

Ward, D. S. *Enki and Enlil.* Retrieved January 8, 2019, from Library of Halexandria: http://www.halexandria.org/dward184.htm.

Ward, D. S. *Sumerian Family Tree.* Retrieved January 8, 2019, from Library of Halexandria: http://www.halexandria.org/dward186.htm.

Wigington, P. *Magical Grounding, Centering, and Shielding Techniques.* Retrieved January 24, 2019, from ThoughtCo. https://www. thoughtco.com/grounding-centering-and-shielding-4122187.

Wikipedia. *Baphomet.* Retrieved January 23, 2014, from Wikipedia. http://en.wikipedia.org/wiki/Baphomet.

Wikipedia. *Luciferianism.* Retrieved January 23, 2014, from Wikipedia. http://en.wikipedia.org/wiki/Luciferianism.

Wikipedia. *Number of the Beast.* Retrieved January 23, 2014, from Wikipedia. http://en.wikipedia.org/wiki/Number_of_the_beast.

Wikipedia. *Satan.* Retrieved January 23, 2014, from Wikipedia. http:// en.wikipedia.org/wiki/Satan.

Wikipedia. *Ancient Canaanite religion.* Retrieved December 28, 2018, from Wikipedia. https://en.wikipedia.org/wiki/ Ancient_Canaanite_religion#Deities.

Wikipedia. *Luciferianism.* Retrieved December 26, 2018, from Wikipedia. https://en.wikipedia.org/wiki/ Luciferianism#cite_note-28.

Wikipedia. *Dagon.* Retrieved January 10, 2019, from Wikipedia. https:// en.wikipedia.org/wiki/Dagon.

Wikipedia. *Enki.* Retrieved January 7, 2019, from Wikipedia. https:// en.wikipedia.org/wiki/Enki.

Wray, G. M. *The Birth of Satan: Tracing the Devil's Biblical Roots.* New York: Macmillan, 2005.

Yezidi Truth. *Yezidi Religious Tradition.* Retrieved December 25, 2018, from Yezidi Truth: http://www.yeziditruth.org/ yezidi_religious_tradition.

In loving memory of Richard Scott Cavenett, my beautiful husband, who lived large and loved deeply. You will always be my shelter from the storm. (1963–2020)

Milton Keynes UK
Ingram Content Group UK Ltd.
UKHW030853100924
1574UKWH00005B/119